Praise for

# A GREAT FLASH OF LIGHT

*"Most of us alive today have been born into the Nuclear Age but are largely unaware or indifferent to its globe-encompassing perils. Bognar's memoir is a thoughtful and charming exploration of nuclear dangers, pulling back the veil of fog covering the severe threats to all life on the planet. It is the story of one man's awakening, while growing up and living in the Nuclear Age, and it contains important insights for anyone wanting to pass the world on intact to their children and grandchildren."*

David Krieger, J.D., Ph.D.
Founder of the Nuclear Age Peace Foundation

*"Frank Bognar has written an inspirational memoir that reminds us in lucid prose about our better angels as a country and in our private quests for fulfillment. It is an all-American story that gracefully combines the virtues of a religious upbringing with the commitments of a morally engaged citizen."*

Richard Falk, S.J.D.
Former American Professor Emeritus of International Law at Princeton University, and United Nations Special Rapporteur in "the situation of human rights in the Palestinian territories occupied since 1967."

*"Frank Bognar gives us a necklace of warm, wryly told family anecdotes with insights into a national history approaching nuclear midnight. He takes us through his heartfelt prayer for John Kennedy in the Cuban Missile crisis, a struggle to conscientious objection to the Vietnam war, and despair at changing the world until his turn toward a nuclear-weapons-free horizon. This is a memoir full of grace pushing back the darkness."*

James W. Douglass
Author of *Lightning East to West: Jesus, Gandhi, and the Nuclear Age* and *JFK and the Unspeakable: Why He Died and Why It Matters.*

# A GREAT FLASH OF LIGHT

One American's Journey Across the Nuclear Age

A Memoir Illuminating a Path to World Peace

Frank C. Bognar

Copyright © 2021 by Frank C. Bognar

All rights reserved. No part of this book may be reproduced or distributed in any form without written permission, except as permitted under copyright law for brief quotations embodied in articles and reviews.

ISBN 978-1-7372260-0-0 (paperback)
ISBN 978-1-7372260-1-7 (e-book)

Library of Congress Control Number: 2021910926

This book is a memoir. It reflects the author's present recollections of experiences over time. Some names and characteristics have been changed, some events have been compressed, and some dialogue has been recreated.

Cover design: Sandy Jones
Editor: Debbie Jenae
Digital Content Editor: Sean Hirshberg

Scripture quotes courtesy of the *New American Bible, revised edition* © 2010, Confraternity of Christian Doctrine, Washington, D. C. and are used by permission of the copyright owner. Accessed via https://www.biblegateway.com, October 4, 2021,

Photographs courtesy of the author unless otherwise indicated in the caption.

Printed in the United States of America.

10 9 8 7 6 5 4 3 2 1
First Edition

Published by Frank C. Bognar

Visit www.greatflashoflight.com

Dedicated to Max, Nathan, and Hayden,

to their generation,

and to generations yet unborn.

*Everything now depends on man: immense power of destruction is given into his hand, and the question is whether he can resist the will to use it, and can temper his will with the spirit of love and wisdom.*[1]

Carl G. Jung

*I can't believe that this world can go beyond our generation and on down to succeeding generations with this kind of weapon on both sides poised at each other without someday some fool or some maniac or some accident triggering the kind of war that is the end of the line for all of us.*[2]

President Ronald Reagan

*Our problems are manmade--therefore, they can be solved by man. . . . No problem of human destiny is beyond human beings.*[3]

JFK

*Never doubt that a small group of thoughtful, committed citizens can change the world; indeed, it is the only thing that ever has.*

Source unknown, but often attributed to Margaret Mead

# Contents

Introduction ............................................................... 1
Genie ......................................................................... 5
1  Roots ................................................................... 9
2  When Johnny Comes Marching Home ...................... 19
3  Journey to the Promised Land ............................ 29
4  Hunkering Down ................................................ 37
5  Bucket Duty ....................................................... 41
6  Day of Rest ........................................................ 45
7  St. Agatha's ....................................................... 53
8  God Bless America! ............................................ 59
9  Spring and the Return of Thomas ....................... 63
10 Television .......................................................... 69
11 The High Room .................................................. 73
12 Brylcreem and Bandstand .................................. 83
13 A Tremendous Flash of Light .............................. 89
14 A Prayer for John Kennedy ................................. 95
15 Great Trouble ..................................................... 99
16 At the Brink ....................................................... 107
17 Moses ................................................................ 119
18 Searching for Wonders Hall ............................... 125
19 A Giant Flying Saucer ....................................... 129
20 Finding My Way ................................................. 139

| 21 | Change of Direction | 145 |
| 22 | A Square Peg | 149 |
| 23 | Close Call | 155 |
| 24 | Miracle | 159 |
| 25 | Crucible | 165 |
| 26 | Land of the Beast | 175 |
| 27 | Years Go By | 187 |
| 28 | Wake Up Call | 197 |
| 29 | A Great Flash of Light | 201 |
| 30 | Epilogue | 205 |

Starting Points .................................................................215

    100 Ideas for Creating a More Peaceful World..........217

    Organizations and Links ...............................................220

    Ten Lessons You Should Learn About
    Nuclear Weapons ..........................................................222

    Treaty on the Prohibition of Nuclear Weapons .........224

    Nuclear Abolition: The Road from Armageddon
    to Transformation ..........................................................234

    President John F. Kennedy Commencement
    Address At American University .................................248

Notes.................................................................................259

Sources Consulted / Further Reading..............................267

Acknowledgments ............................................................271

About the Author..............................................................275

*I have set before you life and death, the blessing and the curse.
Choose life, then, that you and your descendants may live.*

Deuteronomy 30:19

# A GREAT FLASH OF LIGHT

# Introduction

**ON AN EARLY** Sunday morning, a dozen years ago, I sat in a restaurant booth waiting for my breakfast order. I felt a gentle but firm nudge from within that directed me: Write this down. I didn't know what I was supposed to write, only that it seemed important. Having a pen with me but no paper, I pulled a paper napkin from its holder and wrote down these four words: *Citizens of the Earth*.

From those words, over the next months and eventually into years, came a flow of long forgotten memories centered around an abundant life with a loving Catholic family, sibling rivalries, touching moments, and laugh-out-loud antics. But along with the memories came other scattered thoughts, words, and images from life beyond the family—news from Washington and around the world. Sometimes they were serious, other times inspiring, and occasionally even funny—all of this was a strange mix of a compelling brew.

As I followed my normal daily routine, I took a pen and small notepad wherever I went, scribbling down whatever thoughts came to the surface of my consciousness. I might write down two or three ideas one day, and then nothing for weeks at a time. I had no idea what all this meant or where it was going.

As the world continued its journey well into the twenty-first century, 24/7 news reported troubling environmental developments about melting polar ice caps and global warming, and a frightening escalation of shootings and bombings breaking out everywhere in our country—night clubs, theaters, high schools and even a grade school.

Abroad, attacks occurred in marketplaces and village squares. Missiles flew in the nighttime skies over the Mideast taking both military and civilian lives. This acceleration of madness was, like climate change, becoming a mega-issue. From my life experience, I knew enough about history, world wars, the Cuban Missile Crisis, and Vietnam that this alarming trend needed to be taken seriously. Unchecked violence taken to its extreme—organization against organization, country against country—could result in a nuclear exchange that would threaten our global environment and our very lives on earth.

I saw then, as I see more clearly now, that humanity needs to address two of the most urgent and overriding environmental dangers: global warming and a nuclear catastrophe. The latter could be brought on by miscalculation, accident, war, or even domestic violence. While the public seems to be finally awakening to the need to address the man-made factors affecting our climate, that same public seems to know far less about the environmental impact of a nuclear event.

In the early 1980s, Jonathan Schell, the author of the book, *The Fate of the Earth and The Abolition* noted: "A whole generation came of age lacking even rudimentary information regarding nuclear arms and nuclear peril."[4]

His point was brought home to me one day when I stopped by my favorite diner for lunch. A waitress, who was working her way through college, showed me to a booth, handed me a menu, and poured me a cup of coffee.

"What are you reading?" she asked, noting the book I had with me.

"It's John Hersey's *Here to Stay*," I answered.

In his book, Hersey, who had witnessed some of the worst of the world war in the Pacific and the aftermath of the bombing of Hiroshima, warned that for humanity to survive and flourish, it is essential that we take time to learn the crucial lessons of history: "Our only hope is memory," he wrote. "We need to remember the Holocaust; we must remind ourselves of what Hitler stood for; we must not forget Hiroshima."[5]

She read the passage and left me stunned with her response.

"What's Hiroshima?"

## Introduction

I had no idea how I might remind us all, especially a new generation of concerned citizens around the globe, of the consequences that a nuclear exchange could unleash. I went on to recall the encouraging words of Herman Wouk in his magnificent book, *The Winds of War*: "...the most insignificant writer," he wrote, "can serve peace, where the most powerful tribunals can do nothing."[6]

The answer to my writing task lay in the notes I recorded meticulously over the years. As I organized the material, an important story unfolded at a level deeper than the memories of my youth and everyday life. This developing story was building and gaining a perspective from two confluent realities: my everyday life and my experience of what is commonly known as "living under the shadow of the bomb."

*A Great Flash of Light* is the story of how the nuclear age began, how it evolved, and how this nuclear peril has become the most urgent threat to all people around the globe. And most importantly, this is the story of what we can do to eliminate this environmental danger, a hope rooted in a fundamental truth:

We have the power within us to bring about the vital changes needed to save our world and all who live on it.

Frank C. Bognar<br>
Ventura, CA<br>
October 15, 2021

# Genie

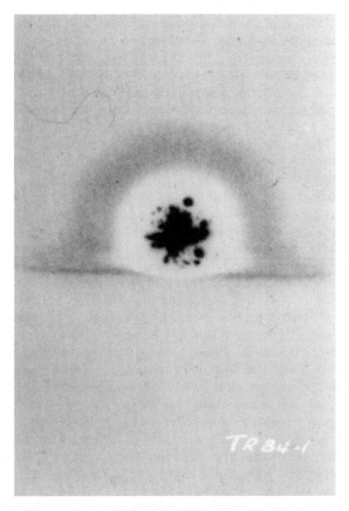

Fig. 1. First Image of the Explosion of the Atomic Bomb,
The Moment of Birth of the Nuclear Age.
(Photo courtesy of National Archives. Photo 434-RF-12A-TR-84-1-5.jpeg)

## A Great Flash of Light

> *...perhaps the genie is out of the bottle and we will not ever get him back in again.*[7]
>
> JFK, May 8, 1963, News Conference

**AT 5:29:45 A.M.**, on the pre-dawn morning of July 16, 1945, the United States of America detonated the world's first atomic bomb.

The place chosen for the test was a godforsaken hundred-mile stretch of New Mexico desert, where the terrain was so stark and noon day heat so oppressive, that centuries earlier, Spanish conquistadors named the trail *Jornada del Muerto*: the Journey of the Dead Man or the Journey of Death. The explosion might be so great that the Army found it necessary to position fifty cameras more than five miles away to record the event.[8]

In bunkers thousands of meters from ground zero, scientists and soldiers alike, wearing welder goggles and waiting in dread, hunkered down in trenches to witness what could be a cataclysmic event. No one knew the enormity of what might happen if or when they split the atom, and that included the theoretical possibility that the entire physical universe could implode on itself.

A strident warning siren wailed in the dark and their anxiety reached a peak as the final countdown 5. . . 4. . . 3. . . 2. . . ground to a halt. Then observers felt a tremendous shockwave that slammed above them, around them, by them, and through them. Looking toward the blast, they witnessed the formation of a massive mushroom cloud which, at the point of detonation, generated heat greater than that on the surface of the sun. Billowing upward in colors of orange, black, violet, purple and gold, some said the rising cloud was beyond the words of poets to describe. Others said it was entering the realm of the gods, and still others said it was like witnessing the end of the world.[9]

The world-renowned physicist, Dr. Albert Einstein, later wrote of this moment: "The unleashed power of the atom has changed everything except our modes of thinking and we thus drift toward unparalleled catastrophe."[10]

Humanity had released an unknown Genie out of the bottle. Once freed from its confines and fueled by humanity's fear, ignorance, greed, and hate, this unfathomable power of darkness was now free to move about as it liked, finding its way to the councils of power where it entered into the hearts and minds of men, inviting them to create diabolic devilry on the global stage. Powerful world leaders would seek to possess this ultimate weapon; aspiring leaders soon followed.

The allure of the atomic bomb lay in its promise to provide a country with ultimate national security from its enemies. No country would dare consider an attack on another that possessed a weapon with such destructive power. This mindset triggered into motion a giant arms race among modern, post-World War II countries. They developed atomic bombs, followed by much more destructive hydrogen bombs, and built guided missile systems to deliver them on their enemies and, if need be, entire civilizations. This nuclear arms buildup became the very cornerstone of the international order of our present day, upon which our future and that of all life on earth rests.

Notwithstanding all that was to come, some witnesses to this July morning felt a deep sense of foreboding that the control of this awesome power might stay just beyond humanity's reach. Might this bomb even turn on its creators and bring a final fire to the earth? That question was relegated to academic status for some future generation to resolve, because the terrifying cloud of atomic fire was already billowing high into the dawning New Mexico sky, giving proof to the morning, and to the ages, that the Genie was out of the bottle and the nuclear age was born.

Chapter 1

# Roots

*Stories are for joining the past to the future. ...Stories are for eternity, when memory is erased, when there is nothing to remember except the story.* [11]

Tim O'Brien

**I WAS BORN** on January 19, 1946, six months after the detonation of the first atomic bomb and five months after the bomb was dropped on Hiroshima at the end of the Second World War. My birthdate places me among the baby boomers, the first generation in history to be born into the nuclear age and live under the terror of "the bomb."

When I arrived, my father beamed with pride at

Fig. 2. My mother said I was the most beautiful baby in the whole wide world.

the birth of a fourth son, and my mother said I was the most beautiful baby in the whole world. Considering there were billions of kids, it was quite an honor. Life was totally open and it looked like nothing but smooth sailing ahead. However, I sensed early on that my ten-year-old brother, Thomas, maybe didn't experience the same deep joy that my parents felt upon my arrival. His new job was to look after me, mom's little trooper, to make sure I didn't get into trouble. I soon realized that none of my five siblings fully appreciated the family's new addition.

My sisters, Margaret and Virginia, both in their teens when I came along, teased me with verbal inflections that only teenage girls can do justice: "Isn't Francis a girl's name?" Occasionally, they tried to boss me around like they were my mother. My three brothers, Peter, George and Tom, were more interested in running through the house as junior detectives solving imaginary crimes they had seen at the movies or heard on the radio. But I'm getting ahead of my story.

---

I was born into a devout Catholic family, the sixth and last child of Peter and Vera Bognar. My mom and dad were immigrants, both from small villages in Hungary, with mom's village a stone's throw from Budapest.

In a world of cell phones, text messaging, and social media, it's hard to imagine my parents living in a time ruled by old world monarchs. History books are filled with photos of kings and kaisers, archdukes and czars posing stiffly with mustaches waxed and uniforms covered with medals and gold braids. They wore helmets adorned with eagles and colorful plumes. Black and white newsreels of the day show them inspecting their troops before staged war games and parading on horseback to cheers from an adoring public. All of this pageantry provided reassuring evidence that their present world order was stable, unshakable, and would live on into the future. Royal subjects obeyed their rulers without question, performed their military duty, and placed their individual destinies, as well as their country's fate, into their monarch's hands. In doing so, the incoming 20th century was undoubtedly destined to be bright.

Unfortunately, things didn't turn out that way. Through their collective arrogance, ignorance, and miscalculations, these same monarchs convinced their subjects to succumb to the allure of war. For the first time, entire civilizations hurled everything they had against one another, destroyed the very order they sought to preserve, and ultimately plunged the entire European continent into a cataclysmic convulsion known as the First World War.

Fortunately, as children, both of my parents had already left Europe with their respective families and came to America prior to the war's outbreak. I only recall hearing two stories about their ocean crossings to America, both from my mother. She, her mother, and sisters left their village riding on a horse drawn cart. A second memory was of her riding on the ship's deck, when passengers were told that they could see two continents at one time—on one side they could see Europe, on the other Africa. My guess is that they were passing through the Straits of Gibraltar as their ship made its way to the Atlantic.

Both families, independent of one another, arrived around the time the magnificent ship, R.M.S. *Titanic*, sunk slowly into the icy black waters off Newfoundland into her deep, silent Atlantic grave. Filled with reverence and awe, they sailed by the magnificent Statue of Liberty in New York Harbor, the very symbol of America, the land of freedom and opportunity. Like millions of others, they passed through the processing center at Ellis Island, barely glancing back at the Europe they had left behind. Filled with hope and high expectations, they gathered what they brought with them, moved through the gates, and on to life in this new world.

I gather my mother made the transition to American life without difficulty. She was an optimist, independent in her thinking, and grounded in what she thought was right—and that meant the new American way. Her sense of independence was evident even at the age of eleven when her family first arrived from Europe. Her parents, who only spoke Hungarian, gave her the task of enrolling herself and her three sisters in the local school. She went into town and visited both the Catholic and public schools. She didn't like the Catholic school, but to please her parents, enrolled her sisters there, while she signed herself up with the public school. As I understand it, her parents, who never learned to speak English, never discovered the discrepancy.

Fig. 3. My Father and Mother on their Wedding Day, 1923.

About ten years after arriving in this country, my parents, now in their early twenties, met in Pinckney, a little Michigan town near Ann Arbor. They fell in love and were married in 1923. As was the custom of the time, my father's role was to be the family's breadwinner, my mother's role was that of housewife and taking care of the home front.

Although they were very different from one another personality-wise, they were compatible. My father was a serious, but loving, deeply caring man especially for those most in need. His seriousness was offset by a playful sense of humor. My brothers have told me that he was, like fathers of that day, a strict disciplinarian. Inside the house, the rules were simple: "No running, no jumping, no horsing around." He also put a willow switch up on the wall as a reminder for my brothers to behave themselves. By the time I came around, he had mellowed a lot. I only remember one disciplinary incident involving me trying to kick down my brothers' bedroom door. Whereas my mom's thoughts and feelings were an open book, his were deep, tightly guarded, and rarely revealed. Although he never discussed it, I sensed there was a deep wound within him from the fractured family life of his youth. That wound, in turn, resulted in his commitment to provide for his family no matter the cost.

While my mother went to school through eighth grade, I don't know if my father went past the fourth. Nonetheless, he was always reading, eager to learn, and applying the knowledge. He wasn't content to stay at one job for any length of time and was always interested in taking on greater responsibilities. He moved upward from worker to foreman to plant supervisor. He had a simple formula. If he didn't know how to do something, he would find out how. That meant reading and improving every day. I think his deepest interest was in history, for which he had a voracious appetite, and one he passed along to me.

As a young man, he became interested in three of the exciting new trends of the "roaring twenties." The first was boxing. His hero was Jack Dempsey, the world's heavyweight champion. The second was riding his motorcycle at high speed. The third was the new and thrilling, but terribly dangerous, field of flying.

Fig. 4. As a young boy, I thought my father (*right*) bore a resemblance to his hero—the great Jack Dempsey. (Dempsey photo source unknown)

Even before Charles Lindbergh made his historic flight across the Atlantic, my dad took lessons in one of the primitive and flimsy "Jennys," an aircraft partially made of canvas and wire, which he said were often referred to as "flying caskets." Rightly so, as in the 1920s, deaths from flying were frequent. Yet, in an effort to show my mother how much fun it was to fly and how flying was getting safer, he invited her to go up on a short flight with him. Remarkably, she agreed to do so. Unfortunately, as she climbed to get into the plane, she was horrified to see that her high heeled shoe punctured the plane's canvas wing. She still went with him on the flight, but the experience did nothing to advance my dad's case that there was nothing to worry about, and he should continue flying.

The Jennys were open cockpit planes, which required that both pilot and passenger wear leather helmets and goggles. They communicated with one another by yelling over the deafening roar of the motor and the force of the wind. In those pioneer days of the 1920's, parachutes didn't open automatically. Parachuting safely to the ground required a number of carefully followed steps. First, it was imperative to summon all of one's courage to crawl out onto the wing. Once that was achieved, the next step was to hang onto the plane for dear life with one hand and wave the chute around with the other hand, in hopes that the onrushing wind would catch and take hold. If you were lucky enough for your chute to fill with air, you could then feel free to jump. Yet a successful jump was based on two pesky fundamental assumptions: first, sufficient time was needed to crawl out onto the wing. Second, the plane had to fly along smoothly enough for its wings to stay level.

Unfortunately, that was not the case after my father, a student pilot, and his instructor sped down a muddy runway. Once airborne and hundreds of feet into the air, a cable snapped, the plane spun out of control, and fell out of the sky. The duo crashed into an orchard below. The plane ended up in shambles. A photo of the event appeared on the front page of the local newspaper, which mistakenly reported that the pilot suffered bruises while my dad escaped injury. Actually, my father suffered severe bruises and a broken nose, and the pilot died sometime later from injuries resulting from the crash.

Fig. 5. My father's plane crash in 1926 as reported in local newspaper.

Shortly after, my mother offered my dad a choice: fly or stay married. "Choose one," she said. He decided to go with marriage.

My father's first job was at a steel mill shoveling coal into furnaces. It was backbreaking work with long hours in unbearable heat. Many workers couldn't stand the heat or keep up the pace, but dad managed to survive it all in order to put food on the table for his growing family. In the process, he became strong both physically and in character, which he would need in the 1920s and '30s when men were rough and fights were common. In boxing, those were the times of Jack Dempsey, Gene Tunney, and James J. Braddock, the famous Cinderella Man.

In 1929, the good times of the roaring 20s came to an end when the stock market crashed, and the country plunged into the Great Depression. Millions of men were suddenly unemployed and wound up standing in soup lines. My father, however, was fortunate enough to keep his job. The reason for his good fortune was that in the 1930s, Huey Long, the powerful Louisiana governor and political rival of President Franklin Roosevelt, courted manufacturers from the north to move to his state and set up factories there. My father, who had been promoted to management in a Detroit glass manufacturing company, was transferred as part of a team to set up a new operation in Louisiana's capital city, Baton Rouge. He knew the heat and humidity of the south was going to be uncomfortable, but he had no inkling of just how intense. He later described it by saying, "I stepped off the train and walked into an oven."

On the new home front in Louisiana, before I came along, my mom had her hands full with cooking, cleaning, washing, and ironing for a family of eight, including my dad's widowed father. She went about her tasks with a cheerful disposition and a bright outlook on life. Her child-raising philosophy was a balance of a warm heart, backed up, if needed, by a painless swat on our backsides with her wooden stirring spoon. If any of us fell and hurt ourselves, she stooped down and kissed the hurt saying, "All better!" and with a pat on the butt, sent us on our way. If we encountered a troubling problem as we grew older, her answer: "Say a little prayer."

Both my mother and father were as respectful of other religious traditions as they were of their own Catholic roots. I don't remember my father ever quoting scripture, and I only recall my mother quoting one, "Ask and you'll receive. Seek and you shall find." Although I didn't know it, the quote was from Matthew 7:7: *"Ask and it will be given to you; seek and you will find; knock and the door will be opened to you."* What she was saying was life requires that we continually ask, seek, and knock.

The kitchen was her domain with its pots, pans, and a heavy, black iron skillet. My father had a special love for her chicken *paprikash*, a red peppery Hungarian dish with fabulously textured dumplings covered with a sour cream sauce. The aromas that emanated from the kitchen came straight from heaven to cast a spell on family members who gravitated toward the stove only to be shooed away. As she brought her creamy creation to a mouthwatering perfection, my father would sneak up and give her a big bear hug along with a peck on the cheek, reminding her she was the best cook in the entire world. She would thank him and tell him to get out of the kitchen. He had to wait like everybody else.

Everyone had to scramble to find their places at our big dining room table. Once situated and hushed up, my father would begin the prayer. "Bless us O Lord, and these Thy gifts. . . ." Only then would mom go from place to place to fill our plates. If someone dared suggest that they didn't like what they were served, her old country school roots kicked in. She knew what it felt like to go hungry, and she minced no words. "You will eat it, and you will like it!" When I think about it, she may have been the *founder* of the old country school of thought. My brothers knew what I would later learn: with absolutely no remorse, our mom would plop a huge glob of mashed potatoes right on top of our peas, carrots, or whatever poor vegetable that had the misfortune of being in the wrong place at the wrong time. And she didn't much care whether red beet juice ran all over my plate and oozed into my mashed potatoes and gravy.

The world began to feel the economic depression as well, and in Germany, the Nazis exploited the poverty and discontentment of the unemployed and blamed the Jews for the terrible conditions. Disturbing reports of Jewish persecutions emerged from Germany, though the Nazis, hosting the 1936 Olympic Games in Berlin, went all out to assure the world that such news was simply not the case. There were other signs that international trouble was brewing. Japan abruptly left the League of Nations, refusing to abide by the league's international guidelines to prevent war. In Italy, fascists under dictator Mussolini, seized control of the country and began its rule with heavy-handed tactics. Fears spread throughout European capitals that diplomacy wasn't working, and that war could break out any time. In September 1939, those fears were realized, when Hitler savagely invaded Poland starting the Second World War.

As the decade of the 1940s began, Hitler continued his aggression by next attacking France. For many Americans, including my parents, the war was something they read about in the newspapers, a conflict on the other side of the Atlantic, and they felt America should stay out of it. They continued on with their normal routines of work, housekeeping, and school.

My father found himself working long hours as a plant supervisor. He always seemed to be on the job. Often, he would just get home, tired from a double shift, when the phone would ring calling him back to deal with another emergency. This non-stop pressure was getting old, but those calls kept coming and even more frequently when the world was turned upside down on the Sunday morning of December 7, 1941.

Chapter 2

# When Johnny Comes Marching Home

*My experience was the war. I can tell you about that.* [12]

JFK

*. . .there can be no world peace unless there is soul peace. World wars are only projections of the conflicts waged inside the souls of modern men, for nothing happens in the external world that has not first happened within a soul.* [13]

Bishop Fulton J. Sheen

Fig. 6. Baton Rouge home, circa 1940

**FIVE YEARS** before I was born, about the time of the attack on Pearl Harbor, our family lived in a fashionable section of Louisiana's capital city, Baton Rouge. Lovely homes on spacious lots with manicured yards dotted all along the winding Jefferson Highway. Our home also included a large, wooded area filled with ancient oak trees; their limbs draped with fine Spanish moss. A charming little brook ran through it all.

My sisters, Margaret and Virginia, were attractive teen girls with dark brown hair and big brown eyes. In the long hairstyles of the forties, they would sometimes wear a flower in their hair which, from photos, had a lovely effect. My sisters went to school with books in hand, wearing convent uniforms of starched white blouses, skirts below the knee, and white socks. Occasionally, they were allowed to wear

Fig. 7. Wartime friends Margaret, Virginia, unidentified friend

the deep red lipstick popular at the time. Naturally, boys would stop by for a visit, but there was always an audience. My mother invited everyone to sit out on the front porch in full view and vulnerable to the taunts of my brothers.

My oldest sister, Margaret, who had fallen in love with a soldier stationed in Seattle, had already left home three years before my arrival. Despite my father's concern that she was too young to marry, he eventually gave in to her wishes and helped her with her luggage as she boarded a train bound to the northwest. She had never been away from home, and now, although scared to death, she stepped onto a wartime train filled with soldiers and sailors for a four day and night journey to Washington state. She was too upset to eat and couldn't sleep from the lurching back and forth as she traveled along the winding tracks across America. Servicemen, as exhausted as she was, were heading off to war, but gave up their seats and slept standing, so she could sit.

My second sister, Virginia, was also a teen bride. Unlike Margaret, Virginia remained at home following her wedding in 1943. Her husband, John, enlisted in the Navy shortly after Pearl Harbor. Following boot camp in San Diego, he trained as a medical corpsman, and then was assigned to the Marines. John shipped out to serve in the 1st Marine Air Division that joined in the heavy combat in the Pacific. He arrived at Guadalcanal just as the Americans launched their first counter-offensive against the Japanese. Immediately thrust into battle, John found himself on the ground attending to the dozens of wounded around him, while keep-

Fig. 8. My sister Virginia and her husband, John: Wartime bride and groom.

ing an eye out for Japanese planes circling above for another attempt to strafe American troops with machine gun fire. At the same time Japanese planes were bombing American ships in the harbor.

Fig. 9. JFK and Crew, Pacific Theater (Corbis Historical/Getty Images)

Fighting in the Pacific, in the area of Tulagi and the Solomon Islands, was future president, John F. Kennedy. As a junior grade officer and PT boat commander, Kennedy suffered a back injury when his craft, the PT109, was rammed and sunk by a Japanese destroyer. Stranded on a small island behind enemy lines, Kennedy managed to keep his crew alive until they were rescued by American forces and returned to safe port. His injury was severe, and he rotated back to the states and was discharged from the service. When Kennedy received a commendation for his courage in saving his men, he was interviewed by a young journalist, John Hersey. Kennedy's story of heroism, adversity, and survival was told in Hersey's book, *Here to Stay*.[14] The journalist and the young war hero went on to become friends and later, in fact, became rivals for the affections of the same woman.[15]

While Kennedy was fortunate enough to survive the war, and return home to a well-deserved hero's welcome, Virginia's husband, John, remained in harm's way. As the battles dragged on into 1944, his letters to Virginia conveyed a deepening desire for the war to end, and a longing to return home to his bride and start a family. Virginia awoke every morning worrying about John and his safety. She lived with the constant stabs of fear, that maybe, at that very moment, he could be suffering some terrible fate. She pushed such thoughts from her mind, only to have them return minute by minute, hour by hour. This cycle of mental anguish never left, save minor moments of reprieve when a letter from him arrived. Then, the anxiety returned, as her mind gave way to a new fear. Did something happen to him after he had written this last letter?

My three brothers, George, Tom and Peter, had very different personalities. Peter, the oldest at age 11, was tall and lean, with an imagination bursting with detective plots from radio programs like the *Green Hornet*. From a single episode, he could produce adventures for the crime-solving trio to roam with abandon across the wooded acreage behind our parent's house. There was one exception. They always had to be alert to the rattling sound of a snake lying hidden in the grass and leaves. George, the second oldest at 9, was the easy-going one of the three. He was ready to follow his older brother's lead on whatever adventure Peter cooked up next.

Fig. 10. My brothers George (*left*), Thomas, and Peter playing in the baking 1940 Louisiana sun.

And then there was eight-year-old Thomas, the youngest and busiest of my brothers. He shared dad's interest in mechanics and electronics, and was forever messing around with wires, batteries, and gadgets.

In 1945, the United States was in the final stages of a world war that had raged on for four years. Like women across the country, my mother went to the grocery store and used her war ration card to buy lard, oleo, some coffee, and a little sugar—all items scarce because of the war effort. Likewise, my father used his gas rationing card for the small amounts of gasoline available stateside.

My father served as an air raid warden during the war. When warning sirens blared, military planes took to the air and flew over the state's capital to see if any lights below could tip off an enemy to bomb a populated area. On the ground, my father, along with other wardens, rode his motorcycle through the city's neighborhoods to make sure homeowners had covered their windows during the blackouts.

A strike by the Nazis was no idle threat. My father came home from work on more than one occasion with the news that Nazi submarines had sunk yet another company ship delivering its cargo off the Gulf of Mexico. Our family folklore includes an intriguing story of a man and woman arrested as German spies in a spacious home only two doors down from our house. I had thought the story was the result of one of Peter's flights of imagination. Now, after the release of highly confidential war documents that revealed how active Nazi submarines were in the Gulf, sinking seventy American ships, I am not so sure.

We were a Catholic family based firmly in the belief that God is personal and loving, and cares deeply about our welfare. Prayer was a way to place our needs and problems before Him and ask for help. Accordingly, our custom was to pray the rosary together every evening. At 7:00 p.m., after all the dinner dishes were stacked and put away, the family gathered together. My dad turned off the radio, dimmed the lights, and lit a small votive candle. Everyone had a set of rosary beads and knelt down. With the candle flickering lightly in the calm of the evening, the family recited the Apostles' Creed together: "We believe in God, the Father almighty, creator of heaven and earth." Then the repetition and rhythm of the Our Father had a quieting effect, "Thy kingdom come, Thy will be done on earth as it is in heaven."

Before each decade of the rosary, we recited our intentions. Each night, the first intention asked that Margaret and Virginia's husbands would return home safely from the war. In her heart, Virginia prayed that she would not be the next bride to go into mourning after receiving a visitor in uniform with a telegram that read, "We regret to inform you. . . ."

What my family didn't know in 1945 was that the United States and Nazi Germany had been in a race against one another for years. Each side worked day and night to be the first to have a super bomb that would determine who would win the war. Leo Szilard, a Hungarian physicist who had escaped from Nazi Germany, was alarmed that the Nazis might be on the verge of splitting the atom. Szilard persuaded Dr. Albert Einstein, the renowned physicist, to warn President Franklin Roosevelt that if the Nazis were successful, they would surge ahead of the Americans in the development of a super bomb. President Roosevelt received the recommendation and authorized the army to proceed with the top-secret uranium initiative later known as the "Manhattan Project." The race against the Nazis was on.

In that same year, a string of historic events took place in rapid succession. On April 12th, radios across the country broadcast the news that President Roosevelt had died of a stroke. The man whose strong, confident, and reassuring voice led America through the Great Depression and the Second World War was silent. The nation was plunged into deep mourning. Only a few weeks later, Hitler, with his enemies only a few hundred yards away, put a gun to his head and committed suicide in his bunker. The shrieks of the madman were at last stilled by his own hand. In the Pacific, however, the war with Japan raged on with terrible consequences for both sides.

In July 1945, the atomic bomb was scheduled for detonation in the New Mexico desert. There were unknown dangers with the project. Chief among them was that no one knew what would actually happen when the atom, the basic building block of the physical universe, was split. Could it be so powerful that it might implode the entire atmosphere of the earth? Could it even result in a chain reaction that would cause the entire physical universe to detonate? There was also the question of what would happen if the bomb didn't detonate, and the Nazis were successful in splitting the atom. Any moral reservations about killing thousands of innocent civilians with one bomb would have to be considered when the business of war was over.

The team of top-secret American scientists and military personnel assembled in the predawn hours of July 16, 1945. Dr. Robert Oppenheimer, the noted physicist who took on the intense, relentless pressures of overseeing the project, was reaching an emotional breaking point. Pacing back and forth in the desert mud, chain smoking cigarette after cigarette, Oppenheimer knew there was no turning back. No matter the unknowns, nor the universal risks and potential consequences, the bomb's moment in history had arrived. He and his team took their places in a bomb shelter, put on their goggles, and braced themselves for impact. The countdown began and the detonation was activated. One observer described:

> Suddenly, there was an enormous flash of light, the brightest light I have ever seen or that I think anyone has ever seen. It blasted; it pounced; it bored its way right through you. It was a vision which was seen with more than the eye. It was seen to last forever. You would wish it would stop; altogether it lasted about two seconds. [16]

Oppenheimer and his staff were witnessing the terrifying birth of the nuclear age. Looking directly at the brilliant light of the blast, the physicist intuitively began to grasp the implications of the threat the atomic bomb would pose for the future of the human race. He recalled a line from a Hindu text of the Bhagavad-Gita: "Now I am become Death, the destroyer of worlds." [17]

After the war, Oppenheimer elaborated about his initial reaction to the detonation:

> When it went off, in the New Mexico dawn, that first atomic bomb, we thought of Alfred Nobel, and his hope, his vain hope, that dynamite would put an end to wars. We thought of the legend of Prometheus, of that deep sense of guilt in man's new powers, that reflects his recognition of evil, and his long knowledge of it. We knew that it was a new world... [18]

News of the bomb's successful detonation was forwarded to the new American President, Harry Truman, who, unlike Oppenheimer, was jubilant at hearing the news.

Hitler was defeated, but the Japanese continued to fight on fiercely. Progress for the Allies was slow and bloody. My brother-in-law, John, was assigned to the assault force preparing for the invasion of Okinawa and the final invasion of Japan, but his letters stopped coming. In Washington, advisors to the newly sworn in President recommended the use of the atomic bomb to avoid the loss of hundreds of thousands of American lives in an all-out invasion of Japan. On August 6, 1945, in a radio broadcast to the nation, Truman announced that the United States had dropped an atomic bomb on Hiroshima.

A few days later, following the Japanese continued refusal to surrender, Truman ordered a second bomb dropped on Nagasaki. Japan surrendered, bringing an end to the terrible world war.

Our family, like families everywhere, was ecstatic over the surrender as they celebrated Victory over Japan Day. Then, slowly, the giant American war machine began to reverse itself, as soldiers and sailors came pouring back home from Europe and the Pacific. Margaret's husband had made it home safely. Now, every night when the family prayed the rosary, the primary intention was for John's safe return.

As afternoon faded into evening on the day of his expected return, there was a knock on the door. Inside, my brothers were on the floor squabbling over a game, while my parents were talking at the kitchen table. Virginia, whose heart was racing, quickly glanced at her hair in the hall mirror as she flew by to answer the door. My brothers dropped what they were doing, and my mom and dad came out of the kitchen.

My sister, who had prayed so long and fervently for her husband's safe return, suddenly stopped at the front door. This was the moment she had been waiting for. She took a deep breath, and opened the door to find, not a naval messenger with a "we regret to inform you," but her husband John.

Dropping his duffel bag, John lifted Virginia off her feet and twirled her around in an embrace of pure joy and immense relief. My brothers moved in on him with an avalanche of questions, pulls, and poundings. My father waded through his noisy, jumping, clinging sons. He looked with pride at his young son-in-law who had served his country against one of its most dangerous enemies and shook his hand firmly: "Welcome home."

"Welcome home," two simple words that perhaps express the most joyful heartfelt feelings of the human experience. In 1945, those simple words were those which wives, mothers, and fathers around the world prayed with heart and soul that they would be able to say to their returning husbands and sons. Millions, in deep sorrow, never got the chance. Never again should the world ever have to endure the suffering and sorrow of a world war.

Despite her best efforts to not cry, when it was my mother's turn to hug John, she burst into tears at seeing how his uniform hung on him, showing how much weight he had lost. He was a shell of the strong, young man who went off to war. But that didn't matter now, she reminded herself, because she and Virginia would prepare home cooked meals that would help him regain his weight and strength. What mattered was that he was home.

In the days that followed, my brothers peppered him with questions about what it was like to be a marine in the Pacific. He told them about living on a ship with a thousand other men, as it zigzagged its way across the ocean to avoid enemy torpedoes. He told them about a beautiful island in the Pacific with tall coconut palm trees swaying in tropical breezes, lush vegetation laced with vibrantly colored flowers, a stream of cascading crystal-clear water, and all of it surrounded by the blue expanse of the Pacific Ocean.

For our family, the scourge of the Second World War, the cataclysmic nightmare of the twentieth century, was over. The brutal dictators—Hitler, Mussolini, and Tojo—were all dead. After all the suffering and grief and sorrow, people all over the world finally breathed a sigh of relief. There would be no bombing raid alerts in the night; no more sons and husbands going off to war; no more dread about letters; and no visits from the War Department bringing shattering news. Soldiers and sailors throughout the world continued to return home in vast numbers. They marched in victory parades, with bands playing, and blizzards of ticker tape falling from the sky on Generals MacArthur, Eisenhower, and Patton. Germany and Japan were finally and totally defeated. The United States, the force for good, had triumphed over the forces of evil. Moreover, America was the sole possessor of the atomic bomb, which meant the world was safe and at peace, and our family was getting back to normal. That, seemingly, was the legacy of 1945.

Only, that isn't the way it turned out at all—not for our family, not for our country, not for the world. What lay ahead was beyond anyone's imagination, as our family was about to find out.

Chapter 3

# Journey to the Promised Land

**WHEN THE OUTCOME** of the world war seemed assured, leaders from the United States, the Soviet Union, Great Britain, and their allies met in San Francisco to establish a new post war organization dedicated to achieving world peace: The United Nations. Its charter was based on the dignity of each individual person and to "save succeeding generations from the scourge of war."[19] Despite these noble aspirations, it was becoming evident that enormous difficulties were besetting the new organization at its very inception—at least to one 28-year-old newspaper reporter and war hero, John F. Kennedy.

Kennedy had been hired by the *Chicago Herald-American* to report on the establishment of this new peace organization from the vantage of someone who served in the war. Kennedy reported early on that there were huge obstacles thwarting any progress, brought on by "deep disagreements among its members. . ."[20]

> We must face the truth that the people have not been horrified by war to a sufficient extent to force them to go to any extent rather than have another war. . . War will exist until that distant day when the conscientious

objector enjoys the same reputation and prestige that the warrior does today. [21]

It is unfortunate that unity for war against a common aggressor is far easier to obtain than unity for peace. [22]

Western diplomats found it hard to understand the mysterious and secretive ways of ambassadors from the Soviet Union. The Soviet dictator, Stalin, who was not attending the conference, was pulling strings from Moscow to obstruct everything the allies were hoping to accomplish. For Americans, Stalin, who had murdered millions of his people, was fast becoming Hitler's successor as America's number one enemy. He was the one who now had the intention to rule the world. The American answer to Stalin's plan of world domination was that it wasn't going to happen, not while America had the bomb.

In Chicago, atomic scientists concerned about the threat to humanity brought on by the existence of the bomb, established a bulletin that would report on the urgency of that danger. In the process, they designed what was to be known as the *Doomsday Clock*. The hand of the clock could be moved forward or back from midnight—the moment when humanity would be consumed by nuclear destruction. Given the state of the world, the clock was first set at seven minutes to midnight.

This international concern was far removed from the life of ordinary Americans who simply wanted to forget the war and get on with life. The traumas of the Great Depression and the Second World War were finally behind us. It would take a while, but the manufacturing changeover back to peacetime production would result in a never-before-seen number of products rolling off the assembly lines: refrigerators, washers and dryers, televisions, and the fast new cars from Detroit in *your* driveway—perfect for the new homes being constructed all over the country. Americans focused on a return to pre-war normalcy and its optimism became the foundation for a new standard of living.

By this time, my dad was tired of his job, of always being on call, and after fifteen years of the heat and humidity of the south, he wanted to move the family back to Michigan and a cooler climate.

And, after working for one company for a huge part of his life, he wanted to be his own boss.

My mother was torn. Moving back to the north would allow her to once again live closer to her sisters, but it also meant leaving behind good friends, her lovely home, and a comfortable way of life. In the end, she felt it was her responsibility to follow her husband. When he talked about buying a farm, she believed that, although he didn't know anything about farming, he would do what he always did: read up on it, learn how to do it, and just make it happen.

And so, after weeks of talking about it, my parents sold their home, bought a farm, tractors, and all the pieces of machinery to make a go of it—all of which required a major part of their savings.

According to family folklore, the transition from Louisiana required several separate moves. My dad was the first to begin the trip. With a new sense of freedom that came from leaving his job behind, he rode his motorcycle 1,200 miles to Michigan to get things started. The rest of the family would follow. With me as an infant in her arms, my mother traveled by train, while my sister Margaret, her husband Ray, and my three brothers came up later.

Cars and trucks were almost impossible to get because of the war, as were tires because of a rubber shortage. My dad managed to find a 1934 truck to transport Virginia, John, their one-year-old baby, and all the family's furniture and household goods.

For those of us who rode by motorcycle, train, and car, we suffered no mishaps. It wasn't the same for the threesome riding in the thirteen-year-old truck. It had no accessories, the seat had no padding, and there were no shocks to keep riders from jarring back and forth like they were riding through the Rockies in a stagecoach.

My dad gave the truck a tune-up as best he could in preparation for the trip. The brakes were in bad shape, so he tightened them as much as possible. Gasoline was still scarce from the war effort, so my father and John bought and stored cans of gas over many weeks and then filled a fifty-gallon drum that they secured on the back of the truck. When John needed fuel on the trip, he could take a hose and siphon the gas from the drum into the gas tank.

When the trip day arrived, John got up before dawn to avoid the steamy heat. With the help of a neighbor, they loaded the refrigerator, stove, beds, and chest of drawers alongside the fifty-gallon gas drum loaded the day before. As dawn broke, John carefully placed the smaller furniture items in the truck along with framed pictures, books, tools, and boxes of clothes and other articles. Finally, between some blankets and a mattress, he tucked my brothers' baseball bats and gloves, and a well-worn football—a reminder going back to the 1920s and the days of the Four Horsemen of Notre Dame. That was it; they had a full load.

Fig. 11. The Greatest Generation

John pulled the ropes one last time to make sure the cargo was tightly secured. Jumping down from the truck, he carefully re-checked each tire. After the brakes, the tires were his main concern, and rightfully so. Blowouts were commonplace, even with good tires on level ground. They would be going up narrow mountain roads with patched up tires in poor condition. All were balding—but that's what was available at war's end. As for the brakes, John knew that as much as my father had tried to tighten them, they too were well worn. Questionable brakes, frayed tires, a fifty-gallon drum filled with gasoline—what could possibly go wrong?

It was time to go. John climbed up into the cab and slid behind the large steering wheel that he would grip for well over a thousand miles. With Virginia sitting beside him and their baby in her lap, he tried to start the truck. It showed no interest in kicking over on this first try. He let it settle for a bit, and then, after pulling on the choke, he tried again. The motor refused to turn once again, this time groaning as if to say, "Leave me alone!" The truck was in no mood to start on any long, ponderous, and hazardous journey. With John's third attempt, though, following considerable coaxing, "C'mon, c'mon, c'mon!" the truck relented, and the motor turned over with a loud bang and a healthy roar.

The young couple knew the challenge ahead, yet they were excited about this new phase of their lives. After adjusting the mirrors, John released the brake and pushed down on the gas pedal as he let out the clutch. The truck lurched forward, and they slowly began their long journey north. On the seat beside them was a large bag containing peanut butter and jelly sandwiches, apples and pears, baby food and bottles, and a large thermos of coffee. They had scraped together a few dollars, which they would use sparingly.

They headed out from the familiar streets of the capitol city as the sun appeared on the horizon. Yet, all around the skies were overcast with the promise of rain. With windshield wipers flapping slowly from the mist, they drove eastward to Hammond, where the drizzle diminished, and the hot Louisiana sun asserted itself on the morning. They turned northward onto a two-lane road and brought their speed up to a modest 35 to 40 miles per hour. John was careful to keep an eye out for deep potholes scattered along the road. As morning changed to noon, they crossed over the state line into the flatlands of Mississippi, and well into the day, they passed Jackson with its capital dome jutting out into the sky. After many more hours of careening back and forth, they reached the northern part of Mississippi where, tired to the bone, they pulled off to the side of the road for a few hours of sleep. They had driven almost 370 hard miles and, with each one, they left behind not only the flatlands, bayous, and Spanish moss of Louisiana, but all in life that was familiar to them. As the sun sank into the west and put an end to the first day of their journey, they knew that their next day's drive up the higher mountains of Tennessee, would bring new challenges. But they would worry about that tomorrow.

The two awoke the next morning stiff, achy, and with cricks in their necks from sleeping in the cramped confines of the truck. They climbed out with a couple of moans and a good stretch to find a suitable restroom facility among the tall weeds at the side of the road. John then used his Navy skills to perform his morning inspection of the truck. He checked the cargo to see that it remained secured. He made sure the radiator had enough water to avoid overheating, and the dipstick indicated they were not leaking oil. He siphoned gas from the drum to fill the gas tank and, once again, did an overall check of the tires. Their condition now worried him most, but so far so good.

Starting the truck and shifting it into first gear, he realized that the trip was going to take longer and be more difficult than he originally thought. They had made a good but modest start, but the tough part was coming up. The truck strained more as they continued over alternating rolling hills and small mountains. As their speed slowed on the inclines, John was forced to downshift the stick shift to lower gears, slowing them to a crawl. A half dozen impatient locals, backed up in pickups and cars behind them, honked mercilessly, until they got their chance to zoom past at racecar speeds while wishing them hearty holiday greetings. The miles and the hours came and went. One mountain replaced another, and then another, and still another. Days passed. John wondered if the brakes that seemed tight at the outset were giving way a bit—or was it his imagination?

They started up a final peak. After the truck strained its hardest to reach the summit, they stopped for a few moments to take in the panoramic view of the valley that lay ahead. Virginia's brown eyes grew bigger as she saw the road's curves, deep canyons, steep drop offs, and the law of gravity beckoning them with a sneer. She held her baby tighter. As they began their descent, they realized they now encountered an opposite, greater problem: how to spare the brakes around the narrow road's sharp curves without going over the side.

Moving downward John tried hard to slow the truck, but almost from the start it picked up speed faster than he liked. They careened down long stretches of road and met curves that were approaching all too quickly. They swerved this way and that; each bend seemed to bring them a step closer to disaster. The cargo in back—especially the gasoline drum—shifted and loosened, alarming them both, but they were helpless to do anything. John gripped the steering wheel tighter, as his eyes darted back and forth from the road to the speedometer. Forty miles per hour, far too fast for their threadbare tires. More potholes! The arrow on their speedometer was inching its way to the right. . . forty-two miles an hour. . . forty-three. . . forty-four!

Speeding downward, they approached a final series of hairpin curves. Road signs warned of another impending danger. Coming up was a low concrete overpass, so low that drivers were advised that some larger vehicles would not make it through. John had measured how high his cargo stood when he loaded the truck, and it exceeded the height allowed by the overpass. Their descent grew faster and faster, swerving around one curve then into another. John pumped the brakes repeatedly, as an arid smell from brakes far too hot filled the cab. Veering into the final turn, John saw the road turn straight. Hitting their top speed, he saw the low concrete span directly in front of them. They weren't going to make it! Virginia clutched her baby. John aimed at the center of the tunnel and said his last prayer. In the final second, he closed his eyes bracing himself for the slam into the concrete, the explosion of the gas tank, and the burst of flames that would reach high into the sky, consuming them all in a fiery death.

They shot under the overpass without a bump or scratch and roared onto the magnificent valley floor. They couldn't believe it! They were alive! They yelled and cheered in relief and disbelief. As the road leveled out, their speed slowed, and they were able to pull over to the side and come to a stop. Adrenalin pumping and out of breath, they jumped down from the cab. John climbed on the back of the truck and re-measured the height of the cargo. The load was inches less than the height of the low hanging overpass! Maneuvering the sharp curves and potholes along the way had shifted the furniture, forcing it to settle down, which enabled them to make it through with inches to spare.

They took time to put body and soul back together and climbed into their truck for the final stretch through the gentle hills of Indiana. They crossed over the state line into southern Michigan and continued northward to the "thumb." The state is shaped like a mitten, and the thumb is a fertile area where wheat, oats, barley, corn, and soybeans are raised among such little rural towns as Cass City, Caro, Owendale, and Sebewaing. They were headed to Gagetown, a small village overlooking the rich farmland of the Saginaw valley, or rather the new farm a few miles from the village.

Thanks to John's mastery of downshift driving and his liberal use of the emergency brake, they arrived safely. Within hours after pulling into the driveway of their destination, two of the tires sagged to their demise.

And so it was, at the end of a world war, a young couple in our family, members of what was later known as the "Greatest Generation," arrived in America's heartland. Perhaps it wasn't as inspiring as the Pilgrims' landing at Plymouth Rock, yet we all made it and in one piece. To this day, the trip to the land my father promised remains a heart-thumping story of inspiration and courage every time it's told at a family gathering and passed down to another generation.

Chapter 4

# Hunkering Down

**MY FATHER ARRIVED** at our new farm and immediately busied himself with inspecting and preparing the tractors and equipment he and his boys would be working with in the spring. He was clearly excited to make this change in his life.

When my mother walked into the old two-story farmhouse, her heart sank. No one had lived there in months. The kitchen had no running water and no cabinet space. A huge cast iron stove sat in the middle of the dining room, a coal bucket by its side. Its job was to heat the whole house in the winter that was about to come. The living room needed new wallpaper and its rug was frayed. She climbed the wooden and splintered stairs to see the drafty bedrooms that would house Virginia and John, my brothers, and our grandpa. There was no way the stove could adequately heat the upstairs.

Outside there was a scattering of buildings: a huge barn to house dairy cattle and store hay, a chicken coop, a garage to repair farm equipment, and a small structure where they could pump fresh water from a well.

Along with no running water, there was no indoor plumbing. My father, who had apparently left out that detail, insisted he would change the plumbing situation as soon as possible, but they had to be patient. They first had to get through the winter.

My mother just wanted to sit down and cry.

In some respects, life in rural Michigan wasn't too far removed from life at the turn of the century. Not everyone had electricity. Some families still used kerosene lamps. Telephones were just being installed, but conversations weren't always private. Many families shared party lines with three or so people in the same town on the same phone line. Anyone on the loop could pick up their receiver and listen in on your conversation. It wasn't unusual to hear someone address a particularly nosy neighbor with something like: "Sandra, I know you're there. Please get off the line." To make your call, you had to wait until the other party hung up. That meant repeated trips to the phone, picking up the receiver, and listening to either people talking or a dial tone.

Out in the fields some farmers still worked their crops with teams of horses. And, although roads were being improved from dirt to gravel, it wasn't uncommon to see a car stuck in mud from washed out roads, and some poor traveler hailing a nearby farmer to pull the car out with a horse or tractor.

As daylight shortened, the autumn leaves fell followed by bitter north winds. Folks faced long cold winter nights with no outside entertainment, save radio programs on Sunday evenings. Families gathered and told stories for hours. Those who lived alone played game after game of solitaire with a well-worn deck of cards. Others found a good book, wrapped themselves in blankets, pulled a lamp in close, and read until sleep knocked at their door.

It was time for us to hunker down until this first winter passed. When night came, the temperature dropped to near zero and everyone bundled themselves up in their warmest pajamas and crawled into bed, burrowing themselves deep into their blankets. One night the temperature dropped so low that a glass of water left out overnight had turned to solid ice by morning.

I slept downstairs on a sofa near the stove. In the middle of the night while the rest of the family slept, my father got up, added coal, and stoked the fire. I felt safe and snug as I watched the bright dancing flickers of orange and heard coals crackling and popping. When he finished, he glanced over to make sure I was warm and snug in my sofa bed. I dozed off feeling the comfort and warmth from the stove, even as the blustering winds howled outside.

Everyone's worst nightmare was having to go to the outhouse in the middle of the night. When that issue arose, it involved some really deep soul searching. The choice? Now or later. To choose now meant leaving a nice warm bed. It meant dressing in sweaters, cap, scarf, coats, pants, and boots to greet the blasts of arctic air outside. It meant a journey in knee deep snow to a distant frozen outhouse, like Dr. Zhivago trudging across miles of snow-covered Siberian tundra. Or hunker down by staying under the covers, tough out the next eight hours or so, and at daybreak, still have to make that same journey. To this day, "It's time to rise and shine" remains one of my least favorite expressions.

When my parents wanted to keep something from us, they switched from speaking English to Hungarian in mid-conversation, and their tone became more serious. This often happened when they received letters from relatives in Hungary pleading for help. Send clothes, blankets, anything!

It was in packing those boxes of clothes and other items that I became more aware that as hard as it was for us, it was far worse for people in other parts of the world. Although I didn't know it, millions of half-starving people, displaced from the war, were walking the roads of Europe, sometimes for hundreds of miles or more, trying to find their way back home. They passed through a continent of devastation and carnage, bombed out buildings, and war debris. Even worse, they didn't know what they would find of their homes and families when they arrived.

Hitler lost the war, and Stalin, in his victory over the Nazi military machine, gobbled up the eastern European countries including Hungary, and our cousins found themselves living under a second and equally cruel dictator. There was a great silence in these conquered countries. The Communists prevented most information from making its way out and to the west. In a postwar address to the American people, Sir Winston Churchill set the stage for the Cold War between the Soviet Union and the United States and its allies stating that a Great Iron Curtain had descended across the continent of Europe.

My parents sent the packages though there was no guarantee they would get through without the Communists confiscating them. The cold of that first winter seemed endless, but the only thing to do was to hunker down and hope that spring would bring better days for us and the people in Europe.

Chapter 5

# Bucket Duty

**THE LONG GREY WINTER** finally ended, bringing bright spring days and my mom's commitment to make the best of a bad situation. She let go of her disappointment and anger, rolled up her sleeves, and set about the daunting task of converting the old farmhouse into a decent home. She scrubbed and painted walls and put-up new pictures and draperies. Outside, she planted pink and red rose bushes that joined with two lilac bushes to emit light fragrances into the spring air.

From an orchard of a dozen apple and pear trees, she canned fruit for the winter months. The apples were both sweet and sour; the pears were juicy and delicious. Opposite the orchard lay a little grove of poplar trees with their silvery leaves fluttering in the breeze where her boys built a clubhouse and fished in a creek that cut across their land. This little brook was a place where she often took off her shoes, dangled her feet in its coolness, and listened to the gurgling sounds of the water dancing over rocks and multi-colored pebbles.

For his part, my dad made good on his promise to install inside water and indoor plumbing. In the spring he plowed the fields and planted the crops. When summer came, my father introduced John and my brothers to their work in the fields. This was a major adjustment for my brothers who were used to going to the movies, buying candy, and being free to play as long as they wanted. Now, in addition to milking, feeding, and cleaning up after the cows in the morning and evening, they spent the day hoeing weeds in rows of bean plants extending nearly as far as the eye could see. The field was a half mile long and ended at a little grove of elm trees, where the crew could rest in its shade for a few minutes before turning around and working all the way back to where they started, then do it all over again. Day in and day out they worked, and in no time, the blisters on their hands turned to callouses.

John realized how hard it was for my brothers to adapt to this new situation. He wasn't a whole lot older than they were. How could he motivate them to adapt, realizing how tedious the work was? He tried to think of different ways to somehow make this new responsibility more interesting or more palatable. He was kind of a motivational speaker before his time. While my father was from the no-nonsense, "Do it because I told you to" school, John believed in the more modern idea that if you could make the work more pleasant, time would go by faster. "Before you know it, the job is done!" was John's sunny life-long refrain. In an effort to lift the boys' spirits, he began with a homemade song: "This is the way we hoe our beans, hoe our beans, hoe our beans! This is the way we hoe our beans, all day long!" You can imagine how far that got.

Nonetheless, John's conversations were a mix of themes: how adversity builds character, how a job well done is a reward unto itself. He told stories. Among them, for the millionth time, he talked about the beautiful island in the Pacific, a tropical paradise a million miles away from this dry and dusty bean field and its baking hot, merciless sun. That's where I came in with their one perk—ice cold water!

Around the age of four or five, I was assigned two backbreaking jobs. Inside the house, I had the chore of churning butter, a much harder task than anyone would think. It involved cranking for hours and hours until the milk thickened into butter. As the hours went by, the cream got thicker, and the cranking got harder. My arm ached, but I just kept on going. That churning gave me the arm I have today—an arm of which both Tom Brady and Patrick Mahomes would be envious.

## Bucket Duty

My backbreaking outside job was to drag a bucket of cold drinking water to my brothers working out in the fields, once in the morning and once in the afternoon. Understandably, I felt I was assigned much more work than was my fair share. When the bucket was filled with water and ice, it weighed a ton and took all my might to drag it along, pushing it with one knee and then the other, the water spilling out this way and that. I'd see the four of them in the distance, doing their work. As they got closer, I could hear them talking, largely picking at one another.

"C'mon, boys," John encouraged in his sunny way. "Look, Frankie's up ahead bringing us some nice cold water! Let's hurry up with our work so we can get there faster and have a nice cold drink!"

Talk about your incentives.

They came closer, suddenly dropping their hoes, and raced toward me to get the first drink. Peter, the oldest, usually got to the bucket first. Grabbing the tin ladle, he gulped away as the others waited impatiently for their turns. Frankly, I felt little appreciation for my services. Perhaps because there was always a harvest of criticism about the quality of my work. "Why do you always take so long to get out here?" was the general theme. They also complained that, by the time I got there, all the ice had melted.

Fig. 12. Bucket Duty

One particular gripe that annoyed me above the rest came from my brother George who, when he dropped the ladle back into the bucket, asked, "And why do you spill half the water before you even get here?" I was not amused. It was true, my coverall pants were always soaked, which made my workday even more unpleasant.

When John told them the drink break was over, they returned half-heartedly to their labor. I picked up my empty bucket and began my long walk back to the house.

"More ice, next time!" said a distant, annoying, high-pitched voice behind me." —Thomas!

"Stupids!" I yelled back.

Finished with my generous but daily underappreciated experience of mercy, I'd return from the fields through the grove of apple trees, arriving back at the house where I'd drop my bucket on the front porch and wipe my feet before going into the house. Mom would take a break to make lunch and turn on the radio to listen to the news from the distant radio station in Detroit, WJR, her one connection to the outside world. That's when we heard the news that shook the western world to its core. America was no longer the only nation that had the atomic bomb! Now Stalin had it too! Stalin had accomplished what Hitler couldn't do!

The American assessment, that Russian scientists weren't capable of building the bomb for many years, was shattered. Other disturbing news came across the radio in those days. China joined Stalin and the Soviet Union in becoming a communist country. It was now known as Red China. Then, came a third alarming report. Communist North Korean Red Army troops began pouring over the border into South Korea and pushed back American forces stationed there.

I comforted myself with the thought that America was still the strongest nation on earth, and that whatever was happening, was happening light-years away. Nevertheless, the total security we enjoyed in America's heartland was punctured and replaced by an ongoing and growing anxiety about just how safe America was. When the family knelt to pray the rosary in the early '50s, we prayed for the success of our crops and for our family behind the Iron Curtain. I don't know if I ever said it aloud, but I prayed for us to be safe from Stalin and the Communists. What I didn't know was that the hand of the Doomsday Clock was moved from seven minutes to three minutes to midnight, and there was more trouble on the way.

Chapter 6

# Day of Rest

**AFTER BREAKFAST**, every fourth Saturday of the month, my dad got out his hand clippers and gave haircuts to each of the boys in the family. He started with Peter, then George, Thomas, and me. Once in the chair, he'd ask how we wanted it cut, which really didn't matter since we all got the same haircut. As I waited my turn, I saw how Thomas squirmed this way and that, wanting to scratch when hair dropped down his back. My dad always complimented me on how perfectly still I sat—not like Thomas. Perched on a board placed high across the arms of the chair, I looked down at Thomas, giving thanks that I wasn't like him nor the rest of men. A dab of Wildroot Cream Oil, a final combing, and I'd hop down from the chair and off to play.

After the haircuts, my brothers spent time in their upstairs bedroom, tossing the football back and forth as they talked about sports and girls. Even though I was ten years their junior, I strongly felt that I should be included in whatever they were doing and have equal access to their room. Frankly, I didn't always feel welcome there; actually, I felt more like a celery string stuck between their teeth.

When I was about five, the issue came to a head. I was dragged before the high court of mom and dad. The location of the court was our large dining room table. My father sat at the head of the table in his special chair that, unlike the others, had arms to it, which symbolized monarchical authority. My mother and Thomas sat to his right while Peter and George sat to his left. I, the accused, sat at the end directly across from my dad, the spot I sensed was reserved for the least of the brethren.

Fig. 13. With my brothers, I felt I was their equal.

Essentially our arguments boiled down to this: while I felt my participation enriched their conversations; they felt I never, ever shut up. I didn't know it at the time, but I was arguing a fact that science has since proven repeatably: the youngest child is inevitably the brightest. Nevertheless, my brothers presented a series of our interactions that made me sound rather intrusive. My futile pleadings fell on deaf ears, and incredibly, the high court ruled against me and in favor of the three stupids! The verdict handed down was that I was to go into their room only by invitation. I looked at Thomas, who smiled back at me with his evil grin.

No invitations were forthcoming.

One day, tired of waiting, I took matters into my own hands. I invited myself in, only to be carried out bodily and deposited in the hall, with the door slammed behind me. I didn't appreciate it one bit. I made a split-second decision and launched an assault to kick the door down. From downstairs, I heard my father's thundering voice, "Whoever is making all that racket up there better cut it out!" Ignoring his warning, I stepped up my kicking campaign. There was no doubt in my mind that the door was going down. Seconds later, my father, who was in no mood for nonsense, bounded up the stairs and delivered a WHAP! WHAP!! to my backside. I yelled to high heaven to protest this continuing gross injustice. "I said to stop it!" he yelled, looking me straight in the eyes. I surmised he didn't want to be bothered again. After making his point, he went back down the stairs, and continued whatever he was doing. After a few seconds, the bedroom door opened a crack, and all three of my brothers peeked through to see what happened or, more to the point, to savor the moment. Each of them stood grinning because I had "gotten it" and they hadn't. Of the three, Thomas's grin was the vilest! I checked to make sure my father was out of hearing range and glared back at Thomas. "Stupid!" I hissed. "Stupids!" I hissed at all of them, knowing that the door's demolition would have to wait for another day.

Fig. 14. St. Agatha's Church (Courtesy Jaime Lynn Photography)

Sunday mornings were altogether different. We dressed in our Sunday best, squeezed into our LaSalle, and drove the three miles into town for mass at St. Agatha's. From a distance you could see the church, with its medieval castle shape and steeples jutting high into the sky. For me, church was no treat. It meant kneeling on hard wooden kneelers. It also meant wearing an itchy, black wool suit bequeathed to me by some cousin lucky enough to outgrow it.

In the summer heat, it was like attending mass in a bed of poison ivy.

We always arrived early and quietly moved to our pew, carefully respectful of the few who were saying their private prayers. The routine was the same every week. We went to the same pew, where my father knelt and prayed his rosary, while my mother sat praying hers, which was made of crystal blue beads. I'm not sure what my brothers did, though I doubt it had much to do with spirituality. I mostly just looked around.

The church walls reached high and were beautifully decorated with red, blue, and gold ornate trim. Large lights hung down from the ceiling, though providing only scant brightness to the congregation below. The lack of light was offset by large, mosaic windows that depicted scenes from scripture and filtered sunlight into a dancing array of colors that added some cheer to the otherwise dark setting. The atmosphere was one of prayerfulness and solemnity. Near the front of the church set perhaps twenty or so red votive candles that flickered and emanated a sweet scent, a reminder that many of the faithful shouldered heavy burdens and were asking the Almighty for help. More of the faithful arrived at their places throughout the church, kneeling with rosary beads in hand, their lips moving silently, praying for intentions known and unknown to others—prayers of the heart. A peaceful calm permeated throughout.

At the front were statues of Mary and St. Joseph. Along the side walls were the Stations of the Cross depicting the story of Christ as He was led to His execution. I was most fascinated by the centerpiece of the church—a gold tabernacle at the center of the altar. Even at a young age, when I fixed my gaze on it, I had a primitive sense that this was a sacred place, where time and space blended in with eternity. The quiet would be short lived as more men arrived and removed their hats, and women, required to wear a head covering in church, adjusted their hats or draped scarves over their heads. As more came in, there were sounds of mothers telling their children to hush. The earlier arrivals, my father among them, realized that their personal prayer time was over, made the sign of the cross, and put their rosaries away.

Just before mass began each week, there was a lighting of the candles on the altar by some brave grade school altar boy. This was no easy task because the tops of the six candles stood high above the altar, almost out of reach of a shorter server. The boy had to stretch as best he possibly could, and only then could he light the candle. Even more crucial was the fact that the brass candle lighter had a wick that needed to be measured just right. If the boy didn't push the wick out far enough, the candle lighter would go out. Then, to the stifled snickers of his pals throughout the church, he'd suffer the embarrassment of having to go back to the sacristy to light the wick again. I remember one sacrilegious exception, when this one kid, with a sly smile of satisfaction, whipped out a Zippo-like cigarette lighter from under his cassock, and with a couple of quick flicks, to his mother's horror, relit the wick on the spot.

When I became an altar boy years later, I had a fear of burning down the church. If the wick was pushed too long, the flame shot out like a blow torch. I could see newspaper headlines around the world screaming in bold print: "CARELESS KID BURNS DOWN CHURCH." "I didn't mean to do it!' says kid, hauled off in handcuffs. Somehow, however, the candles always managed to get lit.

A bell rang to signal that mass was about to begin. Everybody stood as the priest and altar boys came out, genuflected, and the mass began. Praying in Latin, the priest faced the altar while the congregation followed along with their prayer books written in both Latin and English. The priest prayed the *Confiteor*—a prayer confessing sins—out loud, and the altar boys responded, *"Mea culpa, mea culpa, mea maxima culpa."* (Through my fault, through my fault, through my grievous fault.) Soon after, from a distant loft, the choir sang the Gloria: "Glory to God in the Highest and peace to His people on earth."

The priest read the gospel in Latin and then in English. Sometimes I understood a passage if it was simple enough. Other times the reading made absolutely no sense to me. "If you have faith like a grain of mustard seed, you will say to this mountain, *'Move from here to there,' and it will move, and nothing will be impossible for you."* That seemed almost crazy.

Following the gospel, the priest gave a sermon based on the reading. Following that, the mass continued with the offering of the gifts of bread and wine, the consecration, and then communion. The mass was over when the priest turned to the congregation and proclaimed in Latin *"Ite missa est."* It was a phrase that meant either "Go forth, the mass is ended" or "Gentlemen, start your engines!" Which of the two translations was correct, I wasn't sure, but that announcement brought about an immediate and total transformation from the sacred to the worldly in about two seconds. I do know that the priest never had to say it twice. The stampede began.

High powered Detroit cars, billowing exhaust fumes into the sky, roared out of the parking lot in a race to the top of the hill and center of town. I'm pretty sure my brothers felt the same way I did in wishing we could be among the cool ones who got to race to the top. But it was not to be. Our dad had matured, and as a converted Catholic, insisted that we wait uncooly behind until the organ slowly ground out every last everlasting note. He would then nod that we could leave.

What was so important at the top of the hill? A paper boy gave you a choice of a copy of the *Detroit Times* or *Detroit Free Press*, but you had to get there before they ran out. Along with the radio and an occasional newsreel at the movies, the newspaper was our third link to knowing what was happening in the outside world.

Once back home, while mom was frying bacon and buttering toast, my dad and brothers and I shucked our church clothes and tore into the *Times*. Lying on the living room floor, I devoured the comics: *Blondie*, *Flash Gordon*, and *Ripley's Believe It or Not*. When I got better at reading, I moved on to the sports section and even the news. In boxing, Rocky Marciano was on his way to becoming the world's next heavyweight champion. In baseball, Joe DiMaggio was finishing out his career with the Yankees, and a young Mickey Mantle took the Yankee Clipper's place in centerfield.

For those reading the *News*, they read about radiation levels being detected in the eastern United States from four atomic tests in Nevada over two thousand miles away. The good news was that scientists assured us "…there is no evidence that the increased levels of radiation resulting from the atomic tests 'could conceivably produce any damage to humans, to animals, or to water supply.'" [23]

Sunday was a day of rest, and aside from care of the cattle, no work was to be done. Sometimes after my dad took a well-deserved afternoon nap, we would go up into the attic, where he would read to me from history books that transported us from present surroundings to far-away places and distant times, from Civil War years to the Hanging Gardens of Babylon.

Once, after our reading session finished and my dad left, I took a well-worn book down from the shelf. Its pages were so dusty that I could feel the dust going up my nose.

The book, *Nations at War*, published way back in 1917, contained photographs of the fighting in the First World War. I opened to a page with two photos.[24] The first was the front of a magnificent cathedral in Rheims, France. The structure, I guessed, was even bigger than St. Agatha's.

Fig. 15. *Above:* Rheims Cathedral in France before it was bombed.

Fig. 16. *Right:* When I saw this photo of the Cathedral after it was shelled by the Germans, I thought: Oh my God, people can even bomb churches!

(Fig. 15, 16 reprinted from Willis J. Abbot, *The Nations at War* (New York, NY 1917))

The second was that same cathedral taken from the air with its roof and walls demolished by German artillery shells. Something that had taken centuries to build was destroyed in a matter of hours. All this happened in Europe, a place on the other side of the world where some of our family still lived.

My five-year-old mind couldn't wrap around the idea of how something so horrible like that could have happened. How could anyone do that to a church where people pray? Was all of that in the past, or could that happen to us at St. Agatha's? I closed the book, put it back on the shelf, and went downstairs for supper. When the evening ended, and I was tucked into bed, I couldn't get the cathedral's terrible images out of my mind. I also wondered about the verse from scripture: *whoever asks receives; whoever seeks, finds.*

As sleep closed in, I wondered if another great war was possible. And I wondered if there was anything that ordinary people like me could do to stop it. I didn't know it at the time, but I wasn't the only one concerned with those kinds of questions. In Washington, a whole slew of folks at the top were wondering about those questions too.

Chapter 7

# St. Agatha's

Fig. 17. St. Agatha's Grade School (Courtesy Jaime Lynn Photography)

**I GOT OFF TO A ROCKY START** on my first day of grade school. The morning began with me marching confidently down St. Agatha's shining hallway floor to the school's "Baby Room." I carried my new lunchbox and a sharp looking pencil box filled with pencils and crayons. My mom walked behind me as we passed through the new one-story brick building adjacent to the church. The little school had three classrooms to house a hundred kids in grades one through eight. Each classroom was decorated with cheerful bulletin boards that stated educational themes of the semester. The first, second, and third grades were taught in the Baby Room. The fourth, fifth, and sixth grades in the "Middle Room," with the seventh and eighth grades in the prestigious "High Room." The largest room was for piano lessons, school assemblies, and talent shows.

On my first day and every day that followed in the twelve years through high school graduation, I fought with my mom over the merits of eating breakfast. I hated the pasty texture of oatmeal on my teeth, and even as I would protest, my mom in her old country way, plopped down giant gobs of the stuff in my bowl. Across the table was the Quaker Oats man chuckling at me from the box.

"You need a good breakfast that will stick to your ribs!" she said.

Stuffed and unhappy, I boarded the orange school bus, whose driver had no qualms about leaning on the horn repeatedly and unabashedly even if I was two seconds late.

But on this first day, mom and I caught a ride to school with another kid and his mom. So, I sat at my desk, got situated, and looking around, discovered that my mother was nowhere in sight. She left with the other lady! It hadn't occurred to me that she wouldn't stay with me all day. Realizing I had been duped, I started to cry and cry loud. My upset soon slipped into another gear: absolute outrage! I made a commitment to protest by the loudest sustained crying and yelling in the history of mankind. I would go on until either my mother came back, or the school let me out. I must've really created a fuss, because I was still going strong when the morning recess bell rang at 10:20.

As the kids ran out of the classroom to go out on the playground, my teacher, a young nun, came over to my desk and begged, "Please, please, PLEASE stop." It was the first time I had even noticed her. She seemed so nice and earnest in her imploring, that I stopped crying and forgot about the whole thing. What I didn't know was that I was meeting the nicest, sweetest nun ever. Any guy who's attended Catholic school will boast about how he had the toughest nun who ever lived, and that if she and George Foreman traded punches, George would be the one who went home crying. But this was just the opposite.

Her name was Sister Agnes Carmel. She was a young Adrian Dominican nun who managed to teach three grades of kids in one classroom each and every day. Looking back, I really don't know how she did it. She would get us first graders busy, then move to the center of the room to teach the second graders, then the third graders, and back to us. She was beautiful, kind, and as lovely as any woman I've ever met. Even with her veil and layers upon layers of pinned linen, she moved about with such grace. Plus, she played the harmonica and could hit a softball farther than any of the eighth graders! She seemed to love little kids so much and was so joyful in her work.

I was in love.

Thereupon I encountered my first theological dilemma. As a cradle Catholic, I thought I was supposed to believe that Mary, the mother of Jesus, was the most beautiful and perfect of all women. But deep in my heart, I felt Sister Agnes Carmel was worthy of that honor. I had never heard of Mary playing a harmonica or anything about how she handled a bat. And besides, while Mary only had one kid to deal with, and a perfect one at that, Sister had thirty kids, and none of them would have been mistaken for Jesus. So, I guess at St. Agatha's, I broke with church dogma. After all was said and done, Sister Agnes Carmel got the gold, Mary came in second to get the silver. The bronze was, I guess, anybody's guess. Maybe Mamie Eisenhower.

How does a five-year-old boy impress a woman twenty-five years his senior? I'll tell you how I did it. I was a natural speller, and I absolutely killed at the "Spell the Color" game. While we lined up, Sister sat in one of those tiny kid chairs with the color cards in her hand. She showed a card with a cluster of grapes. She said, "Spell purple," and the kid spelled "p-u-r-p-l-e." In the line, I bounced around like a ping pong ball. I couldn't wait for my turn. I could spell any color, and I wanted to make it sound like a melody. I was especially good at O-R-A-N-G-E. It rolled off my tongue effortlessly, like an Olympic skater ever so lightly touching down from a triple jump, then gliding across the ice to a stop. Some days I'd wear my special Roy Rogers shirt, and that combination of my shirt and my spelling must've been powerful indeed because she would smile that lovely smile, and I'd hop to the back of the line where I couldn't wait to do it all over again.

Second grade offered a major hurdle: making my first confession. When you're six years old, what are you supposed to confess? In preparation, I studied the catechism, "We believe in God, the Father Almighty. . . ."

"What's 'Almighty' mean, sister?"

She smiled, probably because she was so impressed with my knowledge of colors.

"It means that with God, all things are possible," she said.

I went down the list of the ten commandments. "Honor thy father and mother" and "Do not take the Lord's name in vain" made sense, but apart from that, I didn't see much connection with the process.

The catechism instructed that there were two kinds of sin: venial and mortal. Stealing a pack of gum was a venial; knocking off a liquor store was a mortal. All that made sense. "Thou shalt not steal." I hadn't stolen anything, except for once I took a dime and three pennies from my sister's dresser, but that was when I was four. Was I supposed to mention that?

There was also the coveting thing. I didn't know what "covet" meant, and I didn't know any of our neighbors yet, so I concluded I probably hadn't coveted any of our neighbor's wives. Of all the commandments, the adultery one seemed the hardest to understand, but I wasn't inclined to dig into the matter any further.

When I asked my mom what she thought I should confess, she said, "Well, you might want to think about not calling your brothers "the stupids."

That was of no help.

My sense of anxiety grew as confession day drew nearer. The church felt extra hot when the big day arrived. Standing mid-point in the confessional line, I waited for my turn. From our practices, I was supposed to push aside the heavy maroon curtain that acted as a door, go in, kneel down, and wait. Jeez, how was I supposed to explain the whole coin thing? The other kids might think I was a big sinner because they had to wait in line until I sorted it all out with the priest.

The kid ahead of me went in and blurted out in a hoarse voice that could be heard everywhere within a two-mile radius: "I did adultery!"

God! Talk about guts! Although I couldn't hear much, I think the priest asked for a little more information.

"I stole a pencil, but I gave it back," explained the kid.

So that's what all the fuss is about with that whole adultery thing!

Having received absolution from the priest, two seconds later the kid shot out of the box like a rocket.

Ok, my turn. I pushed past the curtain, entered the confessional, and knelt down. I could hear the muffled conversation of the kid on the other side. Minutes dragged by, turning into hours, and then days that turned into seasons. The screen on my side finally opened. I heard a kind voice say, "Thank God for this confession, please begin."

"Bless me, Father, for I, uh, have sinned."

My voice, too, was hoarse. I cleared my throat, and then, somehow, my examination of conscience took over. I put forth my best assessment. Swiping my sister's thirteen cents was water well under the bridge, and I discarded it. I felt a sudden strong sense of self when I shared my sins:

"I disobeyed my mother three times, and twice I told Thomas he was stupid."

"I see," said the priest. "Maybe you could work on that."

Yep, that's where I stood. I congratulated myself on a job well done!

I finished with the memorized prayer, "For these and for all the sins of my life, I am especially sorry for disobeying my mother." I felt no remorse for telling Thomas he was stupid. Twice.

I left the confessional feeling strong inside. I had conquered another major hurdle in life and was ready to climb the next mountain. Going on to higher grades in a Catholic school, I formed a worldview that boiled down to this: God was almighty and all loving; the world was made up of the sun, the moon, nine planets, and all kinds of stars; America was the most powerful country in the world; the Catholic Church was the true church; and Roy Rogers was "King of the Cowboys."

From that foundation I grew to realize there would be successes in life, and there would be major disappointments too. I had already suffered one of those. It was Christmas eve. I prayed that there would be a Roy Rogers' fancy gun and holster set waiting for me under the tree. On Christmas morning I awoke to a beautifully wrapped present, and upon opening it, got the thrill of a lifetime—three brand new pairs of white underpants.

I also became more aware that there were bad things in life, like money worries and kidnappers. But the reality that terrified me most was polio. The March of Dimes campaigns showed photos of little kids struck by this horrific disease who had to spend their entire lives confined to an iron lung. I understood it as a disease that came when school let out for the summer. It could strike anyone at any time.

As America slipped well into the 1950s, the economy was booming. General Eisenhower, the former Supreme Allied Commander who defeated Nazi Germany, was elected president. He chose a young politician, Richard Nixon, to become his vice president. Eisenhower and his Republican party won in a 1952 national landslide. There was little good news for the Democrats, save that a little-known John F. Kennedy, a Democrat from Massachusetts, pulled a stunning defeat over a Republican heavyweight and was elected as that state's senator.

That same year the government announced that great advances were taking place in understanding thermonuclear reactions necessary for the creation of a hydrogen bomb. "Such a bomb, which would harness the basic power source of the sun, would be hundreds of times more destructive than the atomic bombs dropped on Hiroshima and Nagasaki."[25] Much more frequent testing would be needed. With us having a bomb hundreds of times more powerful than the atomic bomb, Stalin wouldn't ever dare think of attacking the United States.

We could all breathe a big sigh of relief; a sigh, unfortunately, that was short lived.

Chapter 8

# God Bless America!

**NO ONE SANG** "God Bless America" with more fervor than my mom, and no one loved the flag and our country more. As someone who came through Ellis Island as a girl, she saw this new country as the land of liberty, freedom, fairness, and opportunity for all. America meant having a brighter day, good people helping neighbors, and everybody pulling together to build a better world. She loved her Hungarian heritage, but Hungary was the old country—something of the past. America represented the young and the new.

The split between the old and the new grew wider when, following the world war, her beloved Hungary became subjugated under Russian domination. Winston Churchill described it as if a great iron curtain had descended across eastern Europe. Some were beginning to call the tension between the east and west "the cold war."

In 1953, Bishop Fulton J. Sheen, a Catholic prelate, had a television program entitled, *Life Is Worth Living*. Every week he delivered a half hour lecture on a host of subjects confronting humankind in the context of the modern world. His program was widely popular, even in a time slot opposite "Mr. Television" himself, Milton Berle. Sheen had long preached against the evils of communism, and on one occasion, with his eyes focused directly into the camera, I, as a seven-year-old, heard him declare: Stalin, prepare to meet your God![26] Shortly after, in March 1953, the Kremlin announced Stalin's death. "An elite team of Russian doctors... worked around the clock trying to save Stalin's life after he suffered a brain hemorrhage."[27]

While the news of Hitler's death by suicide was reported throughout the world, few seemed to know the details surrounding Stalin's as described by his daughter. Official reports neglected to include the fact that he had spent thirteen hours paralyzed and alone. The reason was that Stalin's henchmen, puzzled by his absence, were unwilling to disturb him in his private quarters lest they risk his unbridled fury. Instead, they played it safe waiting hours before summoning medical help. His daughter wrote: "At what seemed like the very last moment he suddenly opened his eyes and cast a glance over everyone in the room. It was a terrible glance, insane or perhaps angry and full of fear of death. . . . And then he suddenly lifted his left hand as though he were pointing to something up above and bringing down a curse on us all."[28]

After Stalin's death, it became evident that the genie had not been idle. He remained out of the bottle and hard at work, largely behind the scenes. The Soviets announced to the world that they had successfully detonated the hydrogen bomb. This completely unforeseen news sent diplomatic shock waves through stunned western capitals.

The Doomsday Clock was moved to two minutes to midnight. There was more bad news. The Soviet bombs were small and light enough to be carried by plane and dropped on the United States. That meant the historically backward country, that a few years earlier didn't have an atomic bomb, now had a device a thousand times more destructive and the means to deliver it on the U.S.

How did it happen? Who let this happen? A Red Scare swept the country. Had communist spies infiltrated our government? Senator Joseph McCarthy, who seized the opportunity to make his name a household one, provided a frightening answer with the assertion that the State Department was "crawling with Communists." Day after day, over the radio, Senator McCarthy's fear

---

[26] Sheen actually declared, "Stalin must one day meet his judgment." (see "Life is Worth Living 1953")

mongering accusations of communist infiltration came pouring into homes across America.

Things were also grim on the home front. After years of squeaking by financially, one year's harvest was particularly disappointing, and the anticipated income didn't develop. It appeared my parents wouldn't be able to make their mortgage payment. They were on the verge of losing everything. My father had done his best, but it wasn't enough. In addition to work demanded by the farm, my father found a job that would at least keep food on the table, but that job was forty-five miles away. He got up every day at 3:30 in the morning, sipped a cup of black coffee, and ate a thick slice of homemade bread. He fed hay to the cattle and headed to work on back roads covered with ice and snow. He was consumed with worry. Furrowed lines etched deep into his forehead, and traces of his humor were rarely seen. He became impatient and irritable toward my brothers and me, and more withdrawn. At fifty, his age would preclude ever finding a permanent job, and he wasn't about to take charity. He was boxed in from all sides. Something had to give. It wasn't long in coming.

One day, after finishing his job and clocking out, he left the building, and stepped out onto the ice-covered parking lot. He cleared the ice from his windshield, smiled and told a fellow worker he would see him tomorrow. He got into his car and drove off, traveling his usual route, then turned on to a two-lane highway leading back to the farm. A few miles down the road, at a speed faster than usual, he leaned forward toward the steering wheel and veered straight into the path of an oncoming car.

Chapter 9

# Spring and the Return of Thomas

**ONE OF THE** toughest lessons I've learned in life is that events come at their appointed times; they can't be rushed. A farmer may wonder if rain will ever fall on his crops. A woman may wonder, "When will this baby ever come?" Each will arrive in its own time. It was like the Michigan winters that chilled life to the bone, making it seem that winter would never end. But one day each year, the sun's rays warmed the earth, and a tiny drop of water melted to join innumerable other drops to convert the snow and ice into slush and water that flowed into streams and rivers into the blue waters of the Great Lakes. Every year winter loses its iron grip which serves to remind us that winter doesn't have the last word. Spring arrives, brimming with hope and the promise of new life.
    That was the case with my family's financial crisis. The darkest moment came when my father had either blacked out or fallen asleep at the wheel. Hearing horns blaring and brakes screeching, he came to and swerved sharply, missing a car head on, and ended up on an embankment, shaken but unhurt. No one else was hurt either. He later described this incident as a major conversion point in his life, similar to that espoused by Alcoholics Anonymous of turning one's life over to a higher power. For a lifetime, he fiercely

fought life's battle all alone. Like his boxing hero, the great Dempsey, he fought on even when he was out on his feet. He now realized he could no longer go it alone; he no longer needed to go it alone. No matter what happened, he would turn his worry over to a higher power. He spoke of discovering a scriptural truth:

"Worry is useless, what is needed is trust." Mark 5:36.

Not long after, everything changed for the better. He was offered a great job with the state's largest electrical company, a job he had applied for months before, but thought he had no chance of getting. His age wasn't an obstacle; in fact, he landed the job because of his years of supervisory experience. He was assigned to a team of trouble shooting machinists responsible for creating tools and instruments to keep power lines up and running. He and the job were a perfect match. He hired someone else to work the farm and keep that second income stream flowing. The furrowed lines on his forehead smoothed out, and the financial worry drained from his face. Once again, I saw the dad I always knew. Now on Sunday afternoons, he had time to go out on our lawn and hit fly balls for me to catch and throw back to him. Slowly but surely, my mother and father doubled their mortgage payments and freed themselves from debt. Along with the rest of America in the 1950s, we began to experience a new and unparalleled prosperity: new cars, new appliances, and time to relax and enjoy life. I learned the lesson to persevere during tough times. Things get better.

The following months brought major changes to our family. A few days after my grandpa said goodbye to me from the confines of an oxygen tent, he passed away from cancer. My brothers-in-law, John and Ray, who had been laid off one too many times at the Michigan automotive plants, moved back to Louisiana where they found steady jobs. As for my brothers, Peter joined the Air Force and was stationed at a base a few hours away, while George found a nearby job in a manufacturing factory. Thomas joined the Navy and was stationed across the country in San Diego for basic training. I missed him terribly.

In his absence, I started to think about all the things he had done for me. In the first grade, when some kid took my lunch box and I got it back, Thomas painted my name on it in big bold gold letters, so there'd be no doubt that this lunch box was mine. He taught me how to play games, use a slingshot, and shoot a BB gun.

In the times when there was little money to spend on candy, we found a substitute in our garden, where he and I would sit and talk as we shucked peapods to enjoy the sweetness of green peas—amazing as I look back.

Yes, he had his shortcomings. He was also the one who had assured me that by trusting him tying one end of a string to our dining room doorknob, and the other to my deeply imbedded molar tooth, there would be a quick, pain-free extraction. When the weather turns cold, I feel the throbbing pain to this day. Yet, all in all, I began to think that maybe Thomas wasn't such a bad egg after all.

Despite his many flaws, I continued to miss him. I couldn't believe that he wouldn't be home for Christmas. With my mom's help, I saved up thirty cents and sent him his Christmas gift, a pack of Camels. I knew the store-bought cigarettes would be a step up from the tobacco products he cranked out as a teen with his cigarette making device.

Into the new year, I crossed off each passing day on my calendar as we waited for him to come home on furlough. After an eternity, that day arrived. I stood out on our lawn, while my mom did her housework inside. About mid-morning, I saw a distant figure. As he drew closer, I saw a smiling young sailor in a navy-blue uniform wearing a white cap tipped to the side. I couldn't believe it was him, and I rushed forward to hug him.

"Tom! Tom!!"

"Hey, Potshot!" he said, using a name he had given me when I learned to hit a target with my BB gun. "Hey, how y' doin'?"

Fig. 18. Life is good. My bicycle; Copper, my dog and best childhood friend; and my sailor's cap. I thought I looked like a sailor.

"I missed you!" I said, hugging him, my face squished up against his navy belt buckle.

"Hey, I brought you something," he said, pulling a round white sailor's cap from his bag and smacking it on my head.

"Thanks!!" I said, proudly adjusting my new cap and thinking I looked like a sailor.

I couldn't wait any longer! I was just bursting to tell him the thrilling news that I had been keeping secret for months!

"We got some peas!" I shouted out, beaming, motioning him toward the garden. "That's right! We've got peas!!"

"C'mon! C'mon!" I said, grabbing onto his leg, and pushing, pulling, and shoving him towards our garden. I had dreamed about this moment, with the two of us sitting down like we always did and eating the sweetest peas in the world.

And then I received the shock of my life! He wanted to see our mom FIRST! I was aghast! I couldn't believe it! The old evil Thomas was back!

"Wait. . . wait. . ." he said as he tried to climb the backstairs to the farmhouse, dragging me along as I clung onto his leg with a death grip.

"Ok, ok. Give me just a second to say hi to mom first, ok? And then we'll go see the peas."

I COULDN'T BELIEVE IT! What was he thinking??! He was turning away from our PEAS! I couldn't wrap my five-year-old mind around this horrible, unforeseen turn of events.

"Stupid!!" I said, as he held me at arm's distance while I flailed away at him and tried to kick at his shins. To the squeak of our screen door, he went into the house with me following. Mom turned from the stove, and seeing her son, put down the cooking spoon, wiped her hands on her apron, and with a smile and tears, gave him a mother's—I can't tell you how happy I am that you are home—hug. Sadly, she got first priority over my peas. Then they had to talk, ignoring me while I bounced around trying to get him to speed things up. Even during my bouncing, I couldn't help but notice how enormously proud our mom was to see him in uniform. Then, after a lifetime, he at last came to his senses, and I was able to pry him away to walk out to the garden. There, next to the garden, we sat down and ate some peas just like old times.

His week of furlough flew by all too quickly, and he was off again, before dawn, to serve his country. He would have to hitchhike to Saginaw, catch a bus to Detroit, and fly back to San Diego, and then off to a lifetime of other destinations. I was still sleeping, only to awaken many hours later to clinking sounds under my pillow—an envelope spilling over with nickels, dimes, and quarters that he had saved up as a present for me. I jumped out of bed and rushed to the window to see if I could still get a glimpse of him, even though I knew he was long gone. And looking down the long dusty road, I wondered when I would see him again.

In the months that followed, I often found myself feeling alone as I stood in the field where I had once carried my water bucket out to my brothers, their bickering voices now only echoes in my mind. Gone was our large family; we were now down to three. I looked up at the billowing clouds as they slowly drifted across the blue sky and found myself filled with wonder and worry about everything. How could the world be so ordinary and safe on the one hand, and on the other, in danger of a possible attack happening at any time?

On the radio came the sounds of sirens from emergency broadcasts ending with a notification that this was only a test and what to do in the event of a national emergency. I had also seen maps showing how the Russians would fly their planes over the North Pole to bomb us. I wondered from which direction they would come to deliver their strike. I wasn't alone in wondering. In Washington, at the highest levels of government, they were trying to figure out the same thing.

Chapter 10

# Television

**I WAS SPRAWLED** out on our living room sofa reading *Mad Magazine*, minding my own business, when my mom called from the kitchen.

"Open the door for your brother!"

I glanced up and saw it was George, who was having a tough time carrying a large, heavy box, and couldn't get into the house because the back-screen door was locked.

"Hurry up!" he yelled. His voice had a sharp edge to it that I thought was a bit snotty, more an order than a request. Hey, wasn't he one of my brothers who was critical of my water bucket days? That's right.

"Why can't he open it himself?" I asked.

"This thing's heavy!" he shouted, "Hurry up, you little—"

"Hey, you two! Stop it!" said mom.

And in an obvious gesture of favoritism toward my brother, she said, "Open the door for your brother!"

The inflection in his voice had suggested to me that my services were needed with substantially more urgency than I felt like delivering them. But in an act of mercy, I sauntered on over to open the door. There was my less than happy brother sweating profusely and gritting his teeth as he struggled to maneuver the large, bulky cardboard box through the doorway.

"Look out!" he barked, shoving his way past me.

At age twenty-one and single, he had gotten a full-time factory job. Now, flush with cash, he bought the family a television. When I realized what was in the box, I felt kind of sorry for taking my sweet old time.

"Sorry," I said, but even to me my apology sounded a bit hollow.

He shot me a look that would've killed any ordinary man. Then, he laid the box down with a bit of a thud and proceeded to read the assembly directions. A few minutes later, there stood a one channel, black and white television with a seventeen-inch screen. On that late afternoon, none of us ever imagined the powerful influence this small box would have on our lives and on shaping how we understood our world. With a click of the on-off switch, a man named Buffalo Bob asked: "Hey, boys and girls, what time is it?" And from televisions all over the country the answer came shouting back: "It's Howdy Doody time!"

Then a black and white image appeared of a smiling freckle-faced puppet. The picture faded in and out, sometimes rolling vertically upward or flipping horizontally, but a little practice with the adjustment dials and the viewing was great. Kids at school had told me how cool it was to watch shows every night of the week! Before long, our Sunday night radio programs, which had been such a major part of our lives, just faded into the past. Radio required us to imagine what was happening; now we could actually see what was going on! We continued to say the rosary every night, but we also took into consideration our television viewing schedule. Moreover, we now had a front row seat to watch America, as a new economic power, shift into high gear. Everywhere, manufacturing was booming, especially Detroit, where multitudes of powerful new cars rolled off the assembly lines. Dinah Shore, one of America's most popular entertainers, ended her show with a pitch to Chevrolet and a kiss to the audience -M-WAH!

Programs like the late afternoon show, *Queen for A Day*, provided manufacturers with an unprecedented opportunity to showcase their latest products into homes all across the nation. American materialism was kicking into high gear.

## Television

At dinner time, we watched the local news, weather, and sports, which was followed by fifteen minutes of national and international news from the *Huntley-Brinkley Report.*

In the evenings, *Dragnet*'s musical theme became a part of American consciousness, and westerns flooded the airwaves with shows like *Gunsmoke, Maverick, and Wagon Train.* Before long, like other Americans, we no longer spent the majority of every evening in conversation or reading. And, although we didn't know it at the time, another revolutionary change took place. On a new program called the *Today Show*, as I recall, its host, Dave Garroway, armed with yards and yards of heavy cable, took viewers on a tour around NBC's New York studio and explained that the show was trying out a new concept—to bring the world into people's homes. No one had any idea if the concept would take off, but it did. To our horror, we witnessed huge Soviet tanks roll into Budapest to crush the Hungarian revolution, a crisis over access to the Suez Canal, and reports of how the United States conducted atomic explosions in the Marshall Islands of the South Pacific to study the impact that radioactivity would have on animals and native islanders.

While all these things were happening around the world in 1956 and 1957, I advanced to St. Agatha's Middle Room which housed the 4th, 5th, and 6th grades. That's where we practiced the "stop, drop, and cover" drills designed to protect us in case of a bombing attack by the communists. After the demands of the school week, I looked forward to Friday night when all the pressures were behind me and the whole weekend lay ahead. My mom, in keeping with the Catholic practice of not eating meat on Fridays, fixed my dad and me tuna fish sandwiches and french fries. We now ate on trays in front of the TV. The Friday night fights were on, while my mom, still out in the kitchen, wondered aloud how we could even watch boxing. "Any sport where men just punch each other in the face is stupid!" she said.

One Friday evening in October 1957, our show was interrupted by a startling news bulletin. The Soviet Union had successfully launched *Sputnik*, the first man-made object ever launched into outer space. My dad moved uneasily in his chair and set his dinner tray aside. I was about to ask him a question but thought the better of it. His eyes remained fixated on the television screen. The report was very brief. I sensed an alarming urgency that I hadn't ever experienced before, and a sudden knot in my stomach.

All across the nation, a sense of uneasiness grew into a near panic as the news began to sink in that the United States had fallen behind the Russians in the arms race. What was going on? What needed to be done? Who fumbled the ball, and who should be providing leadership? The engineers at Cape Canaveral scrambled around in a furious effort to get our space program off the ground. The nightly news showed huge rockets put together too quickly, exploding during lift off, sometimes exploding on the launching pad. The growing sense of alarm wouldn't be going away any time soon. It was as if, from that time on, we Americans began to live with a largely unspoken and undefined anxiety about the future. We had no idea that this was just the beginning.

Chapter 11

# The High Room

**IN MY JOURNEY** to the High Room, I first had to endure life in the Middle Room with Sister Grace who, somehow, delighted in having talent shows. I *hated* talent shows! I *despised* talent shows! I *loathed* talent shows! I especially hated being forced into showing off what I had learned from piano lessons.

In the third grade, I had to play a duet with some other kid. We had one essential difference between us: he practiced, and I didn't. The result was a train wreck finale with terrible guttural sounds coming from my side of the piano. Yet, here I was, years later, having my arm twisted once again into sharing with my brethren another of my talents in a so-called "Springtime Talent Show."

This time Sister Grace checked off her list the kinds of talent we'd have the opportunity to share. By the time they got to me and this other kid, there was only one thing left: we were paired up to do a comedy routine. I refused to do it, but was chided by my classmates, and so, contrary to all my instincts, I buckled under social pressure. The clincher was when Mary Lou, a cute strawberry-blond, smiled and said admiringly over my objections, "But you're so funny!" Frankly, I didn't want to disappoint her.

## A Great Flash of Light

I agreed to do a routine similar to Dean Martin and Jerry Lewis, a wildly popular comic duo of the time. My job was to come through with the Jerry Lewis (i.e., the funny) end of it. I think the problem was in the material. I shouldn't have relied exclusively on material from *Catholic Digest*. The audience response was. . . Well, maybe some memories are best left repressed.

But here's the thing: just when I had concluded it was futile to stop the evil of talent shows, a miracle was brewing that would change world history at the Middle Room of St. Agatha's. The miracle appeared in the unlikely disguise of a classmate, Robert, the next kid to perform after I was left bleeding on the altar of disgrace. Robert was this husky kid, jolly to the core, who lived life to the fullest. When recess was over, Robert always came in from the playground out of breath, sweating, and his hair messed up. His brown hair always fell over his eyes, and his flannel shirt was always half stuffed in his corduroy pants, with the other half hanging out. I admired Robert for two things. First, Robert was put on the earth to enjoy life. Second, he shared the same dislike I had about being forced to perform. I had done my part, and now Robert stood in front of the class insisting that he didn't have any talent to share, and, therefore, wouldn't be performing anything for us that afternoon. Sister Grace didn't agree.

"You can sing a song," said Sister Grace.

"I can't sing!" Robert fired back.

He looked anything but jolly. He gazed downward searching for a way out, his hands stuck in his pockets. He shifted his weight from one foot to the other.

"Robert, you can either sing a song or dance some dance," said Sister, keeping the pressure on.

Robert kept looking down at the floor and shaking his head. He held his ground, and wasn't going to sing some stupid song, or worse yet, dance any stupid dance.

"Then," said Sister, her voice now had an edge to it, "Do something. Recite a poem. You have to do something! You're not going to sit down until you do!"

Hang in there, Robert, you hang in there! I thought to myself.

Robert looked up. For a moment his face brightened.

"I know a poem," he said, sensing a possible way out. "But," he warned, as his face grew dark again, "you wouldn't like it."

"Recite the poem!" said Sister, her voice rising.

She was now clearly annoyed. She glanced at the clock on the wall, which indicated it was getting close to the time the buses would be lining up to take us home.

"But you won't like it," Robert shot back.

"You just recite your poem, Robert!" ordered Sister. This was no longer a request.

"OK," Robert repeated, "but you're not going to like it."

"Hurry up!" said Sister sharply, as she sat down in her chair, pleased with Robert now under control.

Robert thus began with gusto. "Da Da Da Da Ta Dat! Well. . .
Yankee Doodle went to town,
Riding on a tractor,
Turned on the gas
And burned his ASS!

"And then," said Robert, as he paused to take a breath, "And then he went to HELL!" said Robert in a hearty burst of laughter.

A collective gasp arose from the class, mostly from the girls. I think what horrified them was the indignation of getting one's very behind fried, which was only the beginning—and then getting everything else plunged into the eternally hot hereafter—which, when you think about it, is probably about as bad as it gets.

A terrible silence descended on the room. All eyes locked onto Sister Grace who was sitting perilously half in and half out of her chair—eyes wide, jaw dropped, veil askew. She couldn't speak and looked like she had gotten the wind knocked out of her. It was taking her some time to take in what she had just heard—the calm before the storm.

"Robert!!!" shrieked Sister, as she finally got her wind back and adjusted her veil.

"Thank you! Thank you!" said a smiling Robert as he took his bows; his difficult task accomplished, the sun now shining, and his very soul refreshed.

"And thank all of you!!!" he said, his hand sweeping grandly across his entire audience.

He ended with a deep final bow.

Inside, I was just bursting with pride that I could call Robert my comrade. Robert, who struck a blow for justice and no more stupid talent shows. Aside from that, though, I was a witness to the fact that Robert was the first kid ever in Catholic grade school history to say the forbidden word "ass" out loud. And forever after, I could tell the world that I was there, and had the privilege of hearing it with my own ears! All the Catholics, and probably all the Protestants in our town that night, would be abuzz at the news as they sat down to dinner, and to be honest, I felt kind of envious. Robert would be the hero of all the story telling. Undoubtedly, his fame would spread all throughout the region. He might even become a legend, kind of a horseman with black mask and cape—half Zorro, half Lone Ranger, and half plucky Paul Revere—riding a magnificent stallion through the countryside in the dark of night, triumphantly shouting with abandon, "Ass!" "Ass!" as loud as he wanted, whenever and wherever he wanted!

"I told you that you wouldn't like it," said Robert, looking back over his shoulder at Sister, with just a hint of rebuke in his voice.

"Go back to your seat, Robert!" ordered Sister.

Like an emperor waving and nodding to the crowds, Robert sauntered back to his desk, chortling along the way, his dilemma resolved, and his spirit revitalized. Sliding into his seat, he made silent eye contact with his band of admiring pals, his fellow chortlers. I was among those, who, at that very moment, were elevating him in our minds to that legendary status attained by only a very select few—Julius Caesar in emperor's robes, Alexander the Great in warrior garb, and now our Robert, with his flannel shirt stuffed half in and half out of his pants.

I don't remember if Sister Grace put Robert to the sword that afternoon, or if he went on to live a long and productive life. I don't know if Sister ever fully recovered from someone saying "ass" on her watch. What I do remember, with some relish and with great satisfaction, was that I never had to participate in another talent show at St. Agatha's—not ever again.

In 1958, right about the time the hula-hoop was the national craze, I finally made it to the High Room and Sister Rose, where I would finish up my eighth and final grade at St. Agatha's. About that time too, I began to have a vague awareness that as we try to make our way, life sometimes has nice surprises in store for us. Maybe even a miracle or two, like when the Brooklyn Dodgers beat the unbeatable Yankees in the 1955 World Series.

## The High Room

In the eighth grade, we continued with our Civil Defense drills of "stop, duck, and cover" in the event of a nuclear attack. Sister would shout "Stop!" and our class would stop what we were doing, drop to the floor, crawl under our desks, and cover our heads as tightly as we could.

In the outside world, NATO nations, citing the widening breach with the Soviet Union, agreed to the stationing of American nuclear weapons in Europe along with intermediate-range missiles.[29] "The Europeans acceded to U.S. suggestions that the military side of the alliance should be strengthened by the addition of nuclear weapons."[30] Fidel Castro's revolutionary forces were taking over Cuba, while families in America could buy a cozy fallout shelter for twelve hundred dollars.[31]

As the 1959 school year came to an end, Sister Rose really kept our noses to the grindstone, and our workload became more demanding. In English, she started giving us book report assignments. Our library was meager, consisting largely of books donated by the townsfolk. Some of them were classics, and others were more for adults than for kids, like *For Whom the Bell Tolls*. I found a book I decided to go with entitled *Lassie Come Home*.

I started to read the story that took place in Scotland during really tough times. Lassie's owner, who ran out of money, found himself forced to sell his beautiful sheepherding dog. He turned his beloved companion over to her new owner who took her to a distant place, leaving the owner heartbroken. That's about as far as I got in the book.

The night before my report was due, I sat at our kitchen table feeling miserable. Looking mostly at a blank sheet of paper, I couldn't believe my mom and dad's coldblooded indifference to my situation. How could they possibly expect me to finish reading the last three quarters of the book and still write my paper all in one evening? Around 9:00 o'clock, my dad turned off the television and yawned a good night, while, in the kitchen, mom, who was putting away the last of the dishes, reminded me of my bedtime. I read as fast as I could, to little avail. I scribbled down a whole bunch of thoughts but soon found myself nodding off. Mom closed the last cupboard door and began turning out the lights. I scrawled out a few more sentences, crawled into bed, and felt a sense of doom, as I fell into an exhausted sleep.

Bright and early the next morning, after catechism, Sister Rose stood before the class and announced that we were going to present our two-minute timed oral reports.

Two minutes! My stomach didn't feel very good. I sat at my desk in the back of the classroom and occupied myself with drawing American fighter jets shooting down Russian MIGs. Then, along with the other kids, I listened to the first kid haltingly read his report. I couldn't make heads or tails out of what he was talking about. The second kid, Norm, was even a worse reader than the first. As Norm stumbled through his sentences, regrettably some of the kids laughed heartily. Actually, it might have only been me. Then, a couple more kids were called on. All the while I felt a knot in the pit of my stomach. Finally, I heard Sister Rose call my name.

"Mr. Bognar."

"Yes, Sister."

I stood up and slowly dragged myself up the long aisle to the front of the classroom. At the blackboard, I turned around and looked out at the sea of faces. The place was packed to the rafters. Sister Rose handed my report back to me and clicked her stopwatch. "Begin," she said. I smiled in a winning way to my audience, cleared my throat a few times to kill as much time as I could, and then began.

"My book report is called 'Lassie Come Home'," I explained.

I coughed and cleared my throat a couple more times.

"Sorry," I said, stretching out a few more precious seconds.

Then I began in earnest.

"This man had this dog. This dog's name was Lassie. She was a very good sheep herder."

I looked out at the class. So far, at least, I felt I was doing as good as Norm, who was a disaster.

"So, anyways, times were really tough, and the man didn't have any pesos."

I put that in for a laugh.

"I mean dollars," I corrected myself, with a sly smile, waiting for the laughs that never came.

I continued, "So, he sold Lassie to this man who lived very, very far away."

I was dimly aware that from about here on out I was skating on thin ice. I knew my knowledge of the story was sketchy, but looking down at my report, I was horrified to discover that there were even fewer sentences left on the page than I had remembered! I read them, not quite sure how they were relevant. I cleared my throat a few more times, followed by a retching coughing spasm, then I looked out at the class.

"Does Lassie make it back home?" I asked, not having a clue.

Then after one final stretched out pause, I crossed the finish line, leaving them with the stirring words: "You'll probably find out if you read this book."

Once again, a terrible silence descended upon the land. I was, pardon the expression, completely screwed. I felt Sister Rose's razor-sharp guillotine blade hanging directly above me, and knew it was on its way. Then, out of nowhere, from high in the sky, came an act of Divine intervention that struck like a thunderous lightning bolt—a veritable miracle, like the parting of the Red Sea!

"Very good!" said a smiling Sister Rose.

My jaw dropped to the floor!

Did Sister Rose just say very good!? If so, that meant I had avoided getting my head chopped off! This was the kind of miracle that makes it into the Bible!

"Do you see, class?" Sister asked, as she stood up from her desk.

"Do you see? Mr. Bognar made his book report interesting by asking us a simple question: 'Did Lassie make it back home?' Didn't that make us want to read the book?"

"Yes, sister," said the class weakly, mainly the girls.

A group of emphysema sufferers could've mustered up more enthusiasm than that.

Slowly, though, I found myself nodding approvingly of Sister's remarkably perceptive observation. I stood there and drank deeply from this cup of intoxicating glory as long as I could, knowing that I'd soon find myself back on Sister's other you-know-what list. Returning to my seat, I couldn't believe my luck, not only had I narrowly cheated death, I also received acclaim from Sister Rose. That, for us boys at least, was unprecedented.

I couldn't have known it at the time, but this triumphant moment was the apex of my academic career at St. Agatha's. Those days at the little brick school were about to dwindle down to a precious few. For eight years I had memorized catechism, received the sacraments, and gained a foundational background in geography, math, English, and the sciences. I had gotten into my share of scrapes out on the playground and learned how to fend for myself. I also learned it was my responsibility to be kind, respectful, and fair toward others. Maybe most important of all, I gained a vague understanding that some scripture verses, which at first glance seemed impossible, somehow contained truths that would be revealed to us when the time was right.

On my last day at St Agatha's, we cleaned out our desks and gathered up our notebooks, pens, and report cards. I got in line with the others to file out of the building to the busses for the final time. My only thought was that long, lazy summer vacation days lay ahead.

I joined in the joyous chant, "School's out, school's out, Sister let the fools out!"

Sister Rose, who had spared me the guillotine, didn't try to stop our noisy chanting. Maybe she felt we earned the right. She came down the line to say goodbye to each of us.

"I'll miss you," she said to me, smiling, straightening my collar, and surprisingly giving me a brief hug.

I felt a sudden lump in my throat. The thought that Sister Rose could miss me had never crossed my mind. I boarded the bus and found my way to the very back seat, nearest the rear window. Other kids followed me aboard and sat in their favorite seats.

As the bus filled, some kids started the chant again, "School's out! School's out!! Sister let the fools out!!!"

Everyone joined in, and this time with added foot stomping, the chant grew even louder. The bus driver closed the door, started the engine, and reminded everybody to stay in their seats. I steadied myself as the bus lurched forward.

I glanced back through the window to look at the school one last time and saw Sister Rose standing alone. She was smiling with an occasional wave. Her fingers glided lightly across the rosary beads that hung at her side. She continued to smile until her face seemed to give way to sadness. As our bus pulled away, I was vaguely aware that I was leaving the school with the Catholic education the Dominican Sisters had envisioned, one that formed my identity as a Catholic and as an American. This was my moral compass, one I would take with me as I went on to high school, college, and into the new decade of the 1960s, with all of its soaring triumphs and deepest sorrows.

Sister Rose stood off in the distance, waving her final goodbye, her image now only a blur. I felt sad then, as I feel now some sixty years later. It had never occurred to me to thank her, or to say goodbye.

Chapter 12

# Brylcreem and Bandstand

**THE SUMMER MONTHS** that followed grade school in 1959 were long, lazy, and wonderful. I think it was around that time that my interests shifted dramatically toward teenage things. I listened to the radio's top 40 songs on a Flint station, WTAC, and had many favorites from teen idols including Elvis, Frankie Avalon, Fabian, and the Everly Brothers.

I still enjoyed occasional solitude. On warm June nights, I sometimes took a blanket and tip-toed out of our farmhouse, taking care not to wake up mom and dad. Once outside, I spread the blanket out on the thick grass of our front lawn. There, breathing in the smell of freshly mowed grass, I laid down and listened to the crickets and locusts all around as they performed their lively, nightly concerts, punctuated off in the distance by a lonely barking dog. I was intrigued by the pulsating lanterns of the lightning bugs, and looking up at the heavens, I marveled at an occasional shooting star streaking across the sky.

The crowning glory of these nights was the firmament—the divine space which resided above all. Even at the age of thirteen, I thought of it as the masterpiece of creation—where God's hand had scattered a billion flickering jewels all across the sky. This was the same sky seen by humankind since time immemorial, leaving each observer throughout the ages with a sense of wonder at the immensity of it all, and the recognition of the absolute powerlessness of the intellect, by itself, to fathom the divine qualities of infinity and eternity. I wondered why there couldn't be more than nine planets in the universe and if it was crazy to think that one day humans could travel to the moon. For my mom, accomplishing such an act might be crossing a sacred line, an affront to God.

It was on one of these wondrous, particularly spectacular starfilled nights that everything came together perfectly; the world made sense, and all converged to become one reality. I asked God if there was some vocation that would allow me to capture these moments and spend my entire life looking up at the heavens to contemplate the mystery of the cosmos: eternity, infinity, and God.

I waited prayerfully for an answer. The answer was not long in coming, but in a manner I had not expected—the high-pitched whine of a platoon of dive-bombing mosquitos. I slapped at the first one and missed. He came in for another try. Missed again. He was joined by a friend, and another then another, bringing my blissful moments to a halt.

"Get away!"

More of his buddies arrived, each accompanied by a friend bigger and uglier than the last.

"Go, get away, stop!"

All of them had nasty intent. I realized that trying to continue with my blissful evening was futile, and, unfortunately, it seemed my vocational question was answered by a weird heavenly chorus. I jumped up, pulled my blanket over my head, and beat a hasty retreat back into the house.

"Everything all right?" my father asked from his sleep.

"Everything's fine, Dad. Sorry I made so much noise."

My winged foes pretty much convinced me that I wouldn't be living a life of contemplation—at least not on their watch. No, I was going to have to venture out into the world and find my way.

By the end of summer, I was determined to do just that. I was excited and ready to head off to high school. Standing nearly six feet tall, I looked in the mirror on my first day and was pleased at what I saw. I had successfully combed my unruly hair back out of my face, and it stayed that way! It was the result of Brylcreem. If you used it, throngs of girls were supposed to chase after you.

With the benefit of hindsight, I think maybe the manufacturers were a bit more enthusiastic about their hair product than "the gals" of Owen-Gage High. If not, kudos to the gals who exhibited remarkable restraint as I walked down the school's hallowed halls. Either way, true to form, I maintained my four years of day-to-day vigilance, and successfully fended off the constant threats of feminine sneak attacks.

But as to my first day at Owen-Gage High, a yellow school bus picked me up and dropped us all off at the front door, where I followed an army of kids all abuzz, trying to find their classes. I was struck by the scent of pine from the freshly polished floors in anticipation of opening day. The school was one of those big, red brick buildings found in the Midwest, built God knows when, and located in the little town of Owendale, some ten miles from Gagetown. From having only a dozen kids in my grade at St. Agatha's, I was now in the big leagues where I joined an immense class of forty-two. At orientation I asked if the school offered Latin.

"We don't offer Latin," said the principal, "but we offer Spanish."

He went on to joke: "It's that old thing—Latin is a dead language, as dead as it can be. It once killed all the Romans and now it's killing me!"

I thought that was hilarious, something I should keep in my notebook of great sayings.

The first day ended, and over dinner, I couldn't stop myself from telling my mom and dad about what an exciting day I had. They were both great listeners. I told them how I felt so free! I wasn't stuck sitting in the same room all day! Now I was meeting all kinds of new kids and had two teachers who were really funny. I enjoyed the energetic stampede of students stomping up and down the stairs to get to their next class before the bell rang. Not getting there in time, I explained, meant getting a tardy slip from the principal's office. I admitted I was afraid I wouldn't be able to find where my classes were. But, of course, I did, and discovered some potentially fun kids in my Spanish class, Algebra was going to be a pain, English was dreary and boring, but Shop was great to have after sitting all day.

My enthusiasm continued throughout the school year. Every day brought something new. After school, the bus would transport us home. I was one of those who lived farthest from the school and the last one to be dropped off. I wanted to make it home in time to watch *American Bandstand*. Dick Clark hosted this teen show from Philadelphia that was doing something new. He asked kids what they thought about music—rather than telling them what they should like—and built a music empire around it. He'd start out by playing a new record that teens could dance to and then asked how they would rate it. I recall comments that generally went along something like this:

"I, uh, gave it, like uh, like a 82."
"Your reason?"
"Well, I, uh, liked it and stuff."
"How about you?"
"Uh, I like gave it a 86."
"Why?"
"Cuz it was good and had a good beat."
My words exactly! Great minds!

My school spirit was heightened by the thump of a football kicked high into the cold starry nights, as the Mighty Bulldogs, or sometimes floundering Bulldogs, took the field against neighboring high schools. When football season ended and basketball season began, the gyms were filled with students and family following the lead of the cheerleaders, clapping their hands and stomping their feet in a rhythm that shook the stands. "We are the Bulldogs, the Mighty, Mighty Bulldogs!"

Friday nights also meant dances. Girls clustered in tightly knit groups around the gym floor, talking, laughing, and making multiple visits to the girl's bathroom. Boys, in their groups, were boisterous as they stood around the refreshment table ordering Coca Colas and daring one another to ask a certain girl to dance. Music and voices filled the dimly lit gymnasium, and the braver couples got out on the dance floor. A number of fast dances, like Elvis' "I'm All Shook Up" would be followed by slow dancing songs with timeless lyrics of deep feelings that could have been written by Shakespeare himself, if he had chosen to become a songwriter and write songs about angels, sock hops, and being treated cruel.

On weekday evenings following the family rosary, mom, dad, and I continued to watch our favorite television programs. One September in 1960, ABC interrupted its usual Thursday night lineup to broadcast the first of four televised debates between Vice President Richard Nixon and a lesser-known young senator, John F. Kennedy. The backdrop to the debates, as the Cold War between the U.S. and the Soviet Union was heating up, were growing concerns on both sides about missiles delivering warheads.

A year earlier, Khrushchev visited the United States. According to one source, when he met with a group of American union leaders, he denounced the fact that America had placed missiles in Turkey that had the ability to hit Moscow. Khrushchev expressed his deep concerns. He asked one of the leaders, Victor Reuther, brother of United Auto Workers president Walter Reuther, "How would you feel if there were Soviet military bases in Mexico and Canada?" ('Who is keeping you from having them?' Reuther answered. 'Set them up.')" [32]

Television analysts said the debates were historic, reminiscent of when Abraham Lincoln debated Stephen Douglas for the presidency a hundred years earlier.

In the mind of many across the country, it was a foregone conclusion that Nixon would be the next president, since the enormously popular Eisenhower, who was not only the general who defeated Hitler in Europe, but presided over eight years of unparalleled prosperity, had endorsed him to be his successor. That all changed in the course of an evening.

It was my first real awareness of John Kennedy, who gave the opening statement. With a slight move to assure the straightness of his tie, the newcomer moved to the podium with grace:

> In the election of 1860, Abraham Lincoln said the question was whether this nation could exist half slave or half free. In the election of 1960, and with the world around us, the question is: whether the world will exist half slave or half free. . . . [33]

With these two sentences, John Kennedy broke into America's consciousness. He was ushering in the decade of the

1960s, a decade of highs and lows like no other, and all of it was just about to begin.

Chapter 13

# A Tremendous Flash of Light

**IF JOHN KENNEDY** wasn't cocky, he certainly wasn't at a loss for confidence. That's what I came away with from the first of the Nixon-Kennedy debates.

> This is a great country, but I think it could be a greater country, and this is a powerful country, but I think it could be a more powerful country. [34]

Kennedy's arguments were clear and forceful, although, I thought in his cerebral presentation, he seemed to lack a sense of warmth. Nixon offered his opening statement:

> The things that Senator Kennedy has said, many of us can agree with. ...but our disagreement is not about the goals for America but only about the means to reach those goals. [35]

The candidates sparred through four debates. In the final one, Kennedy said that the Communists had "made a breakthrough in missiles, and by nineteen sixty-one, two, and three, they will be outnumbering us in missiles."[36] He also pointed out that the Communists were gaining a foothold in the western hemisphere, in Cuba, ninety miles off the coast of the United States—further evidence that America was losing the race to the Communists. [37]

By the end of the debates, Kennedy had presented a disturbing image: America was falling behind the Russians, and a new administration was needed to bring about change.

My father turned off the television and asked my mother what she thought.

"Maybe it is time for a change," she said, and added, referring to the youthful Kennedy, "and even though he is so young, he is a Catholic."

The next day at school it seemed like everyone had an opinion.

"Kennedy's smarter than Nixon!"

"Nixon proved himself—he's got the experience, and he's the guy who stood up to Khrushchev!"

Like two athletes sprinting to the finish line, the two candidates raced neck and neck to the campaign's very end. On the bright morning of November 9, 1960, the announcement was made: John Kennedy had won. Televisions showed JFK's motorcade driving to the Hyannis Port Armory for a victory speech. People lined the streets waving, cheering, and getting a glimpse of the new president-elect. The motorcade halted, and JFK exited from the car with his usual grace. Smiling with satisfaction, he was obviously very pleased at winning a long and hard-fought race. In what was to become recognized as his characteristic mannerisms, he brushed his hair aside, shook hands, and nodded to the cheers and chants of the excited hometown crowd. "Jack! We want Jack!"

Kennedy moved easily through the crowd and disappeared into the armory, where he delivered a gracious speech and an address to the nation:

> To all Americans, I say that the next four years are going to be difficult and challenging years for us all. The election may have been a close one, but I think that there is general agreement by all of our citizens that a supreme national effort will be needed in the years ahead to move this country safely through the 1960s. [38]

## A Tremendous Flash of Light

The following January of 1961, the day after my fifteenth birthday, both faculty and students squeezed into our high school gym, where two black and white television sets were positioned on the gym floor. We were reminded that we were witnessing history. For the first time we students were able to watch a presidential inauguration as it happened. Teachers began shushing everyone, and the talking subsided while the young president took the podium for his address to the nation. Some kids, though oblivious to the historic moment, continued conversations as the new president took the oath of office.

Then Kennedy began to speak. The sound and cadence of his sentences began to build, one on the other, as Kennedy presented his message to a deeper intensity and higher moral plane.

> The world is very different now. For man holds in his mortal hands the power to abolish all forms of human poverty and all forms of human life.[39]

As the speech continued, some students became restless and distracted, with a buzz from the crowd growing louder, again they were shushed. But I heard one teacher say, "Politicians all say the same thing. He's not saying anything different." He couldn't have been more mistaken. A half century later, Thurston Clarke, in his book, *Ask Not*, described it this way:

> Finally, after delivering sentences inspired by the most traumatic and memorable moments of his life, and speaking with an emotional intensity he seldom revealed, and inspiring the audience at the Capitol to cry out like a congregation at a revival meeting, he delivered his master sentence.[40]

> '...And so, my fellow Americans, ask not what your country can do for you, ask what you can do for your country...'[41]

From the noise around me, I missed the first part of the president's clarion call as his speech reached its climax. But I did hear, "ask what you can do for your country."

## A Great Flash of Light

The phrase struck a chord within me, almost as if it were a spiritual calling. Words of fire spoken by a young, charismatic leader; words that reverberated way beyond the inaugural crowd to the nation and around the world. ". . .it was at this moment" wrote Thurston Clarke "that Americans walked with him through a membrane in time, entering the next decade, and a new era." [42] With the inauguration concluded, our crowd dispersed to return to our classes, and Kennedy began his presidency.

In the months that followed, however, not everyone was pleased with the Kennedy glamour in the White House. In Kentucky, the Trappist Monk, Thomas Merton, complained in his journal, "Every time Kennedy sneezes or blows his nose, an article is read about it in the refectory."[43] Yet, the combination of Kennedy's keen mind, movie star-like appeal, and sharp wit created a growing sense of enthusiasm throughout the country.

As I went into my sophomore year, television brought bad news from around the world—from a bloody civil rights struggle in Africa to similar struggles in the deep South. Stalin's hot-tempered successor, Nikita Khrushchev, was determined that the Soviet Union was going to pass the U.S. in both its economic growth and military might. He wasn't kidding. To back up his military claim, in October of 1961, the Soviets detonated their most powerful hydrogen bomb yet—in fact, the most powerful human-made explosion in history, and that undeniable fact shook the confidence and security of the entire western world. [44]

One day at my desk in study hall, I did my best teen slouch to communicate to the world that I was more bored than usual. Apart from a clanking radiator, nothing suggested there was life on our planet. My fingers thumped my desk with a creative rendition of the "William Tell Overture." My eyes drifted aimlessly along the classroom walls until they fixed on a poster of a newly published book. The cover had a menacing look: a vivid black backdrop, a stark white circle in the center, and within that, a black swastika. The title: *The Rise and Fall of the Third Reich*.

"You can be the first to read it," said the librarian, noting my interest.

I opened the book and began to read. In a matter of minutes, I was transported back to another time, one that was exciting and yet frightening.

The author, William L. Shirer, was a young and inexperienced reporter for CBS radio in the 1930s who landed an assignment to broadcast reports on what was going on in Germany as the Nazis were taking power. Through Shirer's words, I found myself jostled among a throng of people in an elaborate hotel in Berlin where the rising dictator was meeting with his henchmen. Shirer, along with everyone else, was trying to get a glimpse of this mysterious man. The whole world was focused on Berlin with an anticipation that a terrible international storm was about to break. Rumors had circulated that Hitler was on the verge of a physical and emotional breakdown.

That's not what Shirer witnessed.

Suddenly, the reporter got more than a glimpse of this strange man: "Followed by Göring, Ribbentrop, Goebbels, Hess, and Keitel, he [Hitler] brushed past me like the conqueror he is this morning." [45]

Adolph Hitler "brushed" by him! My God! What must that have felt like? Did it make his skin crawl? Did he feel a chill run down his spine? These were a gang of evil men who condemned millions to their deaths.

After months of being tormented by indecision, Hitler had just made his decision to attack Poland, the spark that ignited a second World War.

I couldn't stop reading as I felt drawn into the eeriness of this distant place and time, when the powers of darkness fomented and grew until the world exploded in flames. I felt an intense desire to know more about how a terrible man like Hitler came to power, and, most of all, how he could be stopped.

When I finished the book, our librarian suggested that I read another: *Hiroshima*, a book written by John Hersey, the journalist who had written about John Kennedy's ordeal with the P.T. 109. Hersey, an author who was interested in how humans can rise above terrible adversity, went to Japan shortly after the bomb was dropped on Hiroshima and interviewed a handful of civilians who had somehow survived. From those interviews, he provided firsthand accounts of what war was like to the victim in this newly born atomic age. I had only thought of the bombing of Hiroshima from the vantage point of the victors—America won, and the war had ended.

# A Great Flash of Light

I checked out the book, turned to its beginning pages, and read about the morning of August 6, 1945—at exactly fifteen minutes past eight:

> The morning was perfectly clear and so warm that the day promised to be uncomfortable."[46] "...Miss Toshiko Sasaki, a clerk in the personnel department of the East Asia Tin Works, had just sat down at her place in the plant office and was turning her head to speak with the girl at the next desk."[47]

I then read the sentence that was to change my life:

> Then a tremendous flash of light cut across the sky.[48]

This sentence, consisting of ten ordinary words of the English language, described the moment in history when humankind crossed an invisible moral line and created the age of atomic war.

From John Hersey's account, few in Hiroshima seemed to have heard noise from the bomb, yet it was heard over twenty miles away.[49] As I read on, at times I felt nauseous, and on one occasion simply had to put the book down. I had a notion that we Americans were not only the victors but also the victims. I breathed a sigh of relief that this horror was a thing of the past and could never happen again.

What I couldn't have imagined, as I finished the book in 1962, was that in only a matter of months, President Kennedy, in a televised address to the nation, would announce that the United States and the Soviet Union were on a collision course to an all-out nuclear war.

And as events began to unfold, it seemed that no one was able to stop it.

Chapter 14

# A Prayer for John Kennedy

**I WAS A SNARE DRUMMER** in our high school marching band. I like to think I participated in competitive tryouts and brought home the silver, but actually there was only me and this other kid. Nevertheless, in my junior year, 1962, I beamed with pride in being proclaimed second drummer, feeling that I was the complete package. I had the passion, the will, and the rhythm. My one, albeit minor, weakness was that my rhythm wasn't always consistent.

In fairness, the first drummer was a natural and could play those drums like the great Buddy Rich. But I could offer a smile, an eagerness to learn, and my mostly on target rhythm. In our concerts, I always got off to a good start, noting that everyone around me, who wasn't blowing into an instrument, was smiling and seemed content. Then, out of nowhere, I'd come in maybe a second or two late on the beat, immediately work to correct my error, and come in a smidgeon early on the next few beats and so on. What complicated things a bit was when the band started following my beat rather than our leader's baton. Understandably, this he viewed with displeasure. A painful, grimacing, non-verbal look can convey a lot of meaning. "What are you doing??!" Those stares could really cut deep into you.

## A Great Flash of Light

At an autumn concert in our gym, with a packed house of maybe thirty, I felt sharp and ready to go. As I was setting up, I heard a fellow band member sneer, "Try not to drop your drumsticks this time." Some last-minute advice, I guess, about getting back to the basics.

I started out really good. But it was in the third piece, the theme from Exodus, that the band's performance began to sag. Our wind section, which normally played the magnificent crescendo with passion, barely wheezed their way through. It was like a group of allergy sufferers all having attacks at the same time. Not a pretty sight, not music that inspires.

But it was the Christmas concert that was traumatic, painful—call it what you want—just the worst. Once again, the house was packed. It all started when our husky tuba player made a rookie mistake. It happened during that quiet moment in "'Twas the Night Before Christmas," when nary a creature was stirring. Well, unfortunately, our guy turned to the wrong page in his music and powered out a couple of monster blasts that nearly blew off the rafters, leaving two elderly ladies in the front row visibly shaken. Our band leader shot a stink-eye look at the kid, who was already horrified at his mistake and was scrambling to pick up his music that fell all over the floor. I could just imagine what was going on inside the kid's head. You fumbled the ball! You dropped the crucial pass! You let the team down! You're kind of like a big glob of mayo sliding down a new silk tie.

What I remember most from my band experiences though, was a morning when we practiced out on our high school football field, preparing for an upcoming Friday night game. It was a chilly Tuesday, October 23, 1962, a cloudy and otherwise ordinary school morning, except that President Kennedy held a televised address to the nation the night before on a matter of highest national urgency. My mom, dad, and I watched the president on television, as did others around the world. Sitting at his desk he spoke words that remain grim to this day:

> ...it shall be the policy of this nation to regard any nuclear missile launched from Cuba against any nation in the Western Hemisphere as an attack by the Soviet Union

on the United States, requiring a full retaliatory response upon the Soviet Union.[50]

I felt a knot tighten in my stomach, as I do when I think about it now. I knew enough about the history of wars and atomic bombs from reading *Hiroshima* and *Nations at War*, and witnessing Khrushchev's combative tantrums, to know that the world was headed toward some deep trouble. I tossed and turned in my bed until I fell asleep well after midnight.

The following morning, before I awoke, my dad got up and left for work. At breakfast I felt sad, wondering if I would see him again. My mother and I spoke little as we watched continuous news coverage, while my fork moved scrambled eggs this way and that on my plate. Even the aroma of coffee made me queasy in a strange way. The news reports seemed surreal. No information about further developments was available. The public was left in a vacuum, not knowing what might happen next. All anyone could do in these hours of total uncertainty, while the future of the human race was somehow decided, was to wait.

As I finished eating, I heard the impatient blare of the school bus horn. I grabbed my books and lunch and hurried out the door. I looked back at my mother for some reassurance.

"Say a little prayer for the president," she said.

I took an extra moment to remember the kind look of her face, then ran off to catch the bus.

My first class was Band. There was a general sense of tension in the air. Some kids fidgeted as they prepared their instruments. Clarinetists ran up and down their scales as a bass drum boomed and the snares rat-a-tatted. There was a wisecrack or two about what could be about to happen to us, followed by forced laughter. What else could you do? Most seemed oblivious to the lethal turn the world was taking.

We moved from the classroom to the football field. I kept looking toward the southeast horizon—toward St. Agatha's and Detroit where my cousins lived, and then toward Washington, D.C. I looked for a flash of light that would cut across the entire sky. What would it look like, this flash point of a welder's arc, a thousand times more powerful than the Hiroshima bomb? Would we see it, or all be melted before we could register the sight?

The world was at the brink of something, we didn't know what. I couldn't do anything but pray. There was nothing that people around the world could do except pray. The activity of the earth ground to a halt, as together we waited helplessly, holding our breath.

I looked up at the foreboding Michigan sky and wondered: Is this the day the world will end?

I was fifteen years old. And I prayed with every fiber in me, "O God, please help Kennedy."

And in Washington, John Kennedy was going to need all the prayers he could get.

## Chapter 15

# Great Trouble

> *Everything now depends on man. Immense power of destruction is given to his hand, and the question is if he can resist the will to use it and can temper his will with the spirit of love and wisdom.* [51]
>
> Carl G. Jung

> *He [JFK] did not shrink from disclosing the gravity of the threat, but he withheld details of a nuclear strike's full horror.* [52]
>
> Stacey Bredhoff

**IN OCTOBER OF 1962,** although he didn't know it, John Kennedy was approaching the darkest hours of his presidency, and the world was moving into the most perilous moments in its history. How did this terrible situation ever come to be?

Following World War II came the Cold War, when the Soviets and Americans were deeply concerned, if not paranoid, about each other's military intentions, but the threat of nuclear war seemed remote. The ominous clouds of an international storm gathered slowly at first, its swirling winds gaining strength with each development. Suddenly, that remote chance changed abruptly.

October 16, 1962, began much like any other Tuesday morning for the 35th president of the United States. That was until intelligence advisors presented him with unmistakable evidence that the Soviets were hard at work installing missiles in Cuba. If they became operational, the Soviets, for the first time, would have the capability of launching a major nuclear attack on the United States, not from the Soviet Union thousands of miles away, but from ninety miles off the coast of Florida. It was estimated that the Russian technicians could operationalize them in a short period of time, but the devil of it was that no one knew if that meant weeks or maybe days. Whichever it was, the time to remove them was ticking.

After he gathered further intelligence information to validate the reality of the missiles, carefully studied photographic data, consulted members of Congress, and formulated a course of action to remove the missiles, JFK delivered his October 22nd address to the nation announcing a matter of highest national urgency. Seeing his somber image and listening to the dark content of his address was a terrifying experience—one I will never forget.

> Good evening, my fellow citizens: This government, as promised, has maintained the closest surveillance of the Soviet military build-up on the island of Cuba. Within the past week, unmistakable evidence has established the fact that a series of offensive missile sites is now in preparation on that imprisoned island. The purpose of these bases can be none other than to provide a nuclear strike capability against the Western Hemisphere. . . .[53]

For almost two years, along with the American public, I had seen a young leader, confident about the direction his country should take. In his press conferences, President Kennedy responded to questions with a crisp delivery, containing factual answers that were sometimes punctuated with occasional flashes of ironic humor. On this night, however, while his address was filled with facts and information, the lightheartedness wasn't anywhere to be found. The president's message was serious, his tone grave.

GREAT TROUBLE

We really had little grasp of the enormity of the danger nor any idea of what was happening behind the scenes to resolve the crisis.

In the televised debates of the 1960 presidential election, I had seen how boldly candidate Kennedy had severely criticized the Eisenhower administration for failing to stop Communist influence from spreading to Cuba. Now the shoe was on the other foot. As president, Kennedy was fast learning that tough talk by a presidential candidate during a political campaign was one thing; dealing with the issue that could bring about a world war was quite another.

The day after learning of the missiles, JFK telephoned his brother, Robert Kennedy, then Attorney General, and asked him to come to the White House. "He said only that we were facing great trouble," Robert Kennedy wrote in *Thirteen Days*, his account of the Cuban Missile Crisis.[54]

Kennedy assembled a committee of advisors, named ExComm. The committee's task was to meet in secret, examine the developing situation, and recommend to the president the most effective course of action to remove the missiles from Cuba. This

Fig. 19. JFK at ExComm (Corbis Historical/Getty Images)

committee consisted of his top-level governmental officials, including his brother Robert, Vice President Lyndon Johnson, Secretary of Defense Robert S. McNamara, and a dozen others. He also had at hand his military advisors, his Joint Chiefs of Staff, including its chairman, the Air Force Four Star General Curtis E. LeMay.

General LeMay was a tough, cigar chomping, battle seasoned, highly decorated career officer, renowned for his bombing raids on Germany and Japan and his superb organizational ability that established the Strategic Air Command as the Air Force's premier striking force unit.

In the Pacific campaign, on the night of March 10, 1945, LeMay's bombers carried out the firebombing of Tokyo,[55] resulting in 100,000 civilians burned to death at one time. The general didn't seem to feel a lot of remorse about inflicting death and destruction on civilian casualties:

> There are no innocent civilians. It is their government and you are fighting a people, you are not trying to fight an armed force anymore. So it doesn't bother me so much to be killing innocent bystanders.[56]

LeMay would later boast:

> ...we scorched and boiled and baked to death more people in Tokyo on that night of March 9-10 than went up in vapor at Hiroshima and Nagasaki combined.[57]

In the months following the fire-bombing of Tokyo, his further bombing raids went on to destroy sixty-six medium-sized Japanese cities, the size of Cleveland or St. Louis, and kill another estimated 400,000 civilians, largely including mothers, babies, and toddlers since young men were fighting in the war. On August 6, 1945, on orders from President Truman, one of LeMay's bombers, the Enola Gay, dropped the atomic bomb on Hiroshima that killed an estimated 140,000 people and delivered a similar fate to an estimated 74,000 people in Nagasaki three days later.[58]

It's hardly surprising to learn that General LeMay and JFK had an intense dislike for one another. My guess is that much of it stemmed from how they viewed people and how they viewed war.

Kennedy had seen war up close in the Pacific, saw what it could do to people, and hated the whole notion of it. In contrast, LeMay, too, saw war up close, but seemed to have an appetite for the destructive power he could deliver on his enemies.

As the crisis unfolded, LeMay despised Kennedy's careful approach, which the general saw as a sign of weakness. The President disliked how LeMay and other members of the Joint Chiefs brushed aside factors that could bring about catastrophic consequences.[59] Now, as one of Kennedy's chief military advisors, LeMay was intent to provide an overwhelming show of military force in the situation developing in Cuba. His position was strengthened by the fact that the missiles might be ready for launch in a matter of days. It, therefore, only made sense to take them out right away, before they were ready for launch. Any delay would be foolish. Following LeMay's leadership, the Joint Chiefs kept the pressure on Kennedy, insisting that a military strike was needed immediately. To do anything less meant that Kennedy was not meeting his primary responsibility as Commander in Chief of keeping America safe.

Realizing the gravity of the crisis, Kennedy was most concerned about something that the chiefs were not, miscalculation. As a student of history, Kennedy had read *The Guns of August*, Barbara Tuchman's brilliant account of how the early twentieth century monarchic and bureaucratic minds were so restricted by their unexamined assumptions, that they foolishly miscalculated one another's actions and blundered into the horrors of the first world war characterized by trenches, barbed wire, and millions of military and civilian deaths. Kennedy was determined not to repeat their errors. Instead, he wanted to proceed through this nuclear minefield carefully and methodically, examining each assumption and potential consequence as best he could. In particular, he wanted to keep in mind how Khrushchev was viewing the development of events from his vantage point on the other side of the world and the pressures Khrushchev was facing from his military advisors and political opponents.

There were many opportunities for miscalculation. Not only were the United States and the Soviet Union separated geographically by thousands of miles, more importantly, they were also separated by differences in language, history, and cultural values.

Those differences complicated the crisis immeasurably and made its solution immensely more difficult. And to top it all, since the Second World War, each country had developed a total and profound mistrust of the other. The two nations were becoming mortal enemies.

In fact, there were two major miscalculations already at work. From an earlier face to face meeting in Vienna, Khrushchev sized up Kennedy as weak and inexperienced, someone he could handle quite easily. Based on that assessment and other conclusions, Khrushchev decided to take a reckless gamble. He would proceed with a top-secret plan, *Operation Anadyr*, to move Soviet missiles into Cuba. If and when Kennedy found out, Khrushchev reasoned, the missiles would already be in place—the deed already done—leaving Kennedy in a position in which he couldn't do much, if anything, about it. If the plan was successful, Khrushchev could launch missiles at major American cities from just ninety miles away. Khrushchev would thus gain a powerful strategic advantage over the Americans and thereby achieve a major shift in the balance of power. It was an unbelievably bold idea and a terrible miscalculation that would bring the world to the brink.

There was another consideration that undoubtedly weighed heavily on Kennedy's mind as the crisis began to unfold. It was a plan so dangerous and unspeakable that it was labeled "For the President's Eyes Only." The plan was so secret that it has only recently been revealed, a half century after it was proposed to the 35th president of the United States.

Only months into his presidency, Kennedy's military and CIA leaders requested his authorization to launch a future all-out, unprovoked, sneak nuclear attack on the Soviet Union and China.[60] The targets included every major city in the Soviet Union and every major city in China.[61] The goal of the nuclear attacks was to wipe out the Russian and Chinese populations. In addition, the plan acknowledged that millions of Europeans would also die in the first hours from a Soviet counterattack, and scores of millions of Americans would also be killed on the east coast.[62] Despite the number of millions, if not billions, of Russian, Chinese, American, and European casualties, the planners somehow reasoned that the sneak attack was necessary if America's force for good would finally defeat the evils of Communism once and for all.

Kennedy, reportedly visibly shaken, angry, and deeply disturbed by this monstrous and morally unspeakable proposition, abruptly left the meeting, later commenting sharply to Dean Rusk, his Secretary of State, "And we call ourselves the human race."[63]

Chapter 16

# At the Brink

**JUST HOW CLOSE** did we come to the nuclear brink? That was the fundamental question I sought to have answered, not only to understand the reality of what happened during the missile crisis, but more importantly, to prevent future incidents from escalating to a point of no return.

When it was learned that the Soviets were installing their missiles in Cuba, the pressure to authorize an all-out nuclear attack on the Soviet Union again found its way back to Kennedy's doorstep. He would need to draw upon every life experience and resource within himself to deal with this crisis.

In addition to his wartime experience in the Pacific, Kennedy, not yet thirty, also saw firsthand the devastation of the war in Europe. Through his wealthy father's connection, Kennedy accompanied a U.S. governmental task force that traveled throughout post-war Europe to assess the war's damage and report back to President Truman. Kennedy kept an ongoing journal of what he saw in the major cities such as Paris, Frankfurt, and most importantly, Berlin—a city he had visited only a few years earlier.

Of this once thriving capital city of Germany, he noted its complete destruction. The grand city before him was totally devastated with countless numbers of people crushed beneath its rubble.

Fig. 20. JFK signing the quarantine proclamation.
(Cecil Stoughton/the LIFE Images Collection/Getty Images)

Now, as president, Kennedy, deeply aware of the consequences of war, carefully chose not to tip his hand to the Soviets that he was aware of the missile installation in Cuba. He continued to follow his regular schedule of social events and speaking engagements.

In the meantime, ExComm began meetings that ran late into the night. Members were all over the map about what to do. Arguments and exchanges became heated. He sometimes left them to meet on their own, where they might feel free to express their opinions more openly. Robert Kennedy wrote:

> Each one of us was being asked to make a recommendation which would affect the future of all mankind, a recommendation which, if wrong and if accepted, could mean the destruction of the human race.[64]

In the days of fiery debate, two courses of action emerged: an air strike or a blockade. To the Joint Chiefs' chagrin, Kennedy resisted their recommendation for an immediate military strike. Instead, he decided on the naval blockade: an imaginary line drawn around the island, a line which Soviet ships would not be allowed to cross.

The term "quarantine" was used which sounded less bellicose than "blockade." Kennedy's hope was that the quarantine option would avoid a confrontation and allow additional time to figure a way out of the crisis. However, like every course of action, the quarantine opened the door to many unanswered questions. What will happen if the ships cross the line? Would American destroyers dare fire a shot across the vessel's bow? Would they fire a disabling shot at Soviet rudders?

A single act of an assassin's bullet was the spark that set off World War I killing eighty million people. One misstep now could result in three billion lives lost. The president and his advisors had to come up with answers quickly so that naval commanders would know which actions were authorized and which were not. As they did, tensions and practical concerns travelled up and down the chain of command.

At the top, Kennedy's Joint Chiefs were furious over his choice of the quarantine option, which they perceived as weak and indecisive, as opposed to their strong proposal of a military strike to take out the missiles while they were not yet operational.

General LeMay, frustrated with Kennedy's handling of the crisis, was used to getting his way. He dominated meetings, presenting himself as the true American patriot, the only one experienced and knowledgeable enough to make the right calls. He treated those who disagreed with him with contempt, viewing them as weak or even unpatriotic. His arguments were sweeping, dramatic, and convincing, overselling their advantages and minimizing any downsides. His position was based on the premise that the Soviets would not respond to an air strike. And he spoke with an absolute certitude that he was right. With a renewed sense of urgency, the general was determined to impose his will on the inexperienced Kennedy, who had only been a junior grade officer in the war. He would demolish the president's reservations, badger him, and bully him into a position where he would have no choice but to launch a military attack.[65] General LeMay confronted the president, which led to the historic exchange between them:

> LeMay: I think that a blockade, and political talk, would be considered by a lot of our friends and neutrals as being a pretty weak response to this. And I'm sure that a lot of our own citizens would feel that way, too. In other words, you're in a pretty bad fix, Mr. President.
>
> Kennedy: What did you say?
>
> LeMay: You're in a pretty bad fix.
>
> Kennedy: You're in there with me.[66]

After Kennedy's address to the nation, the crisis reached the level of DEFCON-2, one short of launching a nuclear attack. The Joint Chiefs insisted that only an immediate air strike would remove the missiles from the island. Discussions were breaking down. The group was on the verge of physical and emotional exhaustion. Robert Kennedy noted that they came to a point "when we almost seemed unable to communicate with one another."[67]

The problem of communication continued further down the chain of command, when Secretary of Defense McNamara and the Chief Admiral of the Navy, George Whelan Anderson, got into a shouting match. McNamara told Anderson that no action, none, would be taken without presidential authorization. Admiral Anderson bluntly told McNamara, his civilian boss, to leave Navy business to the Navy.[68]

By Wednesday, October 24, 1962, the full threat of the international storm arrived. The young president was confronted with the distinct possibility of nuclear insanity. Robert Kennedy later wrote, "I think these few minutes were the time of gravest concern for the President. . . ."[69]

He looked across the table at his brother:

> . . .His hand went up to his face and covered his mouth. He opened and closed his fist. His face seemed drawn, his eyes pained, almost gray. We stared at each other across the table. For a few fleeting seconds, it was almost as though no one else was there and he was no longer the President.[70]

As for himself, Robert Kennedy wrote, "I felt we were on the edge of a precipice with no way off."[71]

Why, despite the unimaginable pressures to launch a military strike as soon as possible, did the president remain resolute to avoid escalation at all costs? Why, especially, since in the 1960 campaign only two years earlier, he was the candidate who repeatedly hammered the point that America was falling behind the Soviets in missiles? He was the candidate that spoke of a missile gap and insisted that the U.S. must strengthen its military might.

But now he wasn't just a candidate running for president. He was the president, and the decision maker of America's nuclear response. One can't help but wonder what was going through his mind as the crisis deepened. Was he remembering what he wrote in his journal of the images he saw in bombed out Berlin?

> The devastation is complete. . . there is not a single building which is not gutted. On some of the streets the stench—sweet and sickish from dead bodies—is overwhelming. . . the people all have completely colorless faces—a yellow tinge with pale tan lips. . . . Where they

are going, no one seems to know. I wonder whether they do.[72]

Was he influenced by his journalist friend John Hersey's book, *Hiroshima*, the book I had read in high school? Was he remembering the same graphic words I had read that revealed the stories of the victims who lived in the aftermath of the atomic bomb?

> ...The hurt ones were quiet; no one wept, much less screamed in pain; no one complained; none of the many who died did so noisily; not even the children cried; very few people even spoke."[73]

Were Hersey's descriptions shaping Kennedy's decision to renounce a nuclear strike?

> They all felt terribly thirsty, and they drank from the river. At once they were nauseated and began vomiting, and they retched the whole day. Others were also nauseated; they all thought (probably because of the strong odor of ionization, an "electric smell" given off by the bomb's fission) that they were sick from a gas the Americans had dropped.[74]

Did the president remember the passage of the Japanese man who made futile efforts to help victims in the aftermath of the atomic bomb?

> He [Mr. Tanimoto] drove the boat onto the bank and urged them to get aboard. They did not move and he realized that they were too weak to lift themselves. He reached down and took a woman by the hands, but her skin slipped off in huge, glove-like pieces.... Then he got out into the water and, though a small man, lifted several of the men and women, who were naked, into his boat. Their backs and breasts were clammy, and he remembered uneasily what the great burns he had seen during the day had been like: yellow at first, then red and

swollen, with the skin sloughed off, and finally, in the evening suppurated and smelly.[75]

On the other side of the globe, about the time of Kennedy's announcement to the nation, Khrushchev had made a crucial decision that worsened an already perilous situation. Unbeknownst to Kennedy and ExComm, the Soviet leader authorized his commander's forces in Cuba and selected submarine commanders in the Caribbean to launch their nuclear missiles against the United States if the U.S. attacked Cuba.[76] Among other complications, that decision meant it was no longer only two people (Khrushchev and Kennedy) who could launch a nuclear war. Now any one in a handful of people had that authority.

Recon missions continued to fly over Cuba to photograph the Soviets' day-to-day progress in operationalizing their missile sites. On October 27, the White House received news that Cuban antiaircraft fire shot down and killed Air Force pilot Major Rudolph Anderson. This was an act of war. Surely, the generals reasoned, the killing of an American pilot would compel the president to authorize an invasion. They reminded Kennedy that air and ground forces were assembled in Florida on high alert, waiting only for him to act like a president and give the order to attack.

On that same day, in the Arctic, a nuclear armed Air Force pilot mistakenly flew deep into Russian airspace, prompting the Soviets to send up their fighter jets to confront or shoot down the invader. Realizing his terrible mistake, the pilot reversed his course, and flew back to Alaskan airspace with Soviet jets in hot pursuit. Khrushchev sent a scathing message to Kennedy, rebuking him for allowing something so provocative to happen at such a critical time.

Meanwhile, the Joint Chiefs continued to harangue the president that an invasion of the Cuban island was the only course of action. The clock was ticking toward nuclear midnight. Soviet ships approached the quarantine line accompanied by four Soviet submarines equipped with nuclear missiles and the authority to use them. American destroyers, unaware that Soviet subs had nuclear weapons, dropped depth charges around the approaching missile-carrying freighters—not to sink the ships but to harass the accompanying Soviet submarines below. The subs would be forced to stay underwater until their oxygen was nearly depleted and then surface, revealing their location.[77]

One of the four, a B59, remained submerged while American destroyers dropped depth charges all around. In the sub, temperatures rose to between 113 to 140 degrees Fahrenheit. Oxygen was running low, and CO2 levels rose to critical points. Soviet crew members began to have trouble formulating thoughts, and officers began to pass out one after another.[78] Nerves on board were beyond frayed, and the depth charge explosions around the sub shook its crew to the core.[79] "They exploded right next to the hull. It felt like you were in a barrel, which somebody is constantly blasting with a sledgehammer."[80]

Under intense pressure, the physically and mentally exhausted sub commander finally reached his breaking point and exploded in a fury, screaming orders to prepare their nuclear torpedo for firing. "We're going to blast them now! We will die, but we will sink them all—we will not disgrace our Navy!"[81] The second in command gave his authorization, but on this submarine, a third approval was required.

Fig. 21. Vasili Arkhipov, the man who saved the world. (Olga Arkhipova, CC BY-SA 4.0, Wikimedia Commons)

The third officer, Captain Vasili Arkhipov, withheld his authorization.[82] And his refusal, in that one moment, saved the world.

However, there was still more to be done. In the White House, Kennedy's advisors had exhausted all their arguments, dispensed all their wisdom, and spouted all their prejudices.

His Defense Secretary, Robert McNamara reflected:

> . . .I do know that as I left the White House and walked through the garden to my car to return to the Pentagon on that beautiful fall evening, I feared I might never live to see another Saturday night.[83]

Now the president was indeed alone. He faced two options, neither acceptable. If he gave the order to launch an attack on Cuba, events would very likely spin out of control into a total war. If he didn't take action, the Soviets would be able to drop a nuclear bomb on every major American city, and he would have failed as president to protect his country. JFK, having totally run out of options, decided to take a long shot—a roll of the dice—something unthinkable to the ExComm, a move the Joint Chiefs would have considered treasonous.

Remembering how European monarchs had so badly miscalculated one another's moves and intentions which led to the First World War, Kennedy made great efforts to understand the conflict from Khrushchev's point of view. Khrushchev and the Kremlin were reacting to American missiles already installed in Turkey that could reach Moscow. Khrushchev also was facing great pressure from forces within his government and could not afford to have his country lose face on the world stage. Instead of insisting that Khrushchev bend to America's military will, Kennedy struck a deal with him. While others wanted a nuclear war, neither of them did.

Late into the night and unbeknownst to the Joint Chiefs and ExComm, he dispatched his brother, Bobby, to meet with the Soviet ambassador with a backchannel appeal. If Khrushchev would agree to remove the missiles in Cuba, Kennedy would, in six months, quietly remove the American missiles in Turkey. If this last proposal failed, DEFCON-2 would become DEFCON-1, which meant the unspeakable.

The world moved through the darkness of Saturday, October 27, 1962.

The next morning, after attending Sunday mass at St. Stephen's Church in Washington, D.C., JFK received word via Moscow radio that Chairman Khrushchev was ordering the dismantling and removal of all missiles from Cuba. The entire world breathed a sigh of relief.

But not everyone. The Joint Chiefs were livid. They felt their Commander in Chief had betrayed them. Robert Kennedy later reported that one of the generals wanted to go ahead and bomb the island of Cuba anyway.[84]

Khrushchev lived up to his word and removed the missiles from Cuba. Kennedy lived up to his word some months later and quietly removed U.S. missiles from Turkey.

The two world leaders, Kennedy and Khrushchev, were instrumental in escalating a conflict that took the world to the edge: Kennedy with his hawkish rhetoric during the 1960 presidential campaign and permitting harassment of Russian ships during the crisis; and Khrushchev with his miscalculation of Kennedy's resolve and his reckless gamble to shift the entire balance of world power without being discovered. However, those same two leaders, along with Soviet submarine Captain Vasili Arkhipov, had made the decision to turn away from a final act of violence and pull the world back from global catastrophe.

Ten months later, JFK accomplished his proudest achievement: the signing of the limited Nuclear Test Ban Treaty.[85] This document, signed by the United States, the Soviet Union, and United Kingdom, prohibited testing of nuclear weapons in the atmosphere, underwater, or in outer space. Although the treaty was limited—nations could still conduct tests underground—it was a major first step that enabled nations to dialogue more effectively and "paved the way for later arms agreements." As a result, the hand of the Doomsday Clock was gladly pushed back from seven minutes to midnight to twelve minutes from midnight.

At the resolution of the crisis, however, Kennedy wryly commented that the world would soon turn back to its pursuit of self-interests and forget how close it came to disaster. His words were prophetic. Even as the world awoke to a morning filled with opportunity to rid itself of the weapons of darkness, the memories of the crisis and the lessons learned began to fade. National attention turned to other issues and distractions. It was as if the nuclear danger had somehow evaporated. Was the world squandering the rare opportunity to assure that we would never come so close to the end by accident, miscalculation or madness?

Or would it continue efforts to abolish these terrible weapons and the mindset that fuels the need to create them before they become our masters?

## Chapter 17

# Moses

*Through our cleverness we have created nuclear weapons and found a way to live with them. We are willing to risk everything that matters, everything of beauty and meaning, everything and everyone we love.* [86]

David Krieger

**WHEN THE CRISIS** was over, I got back to life as usual, but like many across the country, I had no idea of all that happened or how the situation was resolved and there was no way of finding out. There were no bombs dropped and no war started. It was as if a grand silence descended over the whole incident, but the events of that fall of 1962 sank deep into me. I was determined that one day I would find out what brought humanity to the brink and what helped to back us away.

As the spring of 1963 rolled around, I was finishing up my time in high school. Along with my classmates, I began to feel that stress of not knowing what would come next in life. Could I get into college? I had an anemic grade point average, which reflected my indifference to classes in which I had no interest. I hated filling out college applications and only did so because of the prodding of my buddies. I was thinking about majoring in psychology since I was always interested in people and intrigued by the differences in personalities. My brother, Peter, came home on furlough and got me interested in the Air Force Reserve Officer Training Corps (AFROTC). He emphasized that graduating from that program would allow me to go into the service as an officer instead of a private. I submitted my applications to five universities and anxiously waited for the results.

Although I was concerned about my future, our senior class trip provided an exciting distraction. This was a really big deal. In late spring, along with my classmates, I boarded a tour bus that drove all night through the flatlands of Ohio, the rolling hills of Pennsylvania, and the mountains of West Virginia. We arrived at daybreak in Washington, D.C. After having a quick breakfast at a huge cafeteria, we toured the Capitol and the White House.

I asked a guide what everyone else was wondering: is President Kennedy in the building? I didn't get an answer but was told firmly by White House staffers to keep moving along. In fact, JFK was present in the building and would be presenting an award to astronaut Gordon Cooper. Later in the day, we visited Mount Vernon, ran up to the top of the Washington monument, and witnessed an open car motorcade parade with Vice President Lyndon Johnson and astronaut Cooper sitting in the back of a convertible and waving to the cheering crowds.

Back on the bus, we continued on to New York City and stayed overnight in the Edison Hotel. The next morning, I took the elevator down to the lobby, where everybody was abuzz with excitement. I bought a newspaper and read the front page of the *New York Herald Tribune*, which illustrated the flight of the ball from Mickey Mantle's monster home run that came within inches of going out of Yankee Stadium.

The rest of the day was a blur of activity. I remember going to the top of the Empire State Building, climbing to the top of the Statue of Liberty, and touring the General Assembly Hall at the United Nations. I remember stopping for a moment before the magnificent painting in the Security Council that depicted how humanity had evolved over the centuries, moving from a creature fighting wars to a higher state of being with wars becoming a thing of the past. I thought the painting expressed our new reality; I didn't realize the depiction was aspirational.

Soon after our senior trip, graduation night arrived. As we students began the procession to the "Pomp and Circumstance March," I looked up to see my mom and dad in the gymnasium crowd smiling and waving to me. A lump came to my throat.

Then with high school finished, along with my pals, I waited for news of my college acceptance or rejection. My acceptance finally came, as did theirs. In the fall, we were all headed for Michigan State.

That summer of '63, President Kennedy gave the commencement address at the American University in Washington on the subject of world peace:

> I have therefore chosen this time and this place to discuss a topic on which ignorance too often abounds and the truth is too rarely perceived, yet it is the most important topic on earth: world peace. . . .[87]

The president continued and outlined in depth his vision of peace:

> . . .I am talking about genuine peace, the kind of peace that makes life on earth worth living, the kind that enables men and nations to grow and to hope and to build a better life for their children—not merely peace for Americans, but peace for all men and women—not merely peace in our time, but peace for all time.
>
> I speak of peace because of the new face of war. Total war makes no sense in an age when great powers can maintain large and relatively invulnerable nuclear forces and refuse to surrender without resort to those forces. It makes no sense in an age when a single nuclear weapon contains almost ten times the explosive force delivered by all of the allied air forces in the Second World War. It makes no sense in an age when the deadly poisons produced by a nuclear exchange would be carried by wind and water and soil and seed to the far corners of the globe and to generations yet unborn.[88]

The following day, Kennedy presented his address on civil rights. I was struck by the clarity of Kennedy's message and the controlled passion with which he delivered it.

> We are confronted primarily with a moral issue. It is as old as the Scriptures and as clear as the American Constitution.[89]

Along with the nation, I was stunned by the vivid televised images of police using clubs, fire hoses, and attack dogs on civil rights protestors here in America!

Listening to the moral argument and the power of the president's words, surely everyone in America could now understand the immorality of denying people a drink of water from a fountain, lunch at a diner counter, or the right to vote. Within hours of Kennedy's address, however, the nation was horrified to learn of a young Medgar Evers who was gunned down in his Mississippi driveway as his wife and children waited for him to return from a meeting educating people on their voting rights.

All my understanding of the struggle of the civil rights movement in the south came through television, with one exception. A year earlier, at the age of fifteen, I rode a train to visit my sisters back in the south. As the train made its way through Tennessee, I stared in disbelief at the terrible living conditions of black families. I saw miles and miles of shacks made with tin, pieces of lumber, and cardboard, all of which looked like they would collapse in the slightest wind. I saw children playing in squalor and old people sitting in front of the shacks alongside rusted out, abandoned cars scattered along the railroad tracks.

During my visit, I also had my first encounter with racism. I rode along with a carload of teenagers to see the sights along the Mississippi River. As we stopped at the edge of the river in a remote area, one of the teens explained "some crazy old n* lives here." He added, "He's really crazy. He calls himself 'Moses' and thinks he's a prophet."

As the car screeched to a halt at the river's edge, out from a ramshackle houseboat, as if on cue, appeared a stooped-over elderly man, well into his 70s. He slowly and deliberately walked toward our car. His skin was dark and his hair white. His form resembled that of a bent over Gandhi. He wore a worn-out, white robe and leaned on a walking stick in the form of a cross. I was startled when kids in the car began using racial slurs. Not speaking a word, the old man went about his task of making the sign of the cross on the forehead of anyone in the car who would receive it.

My group of teens continued with jeers and irreverent talk. One pulled away, and another acted as if he was being exorcised, going into a loud, pretend frenzy, feigning a seizure and howling like a wolf.

The man reached over and made the sign of the cross on the center of my shirt with his thumb. I saw that his hands were rough and calloused, his knuckles arthritic. I had never even talked to a black man before. I saw an intense kindness in his eyes, even as the ugliness of the even louder howling and mocking continued. I remained stupidly silent. Then taking cues from those around me, I did something for which I am profoundly ashamed and have always regretted. I committed an act of pure cowardice—I laughed along with the others.

With our 'entertainment' over, the driver of the car screeched out, spitting gravel behind us, as we continued on our mindless way, chattering and laughing. I looked back to see the old man walking slowly to his houseboat on the river, his work completed, and his worn-out garment swaying in the blistering hot breeze. I found the whole experience, which seared itself into my brain, deeply disturbing. I didn't understand it and never talked about it. In looking back, I had encountered the force of unconsciousness and evil, which is at the heart of racism—and I was a part of it because I took the easy way and went along with it. I could not fathom how and why that man would subject himself to such hate; I can't fathom it now. But even at a young age, I knew somehow that this man, Moses, on that day had helped to save my gutless soul.

One year after this experience, Dr. Martin Luther King Jr. was scheduled to speak to an expected crowd of hundreds of thousands at the Lincoln Memorial in Washington. I would later read that Dr. King's speech almost didn't happen.[90] By one account, one of his advisors, who had heard an earlier version of King's speech, had labeled it "hackneyed and trite." As a result, the night before the speech, Dr. King's advisors crafted a new speech entitled, "Normalcy – Never Again." The Normalcy speech was not delivered because as Dr. King approached the podium, the famed gospel singer, Mahalia Jackson, called out to him: "Tell 'em about the dream, Martin."[91]

As the world witnessed, that's just what Martin Luther King did. He spoke of the impossible, the final triumph of humanity over the poisons of racism.

> And when we allow freedom to ring, when we let it ring from every village and hamlet, from every state and city, we will be able to speed up that day when all of God's children—black men and white men, Jews and Gentiles, Catholics and Protestants—will be able to join hands and to sing in the words of the old Negro spiritual, "Free at last, free at last; thank God Almighty, we are free at last."[92]

I knew what he said was true, because I saw it in the kind eyes of a man named Moses.

And as the summer of that year came to an end, the autumn leaves turned to yellow, orange and red. Even with the deep problems of our time, the words of King and Kennedy, so full of wisdom and promise, pointed us in the direction of humanity and world peace. When JFK signed the limited Nuclear Test Ban Treaty with the Soviets, he said the treaty was only a first step.

> I speak to you tonight in a spirit of hope.... [Since the advent of nuclear weapons] all mankind has been struggling to escape from the darkening prospect of mass destruction on earth.[93]

Of all my years, 1963 was the most hopeful. John Kennedy and Martin Luther King provided their passionate visions to the world, that in listening to our better angels, humanity could achieve the impossible. I was willing to try, and it was time for me to venture out into the world.

Chapter 18

# Searching for Wonders Hall

I THINK the hardest thing I ever had to do in life was to leave home. But at age 17, it was time. I loved being at home with my mom and dad. Nobody had a more loving childhood than I did. Yet, the day had arrived. I was leaving behind a rare place of love and security, a place of goodness and kindness where I was accepted and could be myself. I was leaving the farm, with its lovely orchard, plush lawn, and beautiful creek.

My mom packed my clothes neatly into my suitcase while she ran down her list of things not to forget.

"Did we pack your sports coat?"

"Yes."

"Did dad give you your tuition money?"

"Yes, dad gave me my tuition money."

"Don't forget to take your nice new tie."

"Yes, mom, taking my nice new tie is the very most important thing in my whole life."

"You're not being very nice, and you don't have to be snippy."

Mom and I crammed my suitcase full, and my dad carried it downstairs and put it in the trunk with the other suitcases and boxes. Next came the last thing I needed to do, the thing I dreaded most, saying goodbye to my dog, Copper, the companion of my youth. We had walked together in the fields, the woods, and along the creek on thousands of wonderful adventures. He once had the boundless energy of a puppy but now moved slowly, his head bowed down before the cruel god of old age. I brushed his coat, hugged him, and told him to be good, and, after I put it off as long as I could, I said goodbye.

I was leaving behind my best friend.

We three then pulled out of our driveway with my dad behind the wheel, my mom in the back seat, and me riding shotgun. The university was at the other end of the earth, some hundred and twenty miles away, and light years from home. We didn't speak as we drove along, each lost in thought. Slouched in the front seat, I found myself in a dark place, my stomach tied in knots.

"You seem tense," said mom.

"You're right, I'm tense."

"Well, you don't need to be."

"But I am."

I felt strangely disoriented. All that I had known, which seemed so real and permanent, was slipping away from me, evaporating into a mirage that would become my past. Only the memories would remain. All that had been, was no longer. In my darkness, I wondered if this was a central truth of life: all that is real is no more, replaced by new circumstances and only memories of what once was. I felt myself sinking into a depression.

The only bright spot in my thoughts was that I was excited at the possibility of what lay ahead of me. Most of all, I was simply scared because I didn't know if I could make it through college. No one in our family had ever attended. I tried to find some comfort in the fact that my two close high school buddies were also attending. But what about when grades came out at the end of the first semester? What if I found out that I had failed? What would I do then?

The ride to East Lansing seemed endless, save the monotonous hum of the tires continuing to meet the road, punctuated only by an occasional disrupting bump. I was annoyed that my father drove so slowly, but then he turned onto a newly constructed four lane highway heading south from Saginaw to East Lansing. I glanced at the speedometer. Sixty miles per hour, a breakneck speed after a lifetime of traveling thirty-five miles per hour on side roads.

"It won't be long," said my father.

He glanced at me and paused, then punched me on my leg to reassure me. "Don't worry," he said, "you'll be fine."

"You worry too much," chimed in my mom from the back seat. "You're such a worrier!"

I felt my spirits brighten a bit. I always felt comfort in my dad's words, and I was amused at how my mother never hesitated to throw in her two cents about anything. I knew I had a bad habit, in unknown situations, of seeing things only from a dark side, which was always a measure of my fears and self-doubts. My mom's words could sometimes soothe my anxieties.

"Aren't you glad now that you ate a good breakfast?" she asked, leaning forward. "One that'll stick to your ribs?" she added, taking full advantage of a final opportunity to emphasize the importance of a hearty breakfast.

I decided to just be quiet.

"You'll do fine," she said, "and your friends will be there too."

"But they are smarter than I am; they got much better grades than I did, mom."

"They applied themselves," she said, "and now it's your time to do the same."

We drove onto the campus of Michigan State University as the cloud cover began to break. Just as the sun came out, almost as if on cue, my mood surprisingly lifted from dark to almost cheerful. The campus was huge—one by one and a half miles—a thriving metropolis, beautifully landscaped with green grass and shrubs, and bustling with students. There was an immediate, almost crackling excitement in the air, unlike anything I had experienced. We crawled along in a parade of cars as students, old and new, searched for their assigned dormitories.

"Ask that guy over there for directions," said my father, nodding toward a student walking along the sidewalk. I rolled down my window.

"Excuse me. We're looking for North Wonders Hall."

"Straight ahead and on the right," pointed the student. "It's the newest dorm on campus—the incoming freshmen football players are being housed there."

"Thanks so much," I said as I rolled up my window.

We pulled to a stop in front of the dorm and were welcomed by a friendly upperclassman who helped us unload our luggage. Music of the Michigan State marching band filled the air. Their brass section sounded fantastic, snare drums rat-tat-tatting, bass drums booming, and trumpets scaling notes that reached into the high heavens. I felt a bit overwhelmed by the immensity of it all and knew it would take some time to get acclimated to my new setting. But I broke through the barrier I feared. I realized I liked the place. I really liked the place! I liked the newness of it and the promise it offered. I liked the spirit. Students introduced themselves, shaking hands and spontaneously helped families struggling with suitcases. It was a remarkably welcoming place.

In the weeks that followed, among the courses I took were American History, Air Force ROTC, and an overview of the field of psychology. In the bookstore, I also found introductory works to the two giants of psychology who changed the way we view the modern world: Sigmund Freud and Carl Jung. I was ready, at last, to buckle down. What I didn't know was that here at the university I was about to brush up against exciting and record-breaking college football history, and history that would change the world.

Chapter 19

# A Giant Flying Saucer

I PACKED and put away my last suitcase. Now I could relax a bit. At least I knew where my new home was; however temporary that might be, an anxiety I suppose many freshmen encounter. There were two rooms in the suite, separated by a bath, and three students to a room. Other guys came in tossing suitcases on beds, dropping stuff, setting boxes down, making hasty introductions.

"This bed taken?"

"Nope, help yourself!"

"Great news!" I later wrote to a friend back home, "My room is in a brand-new dorm, on the first floor, and closest to the cafeteria!"

I went for a walk across campus wide-eyed and in awe of this new world. From the moment I arrived, I could feel it in the air—something BIG was in the making, something beyond all expectations. But first, there was freshman class registration where thousands of new students milled around in a huge auditorium, going from this table to that to find a class they wanted. If it wasn't available, you had to rush back through the crowds to the other side of the building with the hope that a comparable class was open. If not, you might tear up the whole schedule and start all over again. Some panicked, others burst into tears. It took me five grueling hours to get through the process.

Following registration, I headed to the university bookstore. I was a kid in a candy store. All around me were books of every type, possessing the newest and most exciting ideas of the day. I was held to a strict budget of $5 in spending money per week, but my father said if I needed a book, any book, I could buy it. I took full advantage of that. Next, I attended the freshman orientation session, when our incoming class of about ten thousand packed into a noisy auditorium to hear an address by the university's president, Dr. John Hannah. For a guy whose high school class consisted of some forty kids, a class of thousands was a bit overwhelming.

I anxiously settled into what I thought would be a challenging first year of college. What I didn't know was that this was the year the great Michigan State football coach Hugh "Duffy" Daugherty was making sports history.[94] He was doing something for college football that Branch Rickey had done for professional baseball, when he hired Jackie Robinson to join the Brooklyn Dodgers, the

Fig. 22. From *left:* Clinton Jones, Dick Kenney, Bubba Smith, Coach Duffy Daugherty, Gene Washington, George Webster. (Photo courtesy of Michigan State University Athletic Communications)

first step in integrating the major leagues. Daugherty ignored the unwritten practice of recruiting only so many African American players. Instead, he sent scouts to all areas of the country to recruit the best players, white or black. Many were found in the segregated south, where black players had no chance of playing college ball in their states' universities. Duffy Daugherty was putting together one of the greatest teams in the history of college football, and I had the good fortune to be housed at North Wonders Hall along with the players.

Fig. 23. M.S.U. Running back Clinton Jones #26
(Bettmann/Getty Images)

My new roommate Jimmy Summers, a defensive back, came in from Orangeburg, South Carolina. Clinton Jones, a running back, who had set national records in high school track, came from Cleveland. Ernie Pasteur came from North Carolina. Charles Thornhill, who was built like a short, power packed Greek god, came from Roanoke, Virginia. Gene Washington and Charles "Bubba" Smith came from Texas. Fullback Bob Apisa came all the way from Hawaii. The guys from segregated parts of the country didn't know what to expect when they came north to team up with a bunch of white guys like big, tough Pat Gallinagh and other regular guys like my pals and me. All the southern players who were outcasts from their own states, found that at Michigan

State, they could contribute.[95] All of us, from every section of fractured American society, were thrown into the mix with one another.

Since I was in the room closest to the cafeteria, many of these huge guys, with even bigger appetites from their afternoon workouts, often met in our room before going on to dinner. That's how we got to know one another—with lots of talking, kidding, and bantering. Gales of laughter could be heard up and down the halls emanating from my room.

To be sure, we had to make adjustments. I had never heard James Brown wail, "I Feel Good!" at full blast at the crack of dawn. Nor evidently had guys five floors up, who arrived later in the breakfast line half asleep, asking, "Who the hell was playing James Brown in the middle of the damned night?!" And from the earthy feedback I received from both blacks and whites, I don't think anybody ever really warmed up to my Lawrence Welk album, featuring perky harpsichord tunes that I got from my mom.

With all the orientations and settling in complete, the time had come for me to buckle down. I chose psychology as my major and delved into the material with an interest I had never known before. I memorized the defense mechanisms and was fascinated with how the mind could so cleverly shield itself from disturbing information from the outer world. Like denial, which is an unconscious refusal to acknowledge the existence of painful realities, thoughts, or feelings. Another is projection, which occurs when a person unconsciously refuses to acknowledge one's own negative motives or thoughts but perceives those negatives in another person or groups of people.

The first semester came to an end, and I returned home where I anxiously awaited my grades to arrive in the mail. I needed a C average to stay in college. If my grades were below that, I would drop out and likely get a job in a factory. If I made a C or above, I would know I could do the work. The envelope came. I felt like my whole future was riding on this moment, my moment of truth. I took a deep breath and tore it open. On the report card appeared the beautiful numbers, a 2.17. A modest C grade point average,

---

[95] For an account of Coach Daugherty's historic effort to integrate players into college football, see Maya Washington's brilliant documentary *Through the Banks of the Red Cedar*. (www.mayawashington.net).

for sure, but a solid C, which meant I made it! I screamed and yelled, hugged my mom and dad, and jumped around the room. I made the cut!

Now I had to get a better idea of what career I wanted. My choices were to become an Air Force officer through the AFROTC program or perhaps a psychologist. On a sunny Friday afternoon in November, I entered the university's psychological testing building to take a battery of vocational interest tests to help determine a career path. I was looking forward to the weekend, and especially the football game the next day at Spartan Stadium against the University of Illinois. I sat in an isolated booth with my booklets, answer sheets, and a number two pencil. I began to mark my choices in the little circles. Before long I was immersed in the project and cut off from anything outside my booth.

At the time I was focused on my tests, a government plane was flying high over the Pacific Ocean carrying some of President Kennedy's Cabinet members, including his Press Secretary, Pierre Salinger. They were headed to Tokyo for an economic conference on Japanese/American relations. Salinger was studying materials in preparation for the meetings when he was summoned by the Secretary of State to come forward to the communication center of the plane. There he found Secretary Dean Rusk, assembled with four other cabinet members, "grave-faced" reviewing teletype reports coming over the wire. Some seemed to be written in haste containing fragments, half sentences, and misspellings. Other staff members began to gather. What was going on? Salinger looked over Secretary Rusk's shoulder to read garbled messages. His eyes fixed on one with a spelling error that read:

KENNEDY WOUNDED PERHAPS FATALLY BY VASSASSINS [sic] BULLET.

Salinger kept looking at the words "reading it over and over again.... The words stayed on the paper. They would not go away.

"Secretary Rusk read us the last brief bulletin. 'My God!' gasped Orville Freeman. Luther Hodges started to sag toward the floor.... Then there was an interminable silence as each man became lost in his private sorrow."[96]

## A Great Flash of Light

After what seemed an endless amount of time, confirmation arrived that despite all hopes, the President had been fatally shot. Secretary Rusk made the announcement to all the passengers in the plane. "There was a cumulative cry of anguish from the passengers.... Slowly the sobbing subsided, and those aboard returned to their seats and sat in stunned silence."[97]

They turned the plane back toward the United States. A fitful silence ensued, with everyone on board at a loss with what to do. Someone suggested a poker game—a non-speaking, no joking, dead-serious betting ritual to help anesthetize them and eat up the hours of flight time back to Washington. "It seems now, looking back," Salinger wrote, "almost sacrilegious to have played poker at such a time. But if there had not been that game, it is hard to tell what would have happened on that plane, so high were the emotions."[98]

At the testing center, I finished one test and then the next. With the last circle marked, I handed in my material and gathered my things. The workweek was done. Time for the weekend!

Walking down the steps of the center out into the crisp sunny afternoon, I fully expected to hear the music of the M.S.U. marching band practicing for Saturday's game. But there was no music. I looked all around. Where were the thousands of kids talking about their classes, the weekend, and tomorrow's game?

This was eerie; this was strange. The campus was empty! It was as if a giant flying saucer had landed and with a vacuum, sucked up the entire population from the university. How could this be? It was like living in an episode from the *Twilight Zone*.

I began the mile walk back to my dorm when my sense of strangeness turned into alarm. I picked up my pace to a jog. I saw somebody riding a bicycle, suggesting that maybe I wasn't losing my mind. But the rider, who had a transistor radio, just flew past me with a grim expression on his face. He went by so fast; I didn't get a chance to ask him what was going on. I reached the dorm, where, through the front glass doors, I could see a group of students crowding around, all straining to see a large television set mounted on the wall.

As I walked through the doors of North Wonders Hall on that late November afternoon, I learned the news of the unthinkable act in Dallas that shattered our world of hope inspired by a young president. We now faced a new reality, one in which we had no defense, no recourse. The assassins delivered us a blow so severe, so terrible, and, most of all, so irreversible. John Kennedy was dead. How could that be? Something from our innermost core had been taken from us on that day, something we could never get back.

A deep sorrow settled upon us gathered there that Friday afternoon. Within hours, that sorrow descended on people across the earth. An unfathomable truth forced itself on us that day—he was gone forever—and try as we might, we couldn't comprehend it then, nor in the dark days that followed. And for me, a half century later, not even now.

I regret that I was just becoming aware of him. I had taken for granted that he would always be there. Was he not just here providing a vision of a path to world peace?

Was he not just here announcing the reality of a Nuclear Test Ban Treaty?

> But now, for the first time in many years, the path of peace may be open. No one can be certain what the future will bring. No one can say whether the time has come for an easing of the struggle. But history and our own conscience will judge us more harshly if we do not now make every effort to test our hopes by action, and this is the place to begin.[99]

Was he not just here explaining how world peace was not a distant utopian dream, but a realistic goal within reach of humanity?

> With such a peace there will still be quarrels and conflicting interests, as there are within families and nations. World peace, like community peace, does not require that each man love his neighbor; it requires only that they live together in mutual tolerance, submitting their disputes to a just and peaceful settlement.[100]

Was he not just summoning our nation to a clarion call of peace?

> My fellow Americans. . . . Let us, if we can, get back from the shadows of war and seek out the way of peace.[101]

How could it be, that someone who was just here, handsome and wise, with wry humor in darkest times; a young father, president, peacemaker, and friend—the very symbol of youthful life, the brightest light of our generation—how could he, John Kennedy, be torn away from us in one horrific act of assassination? Now he, like Abraham Lincoln before him, belonged to the ages.

The flight back to Washington took eight and a half hours. Salinger and the Cabinet members arrived shortly after midnight. The attention of the whole world was now centered on our nation's Capital. World leaders sent expressions of sympathy to Mrs. Kennedy, while others from around the globe made hurried arrangements to attend the funeral in Washington. Salinger was driven back to the White House to do whatever needed to be done. "Thought of rest was impossible," he later wrote. "Weariness was replaced by numbness, and I plunged into work, almost like a sleepwalker."[102]

The President's body arrived in the East Room of the White House at 4:25 a.m. The casket was accompanied by Mrs. Kennedy, Robert Kennedy, members of the Kennedy family and some of the President's close associates.[103]

> The rest of the night is a blur.[104] Finally, about 7:00 A.M., we went to sleep. At 8 A.M., the phone by my bed rang. I picked it up. The operator said, 'Mr. Salinger, the President is calling.' And for that instantaneous second, I thought to myself, it was all a dream, he wasn't really dead. And then another voice came on the phone. 'Pierre, this is Lyndon Johnson.'[105]

As the new president, Lyndon Johnson went on to pledge publicly that he would advance the work begun by the assassinated president. While he did very well with Kennedy's domestic policies, in particular with the Civil Rights Act, the reality of what he did with regard to Vietnam was quite a different matter.

Kennedy totally resolved to withdraw U.S. troops from Vietnam. His determination likely began as early as when he and his brother, Bobby, visited that country in the 1950s and saw firsthand how unwinnable a conflict was there. They saw how the

Colonial French forces, trying to keep control of Vietnam, suffered a bitter military defeat because they lost support of the Vietnamese people. When later asked why the president was so averse to sending ground units, Bobby said, "We were there in 1951. We saw what was happening to the French. *We saw it.* My brother was determined, determined, never to let that happen to us."[106]

Publicly, Kennedy's statements suggested the importance of a continued American presence in Vietnam, but in private with friends and associates, he repeatedly expressed his desire to avoid a land war in Southeast Asia, which he saw as disastrous. Buttressed by advice from U.S. Army General Douglas MacArthur and President Charles de Gaulle of France, Kennedy was determined to get out of Vietnam after the 1964 mid-term election. Accordingly, only one month before his death, on October 11, 1963, Kennedy signed a National Security Action Memorandum—a national security directive—specifically NSAM 263, that provided a formal declaration to withdraw 1,000 military personnel from Vietnam by the end of 1963[107] Kennedy's hope was to withdraw the remaining 15,000, following his election to a second term, by the end of 1965.[108]

Another memorandum on the subject of America's role in Vietnam, specifically NSAM 273,[109] was issued one month later. I find this directive both strange and troubling for a number of reasons. First, it totally reversed Kennedy's directive to withdraw from Vietnam. Second, it not only reversed it, it vastly expanded America's role in that country to include a "not only military but political, economic, social, educational, and informational effort."[110] Third, the draft of the memo was dated November 21, 1963, *one day before the murder of the president.* Fourth, this was the very first National Security Action Memorandum signed by President Lyndon Johnson and issued on November 26, 1963— *the very day after Kennedy was buried.*[111]

NSAM 273 opened the door to the decades-long agony of the Vietnam war, the deaths of over 58,000 Americans, and estimates of up to, if not more than, 2,000,000 Vietnamese, many of whom

---

[111] For an in-depth study of the forces that murdered John F. Kennedy, see *JFK and the Unspeakable: Why He Died and Why It Matters* by James W. Douglass.

were women and children. Over the course of a weekend, America made a major turning point in its history. JFK's voice was silenced. The vision of peace he outlined in his American University address to the world was shattered.

Thereafter, little notice was given to the fact that the world continued to live under the threat of the nuclear sword. As the world rang in the new year of 1964, no one could have foreseen how dramatically the America we knew was about to change. Nor could anyone have guessed how further entangled we would become in a distant Asian war, one that would tear our country apart. I couldn't know that this memorandum, this single piece of paper, would eventually drive me to the deepest moral crisis and lowest point of my life.

Chapter 20

# Finding My Way

**AFTER CHRISTMAS VACATION,** it was back to the old grindstone. However, this time we were seasoned freshmen who had survived our first semester. Now we had some idea of what university work required. We learned that some "profs" were tough, others were "a snap," and still others were ones to stay away from, killers when it came to giving out good grades. Although most of my instructors were stimulating and engaging in their presentations, I had one professor whose class was just painful. Each session was like sitting through an evening of bad opera.

The pressure to succeed was relentless, but on a cold February evening in 1964, Ed Sullivan, host of a wildly popular CBS Sunday night variety show, introduced a group of four young mop-top musicians from England and changed the course of musical history. "Ladies and gentlemen, The Beatles!"

Across America, black and white television sets filled with images of screaming teenage girls, crying in unrestrained adoration, and shaking their heads in disbelief that they could be in the very presence of the Liverpool rock foursome. The impact of those images moved like a tsunami throughout the whole country. Local disc jockeys were inundated with an unprecedented number of requests. Everyone was talking about The Beatles. Even Elvis was pushed from the top spot. That Sunday night performance also provided the nation with its first uplifting diversion to help wash away some of the national trauma and sorrow of 1963.

As the world forged ahead into this new year, I celebrated my eighteenth birthday. It was an unsettling time. I had little idea about what my chosen profession might be, or the direction my life should take. I thought I belonged in a people profession, the social sciences, so I declared psychology as my major, and I was excited about that. I had always been interested in personalities, how people can be so different from one another, have such different attitudes, react to situations in opposite ways, and experience the same situation and come out with wildly different conclusions. In short, I was fascinated about what made people tick.

I was intrigued, too, by the study of dreams, in particular the chilling dream of Abraham Lincoln. A week before his death, the president dreamed that he came upon an open casket lying in state at the Capitol rotunda. He looked down to see who the person was lying in the coffin, only to discover to his horror that it was he himself who was dead.

I took a class on the Psychology of Personality. The course wasn't at all what I had anticipated. The focus was on Freud and his book *The Interpretation of Dreams*. I understood how his idea of the unconscious was so important because it opened a much deeper understanding of the human psyche. But his concepts of the Oedipus and Electra complexes made no sense to me. Freud was suggesting that at an early age, from three to five, a child has an unconscious desire for sexual involvement with the parent of the opposite sex. A boy supposedly turns his erotic attention to his mother and has a desire to kill his father, while a girl sees her mother as a sexual rival as she tries to win the approval of her father. The theory went on to suggest that boys fear being castrated by the father, who is stronger than the son. Again, it all made no sense to me. As the final exam approached, I pulled an all-nighter trying to make sense of it all. I wasn't successful. I flunked the course. Not a good thing, when you flat out fail a course in the field in which you are majoring.

## Finding My Way

I also thought about going into the military to keep America the most powerful country on earth. If this was my path, I was determined to climb to the top and become a general. To that end, I pledged the Arnold Air Society, a society of Air Force ROTC cadets. At an orientation meeting, an attractive young brunette, who was the chapter's formal consort and looked gorgeous in Air Force uniform, invited us to consider making a commitment. Her dazzling smile sealed the deal, and along with others, I signed up. Upon signing, I couldn't help but notice that the lovely maiden— I even remember her name, Robin—vaporized into thin air and left us only with the downside of pledging: harassment and humiliation.

First of all, we were now referred to as lowly "Dooleys" and left in the hands of upperclassmen, whose mouths watered as they looked forward to the upcoming hazing process. They would pepper the Dooleys with questions about military information and protocol, and if the correct answer wasn't forthcoming, the Dooley would find himself cranking out push-ups. I tackled a stack of manuals and books in preparation. The first thing was to memorize the Air Force chain of command, which went from the president on down to our unit. The worst part was getting signatures from each and every member of the society. That meant taking on the unenviable task of walking across the busily trafficked campus, in uniform, with pen and signature book in hand, and approach uniformed upperclassmen and ask for their signatures. The worst kind to get were those who were walking to class with their girlfriends and felt that humiliating us poor Dooleys was a great way to show off. The one I feared the most was an upperclassman who spoke with a southern twang and made guys do push-ups until they dropped. To me, he looked like Hermann Goering, and had the charm to match. Having put it off as long as I could, I finally caught up with him.

"Sir, my name is Dooley Bognar. May I ask for your signature on my pledge card, sir?"

The upperclassman stepped forward, scrutinized my uniform up and down, then got right in my face. His breath spoke not of springtime.

"Yes," he said, "by your poor appearance, you surely must be a Dooley."

"Yes sir."

"I don't know if you belong in our society, Dooley. Tell me, can you do push-ups?"

That was my first, actually second, clue that this encounter was not going to be fun.

"Yes sir."

The upperclassman smiled, "Then, son, why don't you give me, say, ten."

"Yes sir."

I put my books down, assumed the push-up position, and with a "one sir, two sir" counted off to ten push-ups.

"Permission to get up, sir?"

He paused as if freeing his great mind to contemplate while I remained in the push-up position. "Permission granted."

"But frankly, Dooley, if I were to be truly honest with you, I don't think you did a very good job with your quote 'push-ups.' Do you think you might perhaps try again? This time, making sure you do them a wee bit straighter?"

"Yes sir, I can, sir."

"What, I couldn't hear you."

"Yes sir, I can, sir!"

"Then by all means, what are you waiting for?"

I dropped back to the push-up position and again counted off another ten. Thank God I had been working on my push-ups since high school.

"Permission to get up, sir!"

I felt a bead of sweat trickle down my back. Clusters of students passed by, late for their classes. Some laughed. I felt foolish.

"I don't know, I just don't know," said Herr Goering, in a deep state of contemplation.

"Gloria, what do you think? Do you think I should give this low life form permission to get up?"

The girlfriend, smacking her bubble gum, said, "C'mon, we gotta get to class!"

"I just don't know. . . I just don't know. Dooley Bognar, while I ponder your request, how about you give me the chain of command?"

I continued with the push-up stance, but now I was sweating and straining.

"Yes, sir! The chain of command, sir! President of the United States: John F. Kennedy. Excuse me, sir. President of the United States: Lyndon B. Johnson, sir!"

"Oh, no, no, no Dooley! It's got to be perfect! Let's start again, shall we?"

"Yes, SIR! President Lyndon Baines Johnson, sir!"

My arms felt heavy. I had enough sense at least to remember that with Kennedy's assassination, Johnson didn't have a vice president, so I hurriedly went down the list.

"Secretary of Defense, Robert S. McNamara, sir!"

"Secretary of the Air Force, Stanley Resor, sir!"

"Air Force Chief of Staff, General Curtis E. LeMay, sir!"

It's amazing to me now, in looking back, how I had the naive impression that every leader in the military chain was in agreement with the directives given by his superior. I hadn't the slightest idea that members were sometimes deeply divided in their views, and that in some cases great animosity existed between and among them.

I recited down the chain of command while my arms began to quake and quiver from fatigue. I was drenched with sweat, which I despised, especially while in a wool uniform.

I was ready to drop.

"Permission to get up, sir?"

I don't know how long I struggled to remain in the push-up position. Finally, in a magnanimous gesture of compassion and a repugnant air of disgust, the upperclassman gave me permission. I had a hard time getting up. He scribbled his name in my pledge book and tossed it back to me, my pen falling to the ground. With a final look of contempt, Goering returned my salute, and waddled on his way with his girlfriend, leaving me to spend my whole day in a sweaty uniform.

The good news was that this was the final task I had to accomplish. I had gotten the signatures of all the upperclassmen. I would no longer have to refer to myself as a Dooley.

In a moving ceremony a few evenings later, I was presented with a blue and gold braid to add to my uniform, as I was inducted into the Arnold Air Society. This was a major step in climbing the military ladder. It seemed that my career path was headed toward becoming an Air Force officer.

My freshman year came to an end, and I packed my bags to return home. I said goodbye to all the guys, wishing them a great summer. I had no idea I wouldn't be coming back to Michigan State, nor would I be pursuing a career in the military. Instead, life threw me a curve to go in a direction that I never imagined.

Chapter 21

# Change of Direction

I RETURNED HOME in the summer of '64 to look for a job to help pay for next year's tuition. I missed the excitement of Michigan State, but it was wonderful to be home again with mom and dad. I didn't notice it right away, but I sensed there was something wrong with my dad. He never complained, but lines in his face had deepened, and there was little trace of his ordinary wry humor. I asked mom about it.

"He's not feeling well. They're running tests on him," she said, once we were alone.

She looked away, and I felt a sinking feeling in my stomach.

I didn't have to look long for a job. A small factory manufacturing automobile parts had opened in town and was hiring. As I walked into the factory, gone were the niceties of university life. Instead, my day was filled with sweat and the acrid, burning smell from the flashes of welders' arcs. Workers had to shout to each other over the pounding of machines shaping iron, the whine of grinders cleaning off slag, and the roar of forklifts transporting manufactured products from one end of the plant to another. Safety was just beginning to be recognized as an employee right, but not in time for some who worked for years on the lines. Walking by, I couldn't help but notice missing fingers, or a hand that had gotten caught when a shirt sleeve or glove couldn't be pulled out of a machine in time. Behind it all was a lineup of railroad cars that transported the automobile frames to assembly plants in Detroit.

Tough men with weathered faces, reflective of their years of hard labor and the trials of life, sized up us newcomers as we first checked in. Some weren't at all hesitant about letting us know how we were viewed. One old man, with a menacing smile, took a drag on his cigarette and spat out "You college boys don't know shit!" If he was talking about life, he was probably pretty much right.

Over the weeks, I found that while there were a few characters to stay away from, most of the workers were decent, fair, and once they knew you, friendly. One way you knew you were accepted, was when they tested you with practical jokes, like sending you to the other end of the factory where you were told to bring back a "left-handed bolt stretcher." If you fell for it and dragged some heavy chunk of iron all the way back across the factory, workers from all over the building would laugh uproariously at your expense. Good thing I had figured it out about half-way back. The other way you knew you were accepted was when you were given a nickname, one that was largely earthy and universally unflattering. The more unflattering, the more you were liked. If it was unrepeatable, you were accepted as one of the guys.

Every morning, with my father already long gone to his job, I got up, dressed, put on my steel toed shoes, grabbed my lunch bucket, and walked into town. With my partner on the assembly line, I unloaded finished painted steel products and transferred them onto railroad cars. My hands grew blisters. My arm, neck and back muscles ached from the heavy lifting, but I grew strong as the weeks went by. I also found myself falling into a deep depression. I was upset that I had flunked a course in my major. I worried that it might eliminate me from pursuing a degree in psychology. I also ended the year questioning my worldview shaped by my Catholic school upbringing. I was still grieving the murder of the president. And what seemed to bring it all home was the sense of alienation I felt from the never-ending and unchanging monotony of the assembly line, and how some men suffer the fate of doing the same thing over and over again their entire lives. My greatest worry though was my dad's rapidly failing health. All this brought to front and center the underlying questions of the meaning of life.

There was this painter, a short good-natured guy, George, maybe in his fifties, a roly-poly guy, shaped like a basketball, probably weighing close to three hundred pounds. Every day he showed up in coveralls and a painter's cap. He sat on top of a huge oil drum, and much in the fashion of Norm sitting at the bar at *Cheers*, exerted the least amount of energy possible as he spray-painted each metal part that emerged dry from the cleaning process. Squirt to the left; squirt to the right; wait for the next one. That's what he did all day! I never met a person who exerted so little effort.

I had no idea where I was headed in life, but the one thing I did know was that I didn't want to end up becoming another George. Over dinner one evening, my mom and dad suggested that I make an appointment to see our parish priest to see if he could help. I met with him one evening after work.

"You know, Francis, it may be that the painter's job that seems so terrible to you, might not seem so terrible to the painter himself. When you go back tomorrow, take another look at things a bit more closely and see if he might not see his job differently than you do."

As I headed out the front door, he added, almost as an afterthought, "Do you think you might have a vocation to the priesthood?"

I was kind of stunned. That had never crossed my mind. I liked girls, a lot, and as a priest, obviously you could not marry. Was this the path I had been searching for? I mumbled a thank you for his time and said something like I would think about it.

I returned to the factory and took another look at my rotund painter friend sitting atop of his oil drum. Same routine: squirt paint on one side, then the other, and wait. But when the mid-morning whistle shrieked for a break, George sprung from his oil drum to the snack bar like a pro-basketball player charging in for a slam dunk. He got first in line. A few minutes later, he came back all smiles, drinking a soda, holding a bag of chips and a bag of peanuts, a Snickers sticking out of his shirt pocket. I took off my gloves and walked over to him.

"Hey, George, do you like your job?"

"Are you (expletive deleted) nuts?" he asked, taking a swig of his soda.

He swallowed hard and said, "I got the best (expletive deleted) job in the world!"

He paused for a moment, and said, "Look, I don't need to think about nothin'. I don't have to lift nothin'. While you bastards are out there bustin' your (expletives deleted) the whole (expletive deleted) time, all I do is sit and laugh my (expletive deleted) off."

Nodding in the direction of a nearby foreman, he whispered, "I just hope the (expletive deleted) don't find out how good I got it, or," he added with a chortle, "they'll stop paying me." We talked some more until the whistle signaled that break was over.

"Well," said George, as he tossed his apple core into a perfect arch that clunked dead center into the trash can, "time to get back to (expletive deleted) work!"

I walked back to my spot and put my gloves back on.

"Hey, George," I yelled over the factory noise, "good talking with you!"

"Yeah, me too." said George as he climbed back up on his barrel and went back to (expletive deleted) work.

I began to feel a bit better. Did I have a calling to the priesthood? I had to find out.

That fall of 1964, Roger Maris and Mickey Mantle hit home runs against the St. Louis Cardinals in a super exciting, nail-biting Cardinals vs Yankees World Series. But I was totally disgusted when my favorite player, Yogi Berra, was fired when his team of Yankees lost the seventh and final game to the Cardinals. Fired after 18 years of Hall of Fame caliber playing that produced 358 home runs and 1,430 runs batted in! After that series, it was pretty much all downhill for the Yankees.

On the world stage China exploded its first atomic bomb, but upon its successful testing, immediately assured the world it would never be the first to use nuclear arms.[112]

And I chose not to return to Michigan State. Instead, I entered a Catholic minor seminary in Saginaw to see if I had a calling to the priesthood. Going in, I knew I was going to have to make a lot of adjustments, especially after all the freedom and excitement I enjoyed at Michigan State. But I had no idea just how challenging it was going to be, and it all began on day one.

Chapter 22

# A Square Peg

**WHEN I ARRIVED** at St. Paul's Seminary in Saginaw, Michigan, I knew that the eight-year path to ordination was not going to be an easy one. The first step involved two years of minor seminary to begin academic training. Step two was to send students out of state for two years for studies in philosophy. The final stage included a return to Detroit for four years of theology. Coming into the system, I knew I could excel in areas like public speaking and writing, but I had no interest in learning Latin, which, of course, was a high priority on the curriculum. I wished I had taken Latin in high school and formed a solid foundation in the language, instead of the jingle I had found highly amusing:

> Latin is a dead language,
> As dead as it can be.
> It once killed the Romans,
> And now it's killing me.

Even more difficult than studying Latin, was adapting to the regimentation of seminary life. I felt as if I were a square peg trying to fit into a round hole. Up to that point, I did what I wanted to do when I wanted to do it. The orientation session provided a manual that mapped out the whole school year, including daily activities: what time you got up, what time you made your bed—at Michigan State I made my bed quarterly—chapel for morning prayer, breakfast, morning classes, Mass, lunch, afternoon prayer, more classes, dinner, recreation, study, evening prayer, and lights out. Talk about multitasking! I felt like a juggler trying to keep a dozen balls in the air. I was always, always running behind in daily prayer. We prayed, morning, noon, and night. Jeez-Louise, did we not JUST pray? I had to keep in mind that I was in a seminary, and for heaven's sake, where else would people pray so much? I struggled with the idea that obedience was such an important value. Students had to get permission from a priest to do anything not on the schedule. After my college freedom, I bristled at having to wait in line to get permission for a Saturday morning walk to a local Kmart to buy some pencils. But I gritted my teeth; I was determined to follow the rule.

While I had difficulty adapting, I was inspired by new knowledge of a deeper spiritual life. Each of us was assigned to a director, a mentor to guide our spiritual journeys. I had the good fortune of having a kind, mild-mannered, middle-aged priest, wise beyond his years, who listened carefully and with empathy. He wasn't a great speaker and often found himself unable to convey an idea or experience that had touched him deeply. But, and most importantly, through his guidance I learned how we, in western countries, largely see our world through the lens of an outdated materialistic worldview.

This view largely assumes that there is only one dimension of reality, the physical one; those things in the universe which we can know through our senses—what we can see, touch, taste, smell, and hear. However, if one dares to go within to delve beneath the surface of our everyday lives, one can experience an unseen dimension. We can't see a human mind, but the human mind exists. We can't see a life force coursing through the veins of the physical universe, but we can see its manifestation when spring brings new life to the earth. This unseen dimension is as real as that of the physical and is not bound by the confines of time, space, and matter. In recognizing the reality of both physical and spiritual, this worldview is open to the possibility that human beings can have an encounter with God. These encounters are not wishful thinking; they are real. And as the spiritual masters, from Christ to Gandhi to Dr. King, have given witness over the centuries, God can intervene in human events.

At year's end, though I grew in spiritual understanding and did well in my other studies, I lagged way behind my classmates in Latin, some who had studied the language through four years of high school. Our final exam was to translate, from Latin to English, Caesar's account of marching into Gaul. For me this task was next to impossible, but I was willing to give it a mighty try.

About a week later, Father Bob, a scholarly man with many God-given gifts, a sense of humor not among them, handed our booklets back to us. My classmates, who were Father's prize students, looked with pleasure upon their grades. He gave them comments like "Great work, Larry!" and "So well done, Vernon!" and "Fabulous job, Stan!" as they went on their sunny ways.

"Can we talk for a minute?" Father asked, as he handed me my booklet. I had no doubt I was cooked.

I opened the booklet and, OH MY GOD! Words crossed out here, whole phrases slashed there, arrows pointing this way and that! Except for maybe my monster nosebleed back in the third grade, I never saw so much red in my entire life!

*"Veni. Vidi. Vici,"* wrote Caesar. (I came. I saw. I conquered.) Talk about egotistical! I tried to spice it up a bit. But Father Bob took extra time to carefully go over what I had translated. I learned that if Caesar had marched into Gaul the way I had explained it, he would have likely gotten his you-know-what kicked. Hey, my bad that my spice breathed some life into an otherwise boring story.

Also, the good father explained, it was highly unlikely that Caesar led his troops into battle with the cry, "Let's win this one for the Gipper!" All for naught. Father Bob recommended that I take two summer classes in Latin at the University of Michigan to get up to speed with my classmates. Geez.

When I arrived at the university, I found its physical layout quite different than at Michigan State. Whereas MSU was largely one tract of land where all activities were held, classes at the University of Michigan were held on campus, and at various locations throughout the bustling city of Ann Arbor. One of my classes was in a large auditorium on campus, another was above a drug store in the city.

# A Great Flash of Light

It was in Ann Arbor that I first felt the initial breezes of a conflict in Southeast Asia, which would ensnare us all into a war and nearly tear our nation apart.

One blistering hot afternoon in August, I was running really late for my afternoon Latin class. I flagged down a taxi, hopped into the back seat, and quickly rolled down the window to get some air. The driver was messing with his radio trying to find a station with the news. He turned up the volume.

"Something real important's going on," he said, pulling away from the curb. "Where you goin'?"

I told him.

He said, "The President's gonna be talking to the congress."

A few moments later, I heard President Johnson speaking about how an American vessel had been fired upon. This hostile act, the President said, threatened the future of Southeast Asia.

"A threat to any nation in that region," he said, "is a threat to all, and a threat to us."[113]

"Looks like we might be in a war," said the cabbie.

"Which country attacked the ship?" I asked, wondering if I had heard right.

"Vietnam," said the cabbie, "some country over there in Asia somewhere."

For a long time, I believed that war began on that hot summer day as I paid the cabbie and hurried off to class. I didn't know that America had already been involved in that war for years. Nor could I have known that I, along with hundreds of thousands of other young men, would slowly be sucked into this vortex that would become known as the war in Vietnam.

All of that was ahead of me. I returned to St. Paul's for a second year. Three months later, my dad was diagnosed with pancreatic cancer. I was stunned by how rapidly this terrible disease could reduce a strong man to one who was totally helpless. I was given permission to leave the seminary to help my mom care for him in his final days. He became so thin, reminding me of images of concentration camp survivors. Despite his pain, he assured me time and again that everything was ok with him, and that I should follow whatever path life would have me choose. He also asked me to remember him at midnight mass every Christmas eve.

## A Square Peg

He passed the day before my 20th birthday. He was what a dad should be, a pillar of strength, a man of wisdom, always there to guide and encourage me, and affirming all things noble. And then he was gone, leaving me with a feeling of great emptiness and a throbbing ache at my core—one that is always there.

On the day of his funeral, my mom was an anchor as friends and relatives stopped by. When the last person left, she and I were alone together in our kitchen. Our house seemed so empty. I looked up from the table to see her bring me a small birthday cake she had baked.

"We only had one birthday candle in the house," she said, her eyes glistening. "He would want you to celebrate your birthday."

We sat at the kitchen table eating the cake in silence; she who lost the love of her life, and I, a father, whose absence I feel even now.

I spent a few more days with my mom, and then on a cold, dismal, and totally miserable January night, I drove back to the seminary on icy roads during a downpour of freezing rain and snow. Exhausted from the emotional ordeal, and cold and wet from the freezing rain, I walked from the parking lot into the seminary feeling as alone as I've ever felt.

The halls were dark and deserted. Everyone was in the refectory having dinner. My footsteps echoed as I walked down the polished floors. I could hear my classmates engaged in conversation beyond the doors of the refectory, but when I walked in, there was total silence. Then one by one, they all stood up, and began clapping, and continued clapping, filling the room with applause. At my lowest point, my classmates lifted me up with a simple act of kindness, one I will not forget.

I worked hard at my studies for the remaining months to make up for the time and work I had missed. Now, at the end of the year, it was time to learn where each of us would be assigned, across the country, to study philosophy. There were thirteen of us. The process was to draw numbers from a hat to determine the order of meeting with the seminary's Rector. If you pulled number 1 from the hat, you went in first and had your choice of all the assignments, assuming the Rector didn't object. He still had the final say. If you picked number 2, you had twelve seminaries to choose from, down to number 13, who got stuck with the choice nobody

## A Great Flash of Light

wanted. In order, we told the Rector which of the seminaries we chose. If he agreed, done deal.

There were two of us left to draw: me and the guy holding the hat. There were two numbers left: 2 and 13. If I picked the 2, and if the Rector approved, I pretty much had my choice of where I would go. If I picked 13, chances were excellent that I would go to the remaining seminary—a horrible place universally known as "the Rock."

"Ok" said my classmate who knew my pick was determining both of our very futures, "you pick." I closed my eyes and picked the number and handed it back for my classmate to read aloud.

"Number 2," he said, "Congratulations, man, good luck!"

"Thanks, guy," I said, "you too."

When it was time for me to submit my choice, I made a last-minute decision and chose Notre Dame Seminary in New Orleans. It was kind of ironic that I would be going back south, some eighty miles from where I was born. I reasoned that if I returned to Louisiana, my mom would soon follow. She could buy a house and live close to my two sisters and their children. I was ready to leave the dreariness of the past year and get away from the ice and snow. And New Orleans, with its French Quarter and jazz bands, seemed like a great place to go.

It was that, indeed, and along with it, came, for me, life's greatest surprise.

Chapter 23

# Close Call

**IT WAS AUTUMN** 1966, and I was driving my brand new Chevelle at high speeds through the hills of Kentucky and Tennessee, the flatlands of Mississippi, and into the city of New Orleans. I wanted to test and enjoy the car's high-powered engine, but even more so, I was eager to get away from another northern winter well before it arrived. I wanted to see lots of sunshine, bask in the warm weather, and listen to the sweet sounds of Dixieland jazz.

I arrived at Notre Dame Seminary to study Philosophy and Theology and found a much more relaxed atmosphere than at St. Paul's. There were few restrictions, and we had more freedom to carve out our own course of study. On weekends, I could visit my sisters and their families who had decades earlier moved back to Baton Rouge. I felt I could breathe again.

In this new and challenging setting, I was introduced to the works of great philosophers and theologians, but even though I found the coursework truly fascinating, I was gradually becoming aware that the path of the priesthood was not for me. I was ill-suited to the formality of much of it. What I disliked most of all was that I felt both family and friends were putting me on a pedestal, in a role that separated me from the closeness, personal touch, and the spontaneity I had always enjoyed before. Relationships with women became distant and proper, and for someone who enjoyed feminine company, I didn't want relationships to be like that. Over the course of a few months, I made up my mind that I would leave, but I also knew I would lose my 4-D deferment from service and run the high risk of being drafted and sent to Vietnam. To stay, when I was pretty sure the priesthood wasn't my calling, would have been dishonest and unfair to everyone. Despite the risk, I had to leave.

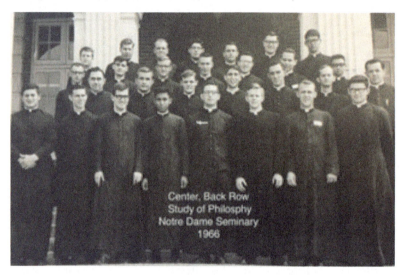

Fig. 24. Philosophy students, Notre Dame Seminary 1966.
Good looking one, center, back row.

It turns out that risk was much greater and much closer than I knew. The war was raging on as President Johnson ordered B-52 bombers to do the very thing to the Vietnamese people that I had feared the Russians would do to us when I was a boy.

In Miami, the young heavyweight boxing champion sent shockwaves throughout the country by insisting the war was unjust.

"I ain't got no quarrel with no Viet Cong," said a young Muhammad Ali.[114]

On leaving Notre Dame at the beginning of 1967, I was reclassified as 1-A, available for service, unless I could quickly enroll at a university. I chose Loyola University just a few blocks away, but I hit a major snag in the transfer. On the morning of the final day of late registration, I called our Dean at the seminary and learned that he had totally forgotten to send my transcripts! Foolishly, I had not followed up to make sure they went through. Loyola's late admissions would close by the end of the day, which meant I had only a couple of hours to complete the process, or I was out of luck!

I drove at breakneck speed the hundred miles to the seminary, picked up my transcripts, and raced over to the university. There I was told I had to get a bunch of signatures to get my application into the Registrar's office before it closed at 4:30. I ran across campus from department to department to get the necessary signatures, asking students along the way if they could point me to the next building. I had to wait in one office for an eternity, only to find that the department head was out of town, and I would need to get the signature from his stand-in—who was across campus.

Exhausted from all the running, I glanced at my watch, only to see that I wasn't going to make it. And if I wasn't registered for the semester, I was going to be drafted!

Nearing 4:30, I got the last signature and with lungs burning, I ran as hard as I could across campus to the Registrar's office in Marquette Hall. My watch said it was past 4:30. Nevertheless, I charged down the crowded corridor, dodging everyone in my way. A woman came out of the Registrar's office and locked its door. Out of breath and hoarse from running, I managed to croak, "Wait! Wait! Please Wait!" Leaning up against a wall, I asked her, between gulps of air, if she would be so kind as to unlock the door and put my application inside. Everything in my life was riding on her answer. She would determine if I was going off to war or not. She looked at me and said, "Of course, I'll be happy to." She took my application, went into the Registrar's office, and placed it on his desk. I thanked her profusely as she came back into the hall and once again locked the door. She smiled and wished me a good rest of the day. Then, totally spent, I leaned back against the wall and slowly slid down to the floor.

That lady's kindness changed my whole life in ways I will never fully know. Whenever I read those bumper stickers that encourage "Random Acts of Kindness," I always say a prayer for her. I sometimes wonder what would have happened if she didn't take my application. Would my name have been added to the thousands of others that are inscribed on the wall of the Vietnam War Memorial?

I had made it into Loyola at a time when everyone was increasingly troubled by the war's continued escalation. And then life sent me another surprise—this one was the best miracle of my life.

Chapter 24

# Miracle

Fig. 25. Mary Ann, love of my life

**THE MIRACLE** appeared at precisely 8:11 on the night of March 10th, 1967. I stood in the lobby of Loyola's girls' dormitory filled with guys picking up their dates for a dance held on a Mississippi riverboat. The boat, named the *President*, was located at the end of Canal Street adjacent to the French Quarter. This was a blind date.

## A Great Flash of Light

Out of the dorm elevator stepped a gorgeous brunette. With a friend at her side and a self-assurance in her walk, she came toward me dressed in a fashionable camel colored dress and high heeled shoes. She had a beautiful face, a cute figure, and gorgeous brown eyes that had a snap to them as they took in all that was around her. When we were introduced, she smiled an engaging smile, and spoke with a lovely voice. Her name was Mary Ann Deswysen, and she was from Miami. As I walked her to my car, a fleeting question crossed my mind, one I had never thought before—could this be the girl I will marry? Thirty minutes later, as we walked up on the plank to board the riverboat, I knew that I was talking with someone who was not only gorgeous but smart and principled. We had a lot in common. She too was steeped in a Catholic school education. She was majoring in sociology and had interesting ideas about the world and what could be done to make it a better place.

We sat out on the open top deck as the riverboat slowly left the dock and made its way up the Mississippi River. The night air was pleasant, and a few stars appeared in a deep blue sky. I was struck by how beautiful my date was as the warm breezes brushed against her hair. We talked easily about a wide range of subjects. Time flew by. Music from the deck below blended in with the gentle splashing sounds of the riverboat's paddle wheel. We made our way to the lower deck and danced to the slow romantic ballads sung by a crooner and backed up by a saxophone player as the riverboat made its way back to its dock.

We disembarked from the *President* and took an elevator to a revolving bar at the top of the tallest building in New Orleans, the Trade Mart. There I had a whiskey sour, while she had a Coke, and we talked on into the night as the lights from the city buildings and boats on the river twinkled below.

It was the first time I had ever been in the International Trade Mart, though I had heard about it in whispered conversations that made mention that the plot to kill President Kennedy had originated in this building. That made absolutely no sense to me, since the President was murdered some five hundred miles away in Dallas. It didn't make sense until twenty-five years later when I saw the movie *JFK*, which linked the CIA's connections in New Orleans with the assassination of the President in Texas.

It didn't take long before I called Mary Ann for a second, third, and fourth date. We spent leisurely hours together walking through the city with its huge oak trees and grand old mansions. In the French Quarter, we stopped to admire the artists painting with oils and pastels in St. Louis Square and sampled the coffee and *beignets* at the Café du Monde. As afternoons blended into evenings, we listened to the sweet sounds of the Dixieland jazz bands freeing their notes to rise high into the air and drift away into the night.

In May we went to a lecture on campus focused on the writings of the theologian I had admired so much, Teilhard de Chardin. The evening ended in a way I hadn't anticipated. As we slowly walked back to her dorm from the lecture, I looked at her face and saw someone who was absolutely lovely. Her white dress with touches of lace contrasted with the tan of her pretty face and thick brown hair which fell lightly across her forehead. Despite my efforts to not get romantically involved with someone, since I still hadn't found my path in life, the words came tumbling out of my mouth. I was in love with her. From that moment on, she was the center of my thoughts. I couldn't think of anything or anyone else. I wanted to be with her the rest of my life.

At a time when we and countless other young couples of our generation hoped simply to marry and settle down to raise a family, Vietnam loomed larger and larger on the world's radar screen. More and more it felt like our generation was caught in some kind of gigantic spider web. Mary Ann and I had to face the possibility that we might not have a life together, but that didn't stop us from sharing every moment. We talked about getting married.

One early morning, we began our long weekend by driving along the Mississippi River to Baton Rouge, stopping along the way for a picnic. We left in high spirits because not only did we have the entire weekend ahead of us, but Bobby Kennedy was visiting our Loyola campus to address the student body on the following Monday. We were thrilled at the idea of seeing him in person. In Baton Rouge, we toured the state capitol building and went to the top of its thirty-four floors to see a beautiful, panoramic view of the city. When we headed back to New Orleans, we felt like we had experienced a perfect day, and a brief reprieve from the cares of the world. And, about that same time, Bobby Kennedy addressed an audience in Indiana:

> I have bad news for you, for all of our fellow citizens, and people who love peace all over the world, and that is that Martin Luther King was shot and killed tonight.[115]
>
> Martin Luther King dedicated his life to love and to justice for his fellow human beings, and he died because of that effort. In this difficult day, in this difficult time for the United States, it is perhaps well to ask what kind of a nation we are and what direction we want to move in. For those of you who are black—considering the evidence there evidently is that there were white people who were responsible—you can be filled with bitterness, with hatred, and a desire for revenge. We can move in that direction as a country, in great polarization—black people amongst black, white people amongst white, filled with hatred toward one another. Or we can make an effort, as Martin Luther King did, to understand and to comprehend, and replace that violence, that stain of bloodshed that has spread across our land, with an effort to understand with compassion and love.... Let us dedicate ourselves to what the Greeks wrote so many years ago: to tame the savageness of man and make gentle the life of this world. Let us dedicate ourselves to that, and say a prayer for our country and for our people.[116]

The Kennedy campaign cancelled the candidate's visit to our university so that he could attend Dr. King's funeral. Mary Ann and I lost our chance to see Robert Kennedy in person.

More and more, our conversations focused on the war and the sense of powerlessness to resist this impersonal, overwhelming, all-consuming destructive force. I had joined the Army ROTC and knew that the majority of us would be commissioned Infantry Officers.

Vietnam raged on into 1968 with more Americans killed, more bombs dropped on the Vietnamese. It seemed that nothing and no one could stop it. The faceless force that devoured everything in its path, now even turned on Lyndon Johnson, the very person who expanded U.S. involvement. In a sudden and dramatic speech, a beleaguered LBJ took to the air waves and declared he would not seek another term as president.

Late one evening, during summer vacation, I watched Bobby Kennedy's televised victory speech for his win in the California primary. Amid the cheers and shouts of the celebration, he rallied his supporters:

> So my thanks to all of you, and now on to [the convention in] Chicago and let's win there. [117]

He gave a victory sign, brushed the hair from his forehead, and left the podium. I moved to turn the television off, when suddenly, on the screen there was total bedlam. People screamed and shouted. It was as if madness had taken over. There were reports of gunshots and Bobby Kennedy lying on the floor. Oh God, no, that can't happen! But it did happen. In America, assassination happened yet again.

Into the night and the following day, the nation waited, expecting the worst. It came the following morning:

> Senator Robert Francis Kennedy died at 1:44 a.m. today, June 6, 1968.... He was 42 years old. [118]

What was this thing, war? What was this thing that was bigger and more powerful than all of us put together—a gargantuan, unstoppable, impersonal whirlpool devouring everything around it to satisfy its voracious appetite? What could stop it? Who had the wisdom to do so? My father was gone. JFK was gone. Dr. King was gone, and so was Bobby.

More violent protests erupted across the nation. The country was tearing apart at the seams.

With my ROTC commitment to join the army after college, this war was no longer an event that was somehow "out there." It was here and now and totally personal. By receiving a commission, I was agreeing to carry out all orders, including orders to kill.

As the school year at Loyola came to an end, the pace of events picked up. Within the span of a few days, young men received their commissions, got married, and went straight into the Army. I was commissioned as an infantry officer, and a few days later, graduated with my bachelor's degree.

At a dinner celebration, one of the student's fathers turned to Mary Ann in conversation and asked casually, "So, Mary Ann, what are you going to be doing while hubby's off to war?"

We were both stunned at the question. Mary Ann tried to answer but couldn't find words. I felt a surge of rage swell up within me. I wanted to grab the guy by the throat.

The man's wife, embarrassed by the gaffe, shushed her husband. "We don't need to talk about such things tonight!" she said.

I wondered if I were to survive this war, if I too one day would grow cold and indifferent to the lives of young couples wanting to share their lives together. Vietnam, like other wars, meant thousands of young brides worrying if their husbands would be returning to them in coffins. On television, the nation watched as more and more of them did.

Mary Ann and I were married a month after graduation on June 7, 1969. We enjoyed a beautiful, tropical honeymoon in the Bahamas, saw an up-and-coming singing couple, Sonny and Cher, at a show on Miami Beach, and spent our last months of pre-military life in Miami. But soon my orders arrived to report to Infantry School in Georgia. And so, on a rainy night, Mary Ann and I packed up and drove the back roads of the deep South to find our way to Ft. Benning, Georgia.

The trip was stressful. Visibility was poor. Thunderous lightning bolts crashed around us, and icy cold sheets of rain pounded our windshield. I gripped the steering wheel ever tighter, while the windshield wipers flailed away in a futile attempt to wipe away the unceasing torrents of rain. We drove deeper and deeper into the darkness of the storm that lay ahead of us. In fact, we were doing more than that—we were descending deep into the heart of a moral nightmare.

Chapter 25

# Crucible

**IN OCTOBER** of 1969, when the war in Vietnam, now under Nixon, escalated further, Mary Ann and I, along with thousands of other young servicemen and their wives, descended on the small southern city of Columbus, Georgia to report for military duty at the vast infantry training center at Fort Benning. Although I recall some pleasant aspects about Columbus, my memories are largely not positive. The one that stuck with me through the years is of the main drag that led to the main entrance to the post. The street was geared up to sell young servicemen anything they could possibly want. Car dealerships, with their banners flapping in the breeze, promised unbelievable deals to meet every soldier's wallet. You could get everything, from the latest shiny model right off the assembly line—with all the bells and whistles—to the 1954 chocolate brown "cream puff" hidden away at the back of the lot. Next to the dealerships were seedy bars with silhouettes of exotic dancers painted on the walls; pawn shops with golf clubs, guitars, and watches in their windows; and joints that promised to get you "cash fast."

 Even after all these years, I recall a used car dealership that took top honors. The owner's name, forever branded in my brain, was "Digger." I guess not a name you'd easily forget. For a publicity stunt, Digger dug a hole about eight feet deep in front of his dealership and publicly vowed to the world that he would live down in the hole and not leave it until his sales goals were met. I couldn't quite grasp how a salesman, spending the majority of his time sitting in a hole, could be executing an effective sales strategy. And it just didn't have a symbolic rallying cry to it, as, say, Gandhi's march to the sea. But I had to give this guy his due—what he lacked in soaring imagination, he made up for in grit. I'm assuming he wasn't sneaking out for smokes when nobody was looking or skulking back home at night to watch TV.

Once we arrived in Columbus, Mary Ann and I encountered the same problem everyone else did: finding a suitable place to stay. We were really at the mercy of the locals, some who were charging exorbitant prices for substandard housing. We pored over newspaper ads for apartments. When we followed up, virtually all of them were out of the question for one reason or another. At one of our stops, an owner in all seriousness showed us a cramped apartment with a broken lamp dangling lifelessly over a dining room table that exuded greasy smells of yesteryear's fried bacon. As we left, Mary Ann described in her typical understated fashion, "Never would I stay there in a hundred million, billion years." I've never had to worry about where Mary Ann stood on anything.

It didn't get too much better throughout the course of the day, and by late afternoon we were totally discouraged. However, at our last stop, we found a small but brand-new trailer in a lovely trailer park near the post. The rent was $125/month, and after all we had seen, it was a find, and we took it on the spot.

Fort Benning, famously known as the "Home of the Infantry," trained thousands upon thousands of young infantry officers and enlisted men before shipping them to Vietnam for immediate ground combat. The post was the third largest military installation in the country and encompassed over 250 square miles.

I pulled up to the military police checkpoint at the entrance gate and was greeted by a sharply dressed officer complete with white gloves.

"Good morning, I'm reporting for duty."

"Good morning, sir. May I see your papers?"

I presented my orders and answered a few questions. I glanced at the post's welcoming sign which read, "With our bayonets we keep the peace." It may have been my Catholic upbringing, but the logic of that statement struck me as rather odd. The officer handed my papers back, wished me a good day, and waved me through.

On the post, troops were marching in platoons hither and yon. Trucks roared about filling the air with noise and exhaust fumes as they transported Army personnel to and from training sites across the miles of complex. 250 feet high parachute jump towers stood tall against the sky. Trainees who wanted to be Airborne qualified were lifted to the top and then released to parachute safely to the ground. Not my idea of a good time.

In a matter of days, and at various weapons sites, I learned about weapon capabilities and their tactical maneuvering. Instructors boasted of the destructive power of the M-16 rifles and the astonishing speed with which the M-60 machine guns could fire off multiple rounds in a matter of a few seconds. I had a lot of experience with guns growing up and felt a thrill in firing these larger weapons with their enormous firepower. But I also shuddered to think of what one bullet or multiple rounds could do to human flesh and bone. I wondered if there was some young man in Vietnam just going about his day-to-day business, who would be dead in a few months as a result of my actions. Or maybe I'd be the one dead as a result of his.

We ran through obstacle courses, jumped over wooden fences, pulled ourselves up and over walls, and crawled under barbed wire. At a grenade station, we learned through careful, step-by-step demonstration how to successfully throw a grenade. To me, those instructors had the worst job on post, because they were the ones who had to stay in the box with the recruits— anxious rookies pulling the pins and throwing grenades for the first time. These newcomers ranged from the athletic and physically skilled, to those who were clumsy and bungling. And things can just go wrong. Again and again, if somehow the grenade was dropped, the message yelled at us was just leave it alone and back away. The instructor, not the trainee, would pick it up and throw it to avoid the confusion of two guys getting in the way of one another, each trying to get to the grenade before it exploded. I managed to succeed with three successful throws. At another station, I sat with a dozen trainees locked within the confines of a suffocating, unbearably hot chamber wearing a gas mask, as a canister of a burning chemical substance was tossed in on us. Not a pleasant experience.

Once assigned to my unit, it didn't take long to find out that guys were all over the map about how they felt about the war. Views ranged from those who couldn't wait "to get into the action," to those who spoke of fleeing the country for Canada. Some felt it was their duty and just wanted to get the whole service thing over with, and others felt they should serve their country, right or wrong. One morning, a fellow officer confided to me that he wanted to go simply to know what it felt like to kill someone. And a stone's throw from where my platoon assembled each morning, Lieutenant William Calley was held in the post's jail awaiting military trial for his role in the horrific My Lai crime the year before, when as many as 500 unarmed Vietnamese civilians including women, children, and old men, were massacred by American forces.

The reality that I was being trained to kill men and might soon be in a situation endangering the lives of women and children was finally sinking into my brain. What puzzled me was that despite all the various views my fellow officers talked about, no one seemed to be questioning the morality of the war itself. I felt a sickening sense of isolation. I was seeing something so huge, so all pervasive, so ugly, so evil, while everyone around me seemed not to see it at all. Was I crazy? Who was I, an absolute nobody, to question the moral judgment of the United States of America? How could I possibly think I knew better than the American president?

Mary Ann wasn't faring much better. She attended an orientation session for the wives of the incoming junior officers and was given the unwelcome news: "It is now your responsibility to work hard to become his second wife," she was told.

Looking back, it astonishes me that the wives of the brass could state something like that as a fact. But tragically, a fact to which many widows of wars can attest.

Our platoon began each day with the challenging task of running up and down the hills of Georgia's red clay as we shouted out into the pre-dawn morning our message to the world:

I wanna be an Airborne Ranger!
I wanna live a life of danger!

I wanna go to Vietnam!
I wanna kill the Viet Cong!

Actually, I hadn't the slightest desire to be an Airborne Ranger, nor did I have the slightest inclination to live a life of danger, and I sure as hell didn't want to go to Vietnam. And like Muhammad Ali, who had his heavyweight crown stripped from him for refusing the draft, I too didn't have anything against any Viet Cong. Ali put it all on the line: his championship, his livelihood, his whole future.

I didn't have to go to Vietnam to experience the racism of which Ali spoke. I already saw it in weapons classes, when instructors spoke of the Vietnamese as creatures less than human. The offensive term they used most often was the "gooks" or sometimes referred to them as "them gooks" or worse. I was sickened by it.

The strange reality known as war, which had previously been theoretical and abstract, was now sinking even deeper within me. And I was haunted by the photo that shocked the world—a Viet Cong soldier being shot in the head at point blank range. This image, more than anything else, revealed the face of war.

This was a war of villagers caught between two opposing military powers, ordinary folk trying to scratch out a living.

How could I go ahead and be a part of this? What should I do?

Life was demanding answers NOW!

I desperately searched for guidance, some wisdom. It was only many decades later when I read what the author Chris Matthews had written that best captured how I felt about that terrible time: "Though I didn't know it at the time, I desperately wanted some grown-up to come along and say we were right, that it wasn't that we were just afraid to fight a war the way our fathers so unquestioningly had."[119]

Conscientious objectors, who opposed the war on moral grounds, opposed all wars. Did I? I had not even heard of that term until now. Would I have not fought off Hitler and his gangsters who were brutal by all measure as they tried to conquer the world? Had I not always greatly admired the courage of RAF British fighter pilots who, in ramshackle planes, risked their lives daily to defend London from the massive German bomber attacks? And how could I not respond to the call of the country, the America of my youth, the country so loved and revered by my mother and father, the country that had given us so much?

I needed a father and felt the pain that my father was gone. Could a member of the clergy help? Mary Ann seemed to think so. "Talk to someone about your moral dilemma," she said. "Find out what the church's position is."

I arranged to meet with a chaplain. It was a mistake. Seeing the chaplain's chest of medals, that would have rivaled George Patton's, should have been my first clue. After hesitatingly telling him the story of my concerns, he turned on me trying to contain his anger, "Let's just say, Lieutenant, that I never met you, and you never met me!"

I felt a knot in the pit of my stomach. That did it for me, I wasn't going to trust any other member of the clergy. But Mary Ann insisted I try again, that I needed to know the church's position on war. This time I made a better choice, a lay priest, who resided in a parish off post. He listened to me carefully and even shared with me that he was struggling as a recovering alcoholic. From what we talked about, it seemed that the church was also split on the morality of war. As we ended our session, he handed me a book and said, "I hope maybe this will be of help."

The book was entitled, *The Non-Violent Cross: A Theology of Revolution and Peace*. The implications of the book were staggering. The author, James W. Douglass, traced the history of how far Christianity had veered off course from its genesis in the Christ, who non-violently confronted the powers of the Roman state, to a church which gradually allied itself with political power throughout the course of history, even to the current B-52 bombers killing thousands upon thousands of innocent Vietnamese villagers in Southeast Asia. With regard to the future, the author also issued a powerful warning. In placing its future in the possession of nuclear weapons, humanity was placing itself on a violent path to its own destruction, as well as that of the earth:

> Military power has put mankind on the cross. The new threat of global suicide has redefined military power at its height as ultimately powerless, because its ultimate use would terminate the life of man.[120]

I was twenty-four years old, and I found it all mind-boggling. Protests around the country intensified as World War II patriots, who had sacrificed so much for the world, clashed with the anti-war demonstrators who felt this new war was immoral. I was torn between the two, and it was tearing me apart. Events reached a climax when Ohio National Guard troops opened fire on protesting students at Kent State, killing four of them. How could this possibly be happening in America?

The question became: Do I participate in a war that I feel is immoral but of which I have no proof? Or do I go with my conscience and against the country that has given so much opportunity to my family and brought so much hope to the world? My decision would impact Mary Ann, in every respect, if I were sentenced to federal prison. In a matter of a few months, I had taken her from her life as a college student, looking forward to a promising professional career, to the wife of someone who could be considered a traitor to his country. I withdrew further and further into myself trying to figure it all out, and this behavior was having an impact on our marriage. She couldn't communicate with me, had no idea where I stood, and felt helplessly caught in this conundrum. And there was yet another very important consideration—we were expecting a baby, whose entire future would also depend on my decision.

I felt my brain was about to explode. It was then that I had one of the strangest and most intense experiences. It came in the form of a dream. The day before the experience, Mary Ann went into labor, and we drove to the army hospital to deliver the baby. It was the army's attitude at the time that husbands were not to be a part of the birthing process. I was instructed to return home, and when the baby came, they would give me a call.

I returned to our apartment, and the level of my anxiety surged to the highest I ever experienced. If it had gotten any more intense, I believe I would have had a heart attack or a stroke. Mentally, physically, and emotionally exhausted, I threw my uniform onto the floor, dropped into bed, and fell into a deep sleep. I felt myself descending lower and lower into a nether world, a dark, ominous region, a set of caves deep within the earth. The place was foreboding; its air was intensely hot, yet I felt cold and clammy, and still I descended its stairs further to find my way. On the walls were tunnels leading in other directions that glowed red and orange, flickering of fires licking at the coal-like walls.

As I reached the cave's floor, the place became baking hot. I heard distant echoes of murmured voices of many souls, living and dead. I couldn't make out what they were saying. The murmurings became louder and were interrupted by bursts of ranting, raving, and insane laughing. Beings blamed each other, cursed one another, and some souls, out of sight, screamed in pain, others howled in frustration—each insisted on its own way, yet all connected to one another in a spirit of damnation. I thought, "This was a place where all wars begin."

How did I ever end up here? Whatever happened to the America I knew that had television shows, baseball, family outings? What about goodness, prosperity, kindness toward neighbors, and just plain normalcy? What forces brought me here? What was the flaw within me that prevented me from going along with what the culture around me saw as morally right?

Some of the beings became vaguely visible as they flitted back and forth in the dark, their faces oddly unrecognizable as they drifted in and out of spirit form. Others lurked behind boulders of coal. I could feel my strength ebbing from me, so that I had no physical strength in my body. I was condemned to this terrible chamber of horror. I was the evil one, the nonconforming traitor to my country, the coward, the guilty one for not falling in line, and not doing my duty. Like jackals, the spirits slowly moved in closer, encircling me, their prey. There was no escape.

In the distance I heard a noise, a ringing—loud, jarring. The heat was unbearable. The ringing continued, slow and relentless. My heart was pounding so hard I thought my chest would explode. I couldn't make sense of what the ringing noise was. Finally, I fumbled to reach for a phone, which fell to the floor. In a clumsy grab, I picked it up.

"Hello?"

There was no answer.

"Hello? Hello?"

A loud stark dial tone.

I put the phone down as the stupor of my deep sleep still held me captive. I couldn't clear the cobwebs from my mind to understand what was going on. Where was I? Why was it so hot?! Who was calling? Groggy and barely able to move, I struggled to drag myself from sleep to consciousness. I laid there unable to clear my mind and shake off the dream. I felt myself falling back into the horrors of the cave.

Another set of jarring rings. I sat up and shook myself awake. As I became aware of my surroundings, the heat and sounds of fury from the dream faded into darkness, and the power of the creatures' grips on me loosened as they slowly retreated and faded back into their nether world.

I tried to make sense of what had happened to me. It was as if I had emerged from a crucible that burned everything away—every argument for and against the war. I didn't know if this was a dream that reflected the nation being torn apart over the war, or if I had visited a chamber in hell itself. There was nothing left of me, save one thing—a conviction that whatever was to come my way—no matter what—I wasn't going to kill anybody in this war.

The phone rang yet again. It was the hospital. I jumped up, got dressed, and drove to the hospital to see Mary Ann. She let me hold our beautiful baby boy. It took me a while to get used to holding such a tiny person. I had witnessed the death of my father, now I was witnessing the beginning of life with my son.

"So, you're Robert Francis," I said.

We named him after a man Mary Ann and I both deeply admired, but never got the chance to meet. We named him after a man who, two years earlier had been assassinated, and was eulogized by his brother Ted Kennedy with these words:

> My brother. . . need not be idealized or enlarged in death beyond what he was in life. He should be remembered simply as a good and decent man who saw wrong and tried to right it, saw suffering and tried to heal it, saw war and tried to stop it. [121]

Our new baby slept peacefully in my arms. I didn't know what the future held in store for him, for Mary Ann, or me, but now it was time for me to speak my truth to power. I had to do it for my son, and I had to do it no matter the price.

Chapter 26

# Land of the Beast

**I MADE THE APPOINTMENT** to declare myself a conscientious objector and resign my commission from the U.S. Army. As I drove onto the post, the traffic was heavier, and everybody seemed to be moving at a faster than usual pace. I took off my cap, as I walked into the company commander's rather stark and drab waiting area and greeted the receptionist. She asked me to take a seat, and I surveyed the ten or so uncomfortable looking army issued wooden chairs lined up against the wall. I evidently picked the most uncomfortable one and switched to another chair equally as bad. I glanced through some well-worn magazines to kill time. Minutes went by and then an hour.

The receptionist continued to peck away at a mountain of paperwork stacked on her desk, pausing occasionally to correct typing errors or answer the phone. After making one correction, she looked up from her typewriter.

"Would you like some coffee?" she asked, nodding to a table with a coffee pot and a couple of Army mugs. "If you'd like some, just help yourself."

"No thanks," I said. "I've already had a couple of cups. Thank you, though."

## A Great Flash of Light

She smiled.

More time passed, and she looked up and said, "You know, I don't think you're going to see him today. I don't think he'll be coming back with all that's going on."

"What's all that's going on?" I asked.

"Surely you've heard that we've just invaded Cambodia," she said, peering at me over her reading glasses.

"No, I'm sorry, I hadn't," I said.

I was stunned by the news. I sat there trying to mull over what it all meant. After a few minutes I got up to leave.

"I'll schedule an appointment for another time," I said, and thanked her.

After all my anxiety and soul searching, I had lost the chance to finally resign my commission! Well, at least delayed for the present. What was I supposed to do now? Maybe just come back in a few days if things settle down? And what was the impact of this invasion—which Nixon was calling an "incursion"? That certainly wasn't going to help my case. "God almighty," I thought, "when does it ever end?"

I telephoned my chaplain friend to tell him the news of our new baby and this latest development.

"Stop torturing yourself any further about all of this," he said, "You've done enough. Go on to your next assignment in Germany, which will give you more time to sort things out. Hopefully, the war will end before too long."

His kind words of guidance were exactly what I needed to hear. For the moment I could just let things go.

In the early hours of the 4th of July 1970, I boarded a jet with dozens of other soldiers bound for Germany. Once on the plane, I walked down the aisle, found a seat, threw my baggage into the overhead compartment, and then slid down into the seat closest to the window. I was dead tired, but more than that, I was upset that I had to leave Mary Ann and Bobby behind until I could find suitable housing without knowing how long it would be until they could come over. I don't remember much after that.

I slept all the way across the Atlantic—the ocean my ancestors crossed sixty years earlier. I woke up to look down on French and German fields, where so much blood had been spilled in two world wars. First came a static war confined to barbed wire and muck-filled trenches that soldiers shared with rats and lice. And then a second war, with Hitler's *blitzkrieg* of armies, tanks, and fighter planes strafing from the air, killing thousands and thousands of soldiers and civilians.

Finally, we landed at the immense Rhein-Main Air Force Base. Here I was standing in the land I had read about in high school in *The Rise and Fall of the Third Reich*. With all my concerns about the war put aside for the time being, I was eager to see what remained of the land left behind by the beast of the 20th century. Hitler's Reich existed twenty-five years earlier, so I was brushing up against history that happened only a short time ago.

A military vehicle arrived to pick up our group of junior officers and transport us to army headquarters in Frankfurt. The driver got on the autobahn, a superhighway with no speed limit, and drove like a madman speeding past everyone. I looked out the window to get my first glimpse of a German building, expecting something like the huge German Reichstag. Instead, just off the autobahn, I saw a Kentucky Fried Chicken.

When I arrived at my destination, I found that my minor in English and some writing skill had landed me a plum job. Instead of being assigned to a platoon right at the border facing eyeball to eyeball with the soldiers of the Warsaw pact, I was to remain in Frankfurt at the V Corps headquarters G-1 Personnel Office. V Corps had a distinguished history in World War II, especially on D-Day, where it was one of the major assault forces that attacked the coast of France. By the time of my arrival, the corps consisted of half of the American troops stationed in Germany.

The building that housed V Corps had been the corporate headquarters for I. G. Farben, a major company that manufactured chemicals that Hitler and his henchmen used to murder millions of people in the concentration camps. Toward the end of the war, the building served as General Eisenhower's headquarters, and because of its size and the importance of the many post-war decisions made there, it became known as the "Pentagon of Europe." My office was on the second floor right above Conference Room 130, which had been General Eisenhower's main office. I know because one of my early tasks was to have a gold-plated plaque struck with the words "Eisenhower Room" affixed to the conference room door—I guess, probably, my major contribution to history.

## A Great Flash of Light

My job as a staff officer was to draft position papers, correspondence, and policies and procedures. My boss was an intense and surly colonel, who had two pencils clenched in his teeth and a third tucked behind his ear. One junior officer pulled me, the newcomer, aside and whispered that there were basically two rules: first, the boss only wanted to see "the guts" of what I wrote, and second, I should get stuff onto his desk fast!

I submitted my drafts, and if he didn't like what I wrote, with pencils in teeth, he'd slide into my office, much like Kramer did years later on *Seinfeld*.

"No! No! No! You're missing the point!!"

I'd write a draft; he'd tear it up. I'd write a second, he'd rip it to fewer shreds.

"But sir..."

Then came his favorite rebuttal: "I don't need to hear your problems, Lieutenant. I need to hear your solutions!"

Day by day, it didn't get better.

"No! No!! NO!!! Get rid of all that!!" he yelled. "Just write glunk, glunk, glunk!"

"Glunk?!" I repeated. "You want me to write about 'glunk?'"

"Exactly!" he said.

I had no idea what the hell he was talking about. But before too long I started to get the hang of the glunking thing, and my stuff began to come back with only a minor correction or two.

The days crawled into weeks. I missed Mary Ann and our new baby terribly. I couldn't wait to bring them over from the states.

After work, with little else to do, I'd go to the movies at the post theater three or four times a week. One particularly memorable scene was in the newly released movie, *Patton*. Against the backdrop of a huge American flag that filled the screen, the academy award winning actor George C. Scott, as General Patton, addressed his troops: "I want you to remember that no bastard ever won a war by dying for his country. He won it by making the other poor dumb bastard die for his country." [122]

The movie reflected Patton's theory that war was the most noble human endeavor, one that offered young men the toughest test of courage and the opportunity to prove themselves as warriors. As impressive as General Patton was on the screen, he and I were not on the same page. If war is such a noble endeavor, why call the young men who fight it "dumb bastards?" My feelings were along the lines spoken by, I believe, a senator whose name I don't remember, but was someone who opposed the war in Vietnam. Simply stated, he said he didn't like old men who make wars for young men to fight.

After a couple of months, I found housing that was more than suitable. Mary Ann and Bobby flew over, and we settled into our new apartment. The German neighbors we met could not have been nicer, nor more hospitable.

My job assignment gave me some breathing room to reflect more on my position on the war and attend night classes to work toward a master's degree. Soon, I found myself in my own element, no longer flailing away at Latin, but excelling in an academic discipline I was interested in, Counseling Psychology—what made people tick, in depth.

I had a welcome break from work, worry, and graduate school one evening when I was invited by a fellow officer to watch a huge sporting event broadcast from the states. It was billed as the *Fight of the Century*, 15 rounds between Smokin' Joe Frazier and Muhammad Ali, the first time two undefeated heavyweight champions ever fought against one another. New York City's Madison Square Garden was the scene. Sports figures, movie stars, and celebrities of every stripe attended. The fight came on German television at 3:00 a.m.

I was rooting for Ali, who in the early rounds seemed to miss a lot of punches. In the fifteenth round, however, the victory was pretty much decided when Smokin' Joe threw a left hook that would've knocked down a building. Yells, groans, and cheers came from apartments around the complex as the blow hit Ali flush on the jaw. He dropped to the canvas so hard that his white shoes with fancy red tassels flung upward. Incredibly, Ali immediately got up at the count of four, and fought to match Frazier blow for blow through the rest of the round. The fight was terribly exciting, and although Ali lost on this night, he would continue his quest to regain the heavyweight crown for four more years until he defeated George Foreman in the *Rumble in the Jungle*. As world champion, he not only became the best-known person on the planet, but also a peacemaker who lived and taught the spirit of universal brotherly love.

Mary Ann and I traveled beyond Frankfurt to other parts of Germany to see first-hand the country that once lived in terror under the shadow of the swastika. I wanted to have a better understanding of how a democracy could have been taken over by such an odd, hate-filled man. How could he gain power over one of the most advanced cultures of Europe? How did it happen? Could it happen again? Could it happen in America?

We saw reminders of the past everywhere. In pawn shop windows, I saw small flags with swastikas that parade watchers waved when Nazi big wigs marched by. You could buy knives that Nazi soldiers carried in battle.

We also met people who shared vivid memories of the war. One family had to evacuate to the countryside as the Allies bombed the city of Frankfurt, and at night, saw the sky lit up from the fire of the bombs. One man told how he had seen Hitler wave to his group from a train making a stop in the city of Mainz, and how he ended up, at age seventeen, serving as a German submariner.

I also had a couple of potentially threatening encounters with a man who claimed to be a former member of Hitler's SS. I didn't doubt that for a minute. Here was a man who was an extension—in the flesh—of a man who ignited a world war. His eyes had a strange, hate-filled, crazed look. He seemed consumed with bitterness, maybe that the war had been lost. Now he was a mean and menacing drunk, swaggering on a street corner, yelling and threatening people as they walked by. Unfortunately, that street corner was where I took a trolley to work.

Early one morning, he began to assault a young woman who operated a small *trinkhalle* where you could buy bratwurst, beverages, and snacks. As he placed his order, he suddenly seized the woman by her arms in an iron grip. She couldn't escape. He lifted her up toward him, I assume in an effort to kiss her. Standing behind him, I said something to the effect of "*Bitte*" or "Excuse me." As he looked back over his shoulder to see who had spoken to him, he caught a glimpse of me in an officer's uniform, and he let the young woman go. The only thing that may have prevented me from being an unfortunate casualty that morning was that I was in uniform, which conveyed a sense of authority. The American eagle on my cap seemed in particular to capture his attention, and while he was distracted, the woman locked herself safely in her *trinkhalle*. I was left with the drunk. We shared a few sentences about military uniforms, and his hostility lessened. I wished him a good day and boarded the trolley, thankful the lady was safe, and that I could get out of there in one piece.

In some sense, one of the more startling moments occurred in the middle of the night, when I was sitting in the lobby of the 97th General Hospital as Mary Ann delivered our second baby, Holly. This hospital had been taken from the Germans and converted into an American medical facility. I glanced up at the high decorative ceiling and saw an eagle. Looking further, I expected to see a shield of stars and stripes on the eagle's chest while arrows and olive branches were held in the eagle's claws. That isn't what I saw. This was the eagle of the Third Reich! Within its claws, the eagle held the globe, and on the globe was a large swastika. A shiver ran down my spine. There, right before my very eyes, was the symbol of the beast: Hitler. His desire to conquer the world and rule the world according to his impulses of insanity, grandiosity, cruelty, and paranoia, were all carried out in an ongoing campaign of mechanized butchery.

We traveled by train to the strange places I had read about in high school. We visited the beer garden in Munich where Hitler started his movement with words of hate and frustration that he crafted into rousing speeches. We saw the huge Nuremberg stadium where he delivered his words at carefully orchestrated rallies, working himself and his followers into a frenzy. And then we saw how words of hate matter and how, if they go unchecked, result in terrible consequences.

It was in a lovely little village perhaps twenty miles from Munich. It was picture-perfect, right out of Hansel and Gretel. The village was Dachau, a virtual stone's throw from the first Nazi death camp that served as a prototype for all concentration camps across Germany. Here, we saw first-hand the terrible consequences brought on by Hitler's words of a master race. Those words put in motion the systematic murder of millions of people, primarily Jews and also many other ethnic groups throughout Europe. This was the manifestation of the inconceivable evil of which history books document. I couldn't and still can't wrap my mind around how the townspeople could go about their daily lives and somehow manage to keep at bay the monstrous, unspeakable reality that was going on all around them.

And, as we walked through the streets of Dachau, I wondered if we Americans weren't doing a similar thing with nuclear weapons. By remaining quiet, were we somehow cooperating with this dark force that can kill more people than even the Nazis dreamed of? We know the weapons are there. We know that if unleashed they can murder us all. We know that our country, Russia, China and six more nuclear armed nations are poised to launch them on a moment's notice. Yet, we don't speak out. Instead, we go about our daily lives in denial about the unspeakable threat that hangs over us. We deny the immorality of it all. We deny that through madness, mistake or miscalculation those weapons can turn on us all. Maybe it's because the whole issue is so big, so powerful, so removed from us, so frightening to us that we don't know where to start. Is it any wonder that we go about our lives in a universal state of denial living under the nuclear sword?

When we returned to Frankfurt, I went back on duty knowing it was time for me to declare that I was a conscientious objector. I dreaded revealing my intention to my boss, a highly decorated infantryman and career officer. However, I put together my paperwork, including my statement and letters of reference that noted my objection to war was valid in Catholic religious tradition. I met with my boss behind closed doors. I stated my objections to the war and how I had struggled to somehow stay true to my country, my religion, my principles, my wife and children, and my commitment as a commissioned officer that I had accepted in good faith. But, having seen what I had seen and read about the world wars and the war in Vietnam and of Hitler's Germany, I could not and would not kill anyone in this war. Therefore, I was resigning my commission. It had taken me a long time, but finally I took my stand.

He listened to what I had to say and reviewed my documents. He looked me straight in the eye, but unlike the chaplain I had sought guidance from earlier, he shared some of his traumatic story of combat. His last assignment was in Vietnam, where he had seen some of the worst carnage of the war: ambushes, charred and maimed bodies of soldiers and civilians, and body bags stacked high on the backs of trucks. He said he respected my position and went on to write me a strong letter of support.

Then as my application was processed, Congress passed a resolution to cut off funding for the war. That meant the Army had to make immediate, deep cuts in troops, discharging those who wanted out. For Mary Ann and me, it meant that the nightmare of

Vietnam was over! Along with Bobby who was a year and a half and Holly who was six months old, Mary Ann and I were rushed onto a jet filled with military personnel for a 4:00 a.m. flight back to America.

Our journey was marred for the final time in the Army's famed "hurry up and wait" fashion. With little sleep from the night before, and after hours over the Atlantic, we finally landed in Charleston, South Carolina at 5:00 p.m. We were told we'd quickly go through customs and take a short bus ride to the post where we would complete the process that night. It took four hours for us to get through customs. We were then hurried onto a bus. The short trip to the nearby post turned out to be a two-hundred-mile trip to Fort Jackson in Columbia, South Carolina. On the bus, the soldiers and their wives comforted their toddlers and babies, who, like their parents, were completely exhausted. But I didn't care what we had to go through, if we could actually be discharged from the whole nightmare that night.

We arrived at 2:00 a.m. in a parking lot in front of a Quonset hut at Fort Jackson. The driver jumped off the bus and unloaded all the luggage, throwing suitcases haphazardly in a huge pile alongside the bus. While husbands sorted through the luggage to see which suitcases were which, wives were trying to comfort their babies, crying from the cold and soaking diapers. Without so much as a single word, the driver, his duty completed, yelled for everybody to back away from the bus, hopped back in, and roared off into the night leaving us behind to breathe in the glory of his exhaust fumes. I went into the Quonset hut to find out what we were supposed to do next. A young PFC stood at attention and responded: "Sir, nobody told us you was comin'!"

We hurried up and we waited, but it really didn't matter. We were back in America! The group piled into a bunch of taxis that transported us to a motel, and I don't remember much else. We woke up the next morning to a day that was bright and sunny. We walked down one of Columbia's streets lined with big, beautiful oak trees. We went to a McDonald's, where I had one of the best meals of my entire life: two cheeseburgers, fries, and a Coke—normal food! Normal! That's what I wanted, NORMAL!

We slept through that entire Sunday, and early Monday morning, I began my last day in the army. I went through the out-processing carrying a huge stack of bureaucratic paperwork. I reached the final station, where I would sign out for the last time and return to civilian life. Upon doing so, I was presented with two additional items to include in the stack of my military records. On the left was an 8" by 10" black and white photo of Richard Nixon. On the right was a form letter from the president telling me I had served my country honorably. I looked at the letter and then at the picture of Nixon. He was smiling. I felt a surge of anger rise from deep within me. A tragic human event could have been prevented had it not been for the weekend of November 22, 1963.

After a moment to let all my thoughts sink in, I crumpled up both the letter and the photo, and slammed them into a nearby trash can. I really didn't need Dick Nixon to tell me how I had served my country.

Richard Nixon would go on to assure the nation that "a just and lasting peace" had been achieved. His address didn't mention the 58,000 American casualties, nor the untold numbers of service personnel coming back with physical injuries and emotional wounds, later identified as post traumatic disorders. Nor did he mention the millions of Vietnamese civilians who were killed, women and children included, to achieve the "just peace."

Make no mistake about it: no matter how it is packaged, at its core, war is a dirty business. When politicians talk glibly about needing "boots on the ground," notice that rarely, if ever, are they talking about *their* boots being on that ground.

I just wanted Mary Ann, Bobby, Holly, and I to get back to a normal life—a life free of war, and thinking about war, and wondering if war could ever be stopped. I just wanted this horrible chapter called Vietnam to be over. I wanted a 9:00 to 5:00 job and a house on a tree-lined street where Bobby and Holly could have fun, grow up strong and smart, and live in a peaceful world.

But Vietnam had provided me with ample evidence that history repeats itself again and again—that wars are inevitable and can't be stopped. Despite all the peace marches, assassinations, sacrifices, and all the suffering, the beast of war continued. Unleashed by a simple memorandum, the war remained unstoppable until it had sufficiently devoured everyone and everything in its path. One of Bobby Kennedy's advisors, Jack Newfield, best described how I felt on that day:

Now I realized what makes our generation unique, what defines us apart from those who came before the hopeful winter of 1961, and those who came after the murderous spring of 1968. We are the first generation that learned from experience, in our innocent twenties, that things were not really getting better, that we shall *not* overcome. We felt, by the time we reached thirty, that we had already glimpsed the most compassionate leaders our nation could produce, and they all had been assassinated. And from this time forward, things would get worse: our best political leaders were part of memory now, not hope. [123]

If war can't be stopped, then a final nuclear war consuming all of us is only a matter of time. Scripture points out that if one lives by the sword, one will die by the sword. Does that not mean, if we choose to live by the nuclear sword, we will perish by the nuclear sword? But I gave up. I surrendered with the thought that I would leave that to others to sort out.

At the hotel, I packed my uniform away. I also packed away all my lifelong questions about the inevitability of war and what I might do to stop it. We picked up our car that had been shipped back to the states from Germany, and our young family of four headed down I-95 to Miami. With every mile we traveled, I left a part of me farther and farther behind. I felt justified in doing so; I had given it all my best shot. Let somebody else do it.

I didn't know it at the time, but this decision to surrender to a sense of hopelessness about stopping war was the great mistake of my life. It meant I was embracing an underlying cynicism that permeates our culture today about the inevitability of war and humanity's future. This was the cynicism, about which JFK had warned us, to which we must not surrender:

> First, let us examine our attitude toward peace itself. Too many of us think it is impossible. Too many think it unreal. But that is a dangerous, defeatist belief. It leads to the conclusion that war is inevitable, that mankind is doomed, that we are gripped by forces we cannot control. We need not accept that view. [124]

### A Great Flash of Light

As we drove southward, JFK's familiar voice grew fainter and fainter. Up ahead of us, normalcy awaited! Sunshine, blue skies, warm weather, and tropical beaches! Miami here we come!

And I for one couldn't wait!

Chapter 27

# Years Go By

*Let man but accumulate his materials of destruction and the devil within him will soon be unable to resist putting them to their fated use.* [125]

Carl G. Jung, Modern Man in Search of a Soul

*If we have them [nuclear weapons], why can't we use them?* [126]

2016 Presidential Candidate Donald J. Trump

**IT FELT GREAT** being back on American soil! I loved Miami, the beautiful and exciting tropical city where Mary Ann grew up. I found a job as a counselor, and Mary Ann found one as a teacher. We bought a house where Bobby and Holly could play in the backyard and ride their tricycles out on the sidewalk. The beaches were only a few miles away, and the kids got beautiful tans from swimming in Miami Beach and across town in Coral Gables, at the magnificent Venetian pool. We also took short camping trips on Florida's west coast, through the Florida Keys, and into Key West. I found being a father was the wonderful experience I had expected it to be. I loved every minute seeing our two smart, talented, and loving children having fun and growing in stature.

Miami grew even more exciting when, in sports, Don Shula and his Miami Dolphins—Larry Csonka, Mercury Morris, Jim Kiick, and Paul Warfield—made football history by winning two Super Bowls with one of them a perfect season—a feat that hasn't been duplicated in nearly fifty years. And then, both the Democrats and Republicans chose Miami Beach for their 1972 national conventions to nominate their respective presidential candidates: George McGovern and Richard Nixon.

Mary Ann went back to graduate school for a master's degree in education. I went back to earn a doctorate in public administration. It was in this doctoral work that I began to access resources that provided information about how razor close the world came to the brink during the Cuban Missile Crisis.

After six years of work and grad school, it was time to move on. With degrees in hand, I took a position with a social service agency in Richmond, Virginia. Shortly after our move, Mary Ann gave birth to our third child, Nicholas. Our hospital experience was totally different from the Army's prohibition of young fathers having any role in the birthing process. This time, while Mary Ann went to weekly Lamaze classes, I confined my approach to attending one class and speed-reading the guidelines outlined in the brochure. With my preparation complete, I felt a surge of confidence in my qualifications as a capable, dependable, and skillful birthing partner. However, in the delivery room, after referring to my brochure, I dared to question Mary Ann's bold assertion that the baby was coming at that very moment.

"Go get the nurse NOW!" she yelled at me. "Don't tell her the baby is coming, you tell her the baby is here!!"

"But, Mary Ann," I tried to explain, "she was just here, and said it was still going to be a while before—"

Following an unpleasant rebuke, from which I still have the ugly bruise marks around my throat, I ran to get the nurse. In retrospect, it appears Mary Ann was right. But for the record, I was simply trying to go by the book. No matter. A few minutes later I got to hold our beautiful baby boy, Nicholas Vincent, and I have no words to express the wonder of the experience, except to say that witnessing a birth is as close to a miracle as one can ever possibly get.

## Years Go By

We settled down to the suburban life we had wanted. Mary Ann continued her teaching career, and the kids attended a neighborhood Catholic grade school.

As the years passed, the presidents came and went—Nixon, Ford, Carter. In 1981, President Reagan was scheduled to make a political speech at a Richmond hotel across the street from my office. Like many people in Dallas during Kennedy's visit, we all stationed ourselves at windows to get a glimpse of the president as he arrived.

"There it is! There they are!" someone shouted, the first to spot the president's motorcade.

From my second story window I saw the fleet of shiny black limousines, accompanied by motorcycle police, slowly driving up the avenue. My feeling of excitement was suddenly replaced by a sense of deep concern. Why were they moving so slowly? As the president's vehicle approached, my anxiety heightened. The scene that unfolded before me was similar to the one in Dallas: a sunny day, shiny black limousines, motorcycle police, and a U.S. president. As the motorcade approached the hotel, the vehicles slowed to a crawl.

My God, I thought, haven't they learned anything from Dallas?

The president's car came to a near stop! What are you doing? GET THAT CAR UNDER THE PARKING DECK FAST! NOW! MOVE IT! MOVE IT! MOVE IT NOW!

But I only thought it. I didn't say anything. This wasn't Dallas. This was Richmond. This was now. Finally, the black, heavily armored car made a slow, sweeping turn and disappeared into the secured area under the hotel's parking deck. I took in a deep breath, maybe the first in five minutes. Everything was fine. Was I becoming an alarmist? I reminded myself that the Secret Service knew what they were doing.

But only a matter of weeks later, in Washington D.C., ninety miles to our north, President Reagan was shot and seriously wounded as he left the Hilton Hotel to get into his limousine. The attempt on his life made a profound impression on him, as did a television drama he had watched entitled *The Day After*, a story of an American family's struggle to survive following a nuclear attack. Reagan commented:

I can't believe that this world can go on beyond our generation and on down to succeeding generations with this kind of weapon on both sides poised at each other without someday, some fool, or some maniac, or some accident triggering the kind of war that is the end of the line for all of us. And I just think of what a sigh of relief would go up from everyone on this Earth if someday—and this is what I have—my hope, way in the back of my head—is that if we start down the road to reduction, maybe one day in doing that, someone will say, 'Why not all the way? Let's get rid of all these things.'[127]

The president, along with his Soviet counterpart, Mikhail Gorbachev, forged a relationship that enabled them to sign the Intermediate-Range Nuclear Forces (INF) Treaty in 1987. This treaty paved the way to reduce the number of nuclear weapons from a high of 70,300 in the mid-1980s to an estimated 13,100 in 2021 of which 91% belong to the United States and Russia.[128] However, once Reagan left office in 1989, it seemed to me that his urgent concern about further arms reductions left with him.

But, while the world largely forgot about the nuclear threat, its destructive power, and its closeness to us, every now and then, the reality of it began to break through what I saw as the world's universal denial. The Genie that John Kennedy referred to in his May 1963 presidential news conference was indeed busy behind the scenes.

In the 1980s, two young researchers, James G. Blight and David A. Welch, came up with a groundbreaking idea later published in a book entitled *On The Brink*. Their idea was to bring together the remaining American and Soviet leaders who were involved in the Cuban Missile Crisis to discuss their experiences, respective vantage points, and reflections of the crisis with twenty-five years of hindsight. The hope was to discover what might be learned to help future leaders avert potential nuclear conflicts.[129] The participants gathered on three occasions. They learned that, despite their best efforts to remain rational as they

---

[128] "Status of World Nuclear Forces" 2021. Nine nuclear armed countries currently possess more than 13,000 nuclear weapons, of which an estimated 2,000 are on high alert, that is, ready for launch in minutes.

worked to resolve the crisis at that time, all of them had operated on a number of mistaken assumptions that brought us all within inches of what would have been the cataclysm of history. It was chilling to learn how little control political leaders have when events they've put into place begin to spin out of control.

Also, in the 1980s, I gained additional insight into how close we came from a book by Robert S. McNamara, who served as JFK's Secretary of Defense during the crisis. In *Blundering into Disaster*, McNamara sounded the alarm on the need to dismantle nuclear weapons or risk our very existence on this planet.[130] He expressed deep concern about how Americans have placed their faith in more than a half dozen widely accepted, but unsubstantiated myths, all revolving around the notion that nuclear weapons keep us safe.[131] To the contrary, our possession of nuclear weapons cannot go on indefinitely without incurring horrible consequences. He stated that as Secretary of Defense, on three occasions, the United States and the Soviets came extremely close to escalating into a nuclear conflict.

> In no[t] one of the three incidents did either side intend to act in a way that would lead to military conflict, but on each of the occasions lack of information, misinformation, and misjudgments led to confrontation. And in each of them, as the crisis evolved, tensions heightened, emotions rose, and the danger of irrational decisions increased.[132]
>
> It is correct to say that no well-informed, coolly rational political or military leader is likely to initiate the use of nuclear weapons. But political and military leaders, in moments of severe crisis, are likely to be neither well informed nor coolly rational."[133]

In fact, the continued reliance on nuclear weapons can lead, he argued, "to **certain** destruction of our civilization...."[134] [emphasis mine]

I also read a book that underscored McNamara's warning about the nuclear danger, this time from a theological vantage point. *The Nonviolent Coming of God* was written by the same author as *The Non-Violent Cross*, which had made a profound impact on me at Fort Benning. In this second book, theologian James W. Douglass wrote that our challenge now, firmly placed in humanity's hands, is to choose one of two paths, either a future dependence on nuclear weapons or one of nonviolence to save life on earth:

> Jesus proclaimed the urgent necessity of choosing collectively between a nonviolent humanity found in God and the looming alternative of self-destruction by violence.[135]

With all of these dire warnings about the very existence of humanity, I returned again to the haunting question I had pushed out of my mind for years: what can an ordinary person do to help stop a nuclear war? I had no answer, but I kept coming back to the fragment of scripture that I had first heard at mass at St. Agatha's. It was Matthew 17:20: "If you have faith the size of a mustard seed, you will say to this mountain, 'Move from here to there,' and it will move. Nothing will be impossible for you."

Life went on, and more presidents came and went: the elder Bush, Clinton, and George W. Bush. As we moved into the 21st century, our two oldest, Bobby and Holly, were adults, and on their own. Nicholas was finishing college with a desire to move to Hollywood and play with his brother Bobby's band, *The Piper Downs*.

Following the 9/11 attack on New York's World Trade Center in 2001, our family situation changed still further. Mary Ann and I, along with Holly and her husband Sean, decided we would also move to the west coast. I accepted an offer as a director of a Catholic Charities' agency in California. Mary Ann followed some months later. Holly, Sean, and their two children followed still later, ultimately finding a beautiful section of San Antonio, Texas, where they decided to stay.

Now living in California, bad news came in from just everywhere. Global temperatures were rising, the polar ice caps were melting at a much faster rate than previously understood. We witnessed nightly news reports of bloody violence that was spreading like an epidemic in America and throughout the world. In our country, a gunman entered a grade school and murdered little kids cowering at their desks. In the Middle East, bombs went off in crowded marketplaces. Gunmen opened fire in churches, universities, and nightclubs. Terrorists executed their victims by beheading them and broadcast those videos to the world. I wondered how long before the violence reaches international levels to the point of a nuclear exchange.

If words matter, there was trouble. Nations now openly threatened to destroy one another—Iran and Israel; India and Pakistan. A new threat appeared of terrorists hacking into computer systems and gaining access to nuclear codes. It was as if the whole world began to race down the path of madness and revenge, events spinning out of control toward an outbreak of total global violence—threatening it and acting on it. Would a final use of nuclear weapons not be the logical last step? Yet, in the presidential debates of the 2016 election, when so much attention was paid to superficial nonsense, the possibility of worldwide violence escalating into a nuclear war was given no serious consideration, despite the Doomsday Clock set at three minutes to midnight. The presidential candidates and the American public seemed to have forgotten President Reagan's words:

> I can't believe that this world can go beyond our generation and on down to succeeding generations with this kind of weapon on both sides poised at each other without someday some fool or some maniac or some accident triggering the kind of war that is the end of the line for all of us.[136]

But the rising of international tensions to the level of nuclear confrontation didn't take long. In 2017, with the American presidential election finalized, President Trump and North Korea's leader Kim Jong-un got under one another's skin, each threatening the other's country and its people. They spoke, I thought, glibly and recklessly of launching nuclear attacks that put over seventy million people in the crosshairs of a nuclear exchange—citizens of North Korea, South Korea, Japan, Guam, Hawaii, and major U.S. cities on the west coast.

Speaking at the U.N. on September 19, 2017, Trump declared:

> If it [the United States] is forced to defend itself or its allies, we will have no choice but to totally destroy North Korea.[137]

Those threats became terrifyingly real on the morning of January 13, 2018, when a statewide text message was sent from Hawaii's emergency alert system.

"BALLISTIC MISSILE THREAT INBOUND TO HAWAII. SEEK IMMEDIATE SHELTER...."

Reactions of islanders ranged from disbelief to numbness to shock. They were saying—What?! Missiles?? Could this possibly be happening? Was this a hoax or was this an actual launch from North Korea in an escalated response to the rhetoric and ongoing threats from the president of the United States?

A third sentence of the alert provided an unequivocal answer: "THIS IS NOT A DRILL." [138]

In a panic, parents shouted in a frantic effort to awaken their families still sleeping and run for their lives. Only there was nowhere they could run, and nowhere to hide. That meant that within minutes, they, their families, and their island paradise, like the *hibakusha*, the victims of Hiroshima and Nagasaki in 1945, would be baked by a heat greater than the surface of the sun. Then, 38 minutes later, at 8:45 a.m., state authorities issued another bulletin—false alarm. It was all a mistake—a clerical error, maybe a software mix-up or someone pushed the wrong button. For the islanders, this day in 2018 was not to be their doomsday. But the reality of the nuclear threat remains, leaving us to wonder what we can do to prevent the real thing from ever happening.

How did we arrive at this moment in history, when this danger has now become arguably our greatest *environmental* threat—one that endangers the lives of the seven billion of us inhabiting this small planet? What climate change can do to our planet over decades, a nuclear catastrophe can bring on in an afternoon.

In 2019, President Trump unilaterally withdrew from the Intermediate-Range Nuclear Forces (INF) Treaty and the safeguards signed by President Reagan and Gorbachev in 1987 to reduce the size of their countries' nuclear arsenals. Not to be outdone by President Trump's decision, Russian President Vladimir Putin also immediately pulled his country from the treaty. The leaders of two major nuclear armed nations had chosen to engage in what they seem to perceive as a game. Even worse, there is no rule book, no refs to make judgment calls, no penalties, and no regard for the decades of peacebuilding. This game is about two men doing whatever it takes to "win" with no real consideration of destruction or loss of life.

The words of threat ramped up further—fire and fury; bombs destroying an area the size of Texas; and reducing the U.S. to a pile of radioactive ash. Meanwhile, almost unnoticed, the Board of Atomic Scientists had moved the hand on the Doomsday Clock to two minutes to midnight.

I kept mulling over that haunting question: what can anybody do about it? Author Jonathan Schell gave his answer some thirty years ago in his book *The Fate of the Earth and The Abolition*:

> At present, most of us do nothing. We look away. We remain calm. We are silent. We take refuge in the hope that the holocaust won't happen, and turn back to our individual concerns. We deny the truth that is all around us. Indifferent to the future of our kind, we grow indifferent to one another. We drift apart. We grow cold. We drowse our way to the end of the world. . . . [139]

Totally at a loss with not knowing what to do, I found myself also drifting off until fate intervened in an unexpected way.

Chapter 28

# Wake Up Call

**I HEARD** a woman's muffled voice. "Sir, you need to lie perfectly still."

I despise the feeling of being confined. Maybe everybody does. But I had no choice. I had to do this MRI thing. Lying flat on my back, my arms tucked tightly at my side, and feeling totally helpless, I heard a steady hum as I was slowly moved into the confines of a futuristic looking metal tube. Entering the machine, I wondered if I would feel claustrophobic. When I was fully inside, I got my answer. I felt a shiver come over me from the machine's cold metal. The whole interior was bright white, but what got to me was that the tube's metal ceiling was almost pressing against my face, like I was restrained in a coffin with no escape.

"Hold it," said the voice.

I heard a wwwwhhhhhrrrrr sound and a click. I just laid there in the silence. I don't know for how long. I felt a sudden need to scratch my nose. Aw geez, not now! I couldn't scratch it, since I couldn't move. So, I tried just to ignore it. But the more I tried to ignore it, the more I wanted to scratch it, so that scratching became the sole focus of my attention.

Mercifully, another wwhhhrrring sound came, along with a click, and as my focus shifted back to the procedure, I forgot about the whole scratching thing.

I felt isolated. The technician spoke to me through headphones placed over my ears. Her voice was distant. I couldn't make out what she was saying. My hearing is bad, and her English was less than perfect.

For God's sake, man, people go through this every day. Relax, relax!! More wwwhhhrrr sounds and clicks. How long is this thing going to drag out? When there was a pause, I thought maybe I could move, just a teeny bit.

"Sir, if you don't lie still," said an annoyed voice, "we'll have to invalidate the results, and you'll have to come back another day!"

Sorry. I just thought it would be fun to move, since I wasn't doing anything else except laying here and decomposing. And so, it went on. I don't know how long it took to finish the whole thing, but finally the humming sound returned, and I was moved out from the machine. I got up, got dressed, and put my shoes on.

"A piece of cake!" I said to the technician in response to her snippy attitude.

"Yes, a piece of cake!" I repeated, a little louder, as I finished putting on my belt, grabbed my jacket, and scrambled to get the hell out of there.

I then drove home to tell Mary Ann what was happening. I had gone for my routine physical earlier that day. My doctor said for a guy in his mid-sixties, I was in decent shape. But finishing up, he asked if anything else was going on. I couldn't think of anything. But then I remembered that a few days earlier, I felt a bit disorientated. We went over it a couple of times. His relaxed mood left the building. He wrote on his pad.

"You need to go for an MRI," he said.

"An MRI?" I asked. "Why?"

He paused, and said, "You may have had a slight stroke."

He looked directly at me, "You need to go now."

I worried in the days that followed the MRI, as Mary Ann and I waited for the report. I had all kinds of questions. If I had a stroke, did that mean I was more likely to have another one? What if I die before I accomplish the work I was put on earth to do? The subject of death quickly moved to the forefront and remained there, pervasive in my thoughts.

One day, as I was carrying groceries in from the car, I passed by the television, which was broadcasting an annual appeal for PBS. Their guest speaker was the author, Wayne Dyer, whose presentations I always enjoyed and whose wisdom I always revered. I put the groceries on the counter and paused to hear what he was saying. The words he spoke next seemed to be a message directed right at me.

"Don't die with your music still in you!" [140]

"Don't die with your music still in you." What is that supposed to mean? The words stuck with me as I waited for the MRI report. I got the results back. I had not suffered a stroke. But even with a new medical lease on life, I still felt deeply troubled by the question about my life's unfinished business. What part of me had I left behind? What was of utmost importance for me to do? Was there music still in me?

As I mulled over these questions in the weeks that followed, I understood that I still had music within me. When I left the army, I left everything about war behind. Now on the news, I began to see world leaders recklessly threatening one another's country—the same dynamics that led to two world wars. In my view the world was heading into dark and perilous waters. In my remaining time on earth, I had to find a way to join with others to help sound the alarm, and actively search for a path to world peace.

Chapter 29

# A Great Flash of Light

*"If, as Merton saw it, the problem of war is, at its root, a spiritual problem, the solution must also be spiritual in nature.... What was needed was a spiritual transformation—a "complete change of heart.... For Merton, spiritual transformation involves a conversion to non-violence."* [141]

Christine M. Bochen, William H. Shannon

*Our problems are manmade—therefore, they can be solved by man.... No problem of human destiny is beyond human beings.* [142]

JFK

*Blessed are the peacemakers...*

Matthew 5:9

**WHEN I LEFT** the service and gave up any hope for peace, many others throughout the world did not. Even over decades, when events seemed utterly hopeless, they persevered. President Kennedy believed:

## A GREAT FLASH OF LIGHT

> Peace is a daily, a weekly, a monthly process, gradually changing opinions, slowly eroding old barriers, quietly building new structures. And however undramatic the pursuit of peace, that pursuit must go on.[143]

Thousands of concerned citizens around the world established organizations like the Nuclear Age Peace Foundation, Physicians for Social Justice, and Pax Christi. For decades these organizations addressed the existential issue of how to help save the world before it slid into unspeakable consequences from a nuclear catastrophe.

In 2007, multiple organizations joined to form the International Campaign to Abolish Nuclear Weapons (ICAN). The work of this coalition culminated in an important international agreement, the Treaty on the Prohibition of Nuclear Weapons. Ratified by the required fifty-four state parties to the United Nations, the treaty now has become international law, which prohibits nations from developing, testing, producing, manufacturing, transferring, possessing, stockpiling, using or threatening to use nuclear weapons or allowing nuclear weapons to be stationed in their territory.[144]

However, even though it has become international law, nine nuclear armed nations still strongly oppose the treaty. Chief among them are the United States and Russia, which together possess 90% of the world's more than 13,000 nuclear weapons.

As of the publication of this book in 2021, the breakdown of the weaponry is as follows: [145]

|  |  |
|---|---|
| Russia | 6,255 warheads |
| United States | 5,550 warheads |
| China | 350 warheads |
| France | 290 warheads |
| United Kingdom | 225 warheads |
| Pakistan | 165 warheads |
| India | 156 warheads |
| Israel | 90 warheads |
| North Korea | 40–50 warheads |

## A Great Flash of Light

There are five nations that host U. S. Nuclear Weapons:

| | |
|---|---|
| Turkey | 50 missiles |
| Italy | 40 missiles |
| Belgium | 20 missiles |
| Germany | 20 missiles |
| Netherlands | 20 missiles |

We are at a crossroads. We must make the most crucial decision of this or any generation, one that will decide the future of the world. The choices are to continue possessing and developing nuclear weapons with a willingness to launch them against one another, or to abolish them.

Carl Jung observed:

> The only thing that really matters now is whether man can climb up to a higher moral level, to a higher plane of consciousness, in order to be equal to the superhuman powers which the fallen angels have played into his hands. [146]

It was to this moral level that Kennedy sought to lead us:

> For in the final analysis our most basic common link is that we all inhabit this planet. We all breathe the same air. We all cherish our children's future. And we are all mortal. [147]

As people, citizens of the earth, we can leave behind the terrifying darkness of the nuclear age and replace it with a great flash of light, like that of a thousand suns; not a final nuclear blast, but a birth of a new global humanity filled with grace, truth, and unconditional love.

Our existential moment of decision is here.

*I have set before you life and death, the blessing and the curse. Choose life, then, that you and your descendants may live.*
*Deuteronomy 30:19*

Everything we treasure, and everyone we love, depends on our choice.

It's our call.

Chapter 30

# Epilogue

**RETIREMENT** means no more getting up early and rushing out into heavy morning traffic! Instead, each day begins with a cup of freshly brewed coffee and the realization that "Every day now is Saturday!" On the sad side, it means giving up some of the dreams of youth. For me, it's a slowly fading dream I'll never be starting quarterback for the Tampa Bay Bucs.

Aside from that, it's all been good. Mary Ann and I are free to do things and go places we've not had time for. Pacific coast sunsets are fifteen minutes away, and Hollywood movie studios, Dodger Stadium, and Disneyland are an hour away. We even attended the ball game of Vin Scully's last broadcast from Dodger Stadium.

We continue to enjoy the company of our three children as adults. Holly works tirelessly with animal rescue. Bobby and Nick, apart from their jobs, team up to play musical shows in L.A.

and Hollywood as the *Bognar Brothers* and with Bobby's spirited band, the *Piper Downs*.

Retirement has also given me time to focus on peacemaking efforts even as the world moves nervously to one and a half minutes to midnight. I've kept in mind John Hersey's warning that it's essential we remember the past in order not to repeat it.

On August 6th of every year, I attend a Hiroshima memorial service sponsored by the Nuclear Age Peace Foundation in Montecito, California. Under a gigantic tree, those gathered remember the victims of the first atomic bomb. At the base of a great tree are hung multi-colored paper cranes representing the souls of those killed in that first great flash of atomic light.

Here I first heard the story of Sadako Sasaki, a young Japanese girl who somehow survived the initial Hiroshima blast. However, a decade later she was dying from leukemia brought on by the radiation exposure. While she was hospitalized, she learned of a Japanese myth that involved the tradition of *origami*. According to the legend, a crane is believed to live 1,000 years, and if you folded 1,000 paper cranes, you would be granted a wish. As she dealt with her sickness, she completed the task with a wish that she would get well. She did not. She set out to achieve a second goal to fold another 1,000 but this time with a different wish. Soon her health went into severe decline. She died having folded another 644 paper cranes. After her death, her family and friends completed the rest hoping she would receive her new wish:

> *I will write 'peace' on your wings,*
> *and you will fly all over the world.* [148]
>
> Sadako Sasaki, 1943–1955

Fig. 26. Painting of Sadako Sasaki sending a spirit of peace throughout the world. (Painting by Steve Simon/Photo courtesy of Steve Simon, steve@stevesimon.com)

Fig. 27. Hiroshima Remembrance Day, Motoyasu River in Hiroshima, Japan (Kiyoshi Ota/Getty Images)

Since then, on the anniversary date of the Hiroshima bombing, thousands in that city gather to set cranes and lighted candles afloat on the Ota River and watch the current carry them down to destinations unknown. Today, millions of people around the world fold cranes in memory of Sadako Sasaki. May her wish help us recognize our common humanity and make an active commitment to choose a path to peace.

When COVID-19 hit in 2020, Mary Ann and I self-isolated. This self-isolation gave me ample time to reflect on the life I've lived. I think back with pleasure, about my first-grade teacher, Sister Agnes Carmel. Some years ago, on her golden anniversary of becoming a nun, I wrote her a letter and spilled the beans about our one-sided first grade romance of long ago.

"Dear Sister Agnes Carmel," I wrote, "This is a long overdue love letter...." I explained how I tried to impress her with my slick spelling of the colors, especially O-R-A-N-G-E. They said they found my letter among her personal effects when she passed away some time ago. I couldn't help but think of her sweet smile, and how, with her there now, heaven is even a happier place.

Almost all in my birth family are gone now, leaving Thomas and me. The last one to pass was my brother-in-law, John.

## Epilogue

When I went to meet him for the final time in an assisted living facility, a staff member said, "Oh, you mean Mr. John! That man has just got the sunniest disposition! He's always going around talking to just everybody, cheering everybody up!"

"He's the one," I said, as I smiled, remembering his efforts to motivate my brothers as they worked in the fields.

Well into his eighties, he didn't recognize me as I greeted him, and I wasn't sure how much he understood when we talked. He faded in and out a couple of times, asking me who I was. I then mentioned my brothers, the farm, and me bringing water out to the fields with my bucket. His face brightened.

"That was YOU?!" he asked in surprise.

"Yeah, that was me."

We had lunch in the cafeteria. He ate very little.

"Be sure to eat your ice cream, Mr. John," said an orderly. "You need to keep your strength up."

He stirred his ice cream and put his spoon down. His head began to bow, and he murmured something about the beautiful island in the Pacific, the one he had talked about his whole life—that perfect paradise with blue skies, palm trees swaying in the breeze, and the crystal-clear stream cutting through the heart of it all. He was getting tired, but I hoped he'd say more. This was the last chance we'd ever have to talk, and the last time I'd ever have to understand the significance of that far away perfect island.

Then, I think I finally understood what he had been trying to say all these years. The island was a paradise, and everything he described about its beauty was true. But the name of the paradise island was Guadalcanal.

Fresh from the states, he was thrown into one of the bloodiest battles of the Pacific. High in the blue skies, Japanese fighter planes strafed the American forces below. Like all the young marines around him, he dove for cover as machine gun bullets and explosions brutalized dozens around him. He got up to patch the wounded and saw first-hand the terrible things war machines do to faces, heads, and flesh. The Japanese plane returned for another kill. The air was filled with the whine of the plane, the endless bursts of machine gun fire, screams of men, and explosions powerful enough to blow out eardrums. More sounds of return fire and young marines all around him: bloodied, disemboweled, blind, burned, and disfigured. In contrast to the chaos and carnage, the dead lay still, no longer concerned about what harm might come to them.

John's beautiful memory of the paradise island screened out the sights, sounds, and horrors of war. We didn't know about post-traumatic stress disorders seventy-five years ago. The wounds of war run deep and last a long time. When he grew tired, I wheeled him back to his room, helped him into his bed, and covered him with his blanket. He fell asleep almost immediately. I kissed him on the forehead. He passed away some months later.

Three years ago, I visited Thomas at his home in Washington state. He's still going strong at 86. We had a grand time staying up late into the morning hours drinking black coffee, one-upping each other, and reminiscing about the good old days. "Hey, do you remember that time…" In the middle of talking about our lives on the farm, I was flabbergasted when he said offhandedly, "I never got what you thought was so great about those peas."

Fig. 28. Thomas and I today. (I'm the taller one over there on the left.)

One thing I couldn't help but notice on my visit was that everybody around Thomas always thinks he's all kinds of "cool." His kids and grandkids adore him. All his friends respect and admire him. People at his church want to talk to him. And even my mother in heaven, I think, is saying, "Say something nice about Thomas in your book." So, with her twisting my arm, I am compelled to admit there is no man walking on the earth with greater integrity, no country ever had a greater patriot, and no man ever had a finer brother.

I hope you're happy, mom!

## EPILOGUE

As life goes on, it's impossible to predict what the future will bring. I haven't a clue as to what is next, but I'd like to go back to Michigan one final time, to see my childhood home. I'll fly out, rent a car, and first visit the farm. The buildings I knew then are long since gone, taking with them the familiar sights of my youth—my dad working on his lathe, my mom hanging clothes on the clothesline, my dog Copper chasing after birds, and kids playing "red rover" on our huge front lawn.

I want to walk down to the creek, put my feet into the cool water, and hear the gentle splashing that's gone on for hundreds of years and will likely outlive us all. I want to look out at the fields of grain, as summer breezes sway the golden wheat this way and that. I wonder if on the horizon, I'll get a glimpse of my brothers working in the field and me walking towards them lugging my water bucket.

I'll drive into Gagetown and walk to the top of the hill, where St. Agatha's church still stands on the crest overlooking the Saginaw Valley. This is the town where teens had sometimes complained that "nothing ever happens here" when, actually, it was here that one of the most important events in history took place.

### PEACE HAPPENED HERE.

A nuclear bomb didn't fall on St. Agatha's and people didn't die here.

Peace happened here because John Kennedy and Nikita Khrushchev, who nearly started a nuclear war, pushed back on the forces of darkness, and chose instead to avert a final war.

Peace happened here, as the Doomsday Clock was about to strike midnight, because a Russian submarine commander, Vasili Arkhipov, with American depth charges exploding all around him, chose not to launch the nuclear armed torpedo that would have set the whole world on fire.

Peace happened here because Kennedy, Khrushchev, and Arkhipov chose a path to peace. They chose the opposite of the Kaiser's choice that decimated the magnificent Cathedral of Rheims. They chose the opposite of those who chose atomic war that destroyed Hiroshima and then Nagasaki.

Peace happened here and around the world. Washington, D.C. still stands, so does Moscow, as does Havana and New York. Today, Miami thrives in all her tropical beauty because Miami wasn't bombed in the Cuban crisis. Mary Ann was not an atomic burned victim but grew up to become the love of my life.

I look around the world and know that Paris and Beijing stand, as do Cairo, New Delhi, and Tehran. Across this beautiful blue marble of a planet, the land is not a scorched earth, poisoned by radioactivity, but a world once again teeming with life and filled with promise, where people enjoy "the kind of peace that makes life on earth worth living."[149]

Fig. 29. St. Agatha's today. "Peace happened here."
(Photo courtesy of John Garman)

At the top of the hill, St. Agatha's church stands tall and beautiful, as observable evidence of peace, proof to the world that war does not have to have the final say in history. People do. We do.

# Epilogue

I want to go into the quiet, darkened church, and hear my footsteps echoing throughout as I heard so many times as a boy. I want to kneel in the same pew where my family prayed every Sunday. I'll watch the flickering candles and call to mind all the family and friends who walked with me in witness to this extraordinary age.

I'll think back over my life and what I've done with it and wonder if I made a difference. When I look at the grand scheme of things, that question dissolves into nothingness. I was a grain of sand on a beach with untold trillions of other grains of sand. But I still wonder somehow if I made the world a better place. Was I kind? Did I offer encouragement to others? Did I help to lift people up? Did the good things I did outweigh the bad? Will I long be remembered by those who knew me? Will they be at my graveside when it's time to say goodbye? Will they stay to join in the final prayer, "We commend into Thy hands, O Lord, the soul of Thy servant, Francis?" Or before the prayer is finished will they decide to split, and stampede off to get pizza?

I will think of Kennedy, the hero of my youth, a man of heroic deeds, as well as shortcomings, and human failings. His life touched every creature walking on the earth today. Every flower that greets the sun in the spring does so because of the life of JFK, as does every youngster who plays soccer, every college graduate earning a degree, every couple exchanging vows, and every parent cradling a newborn baby. As I once joined the world in a prayer for John Kennedy, I'll pray for the seven billion of us who inhabit this planet today. May we, the citizens of the earth, awaken to the beauty around us, God's masterpiece of creation, and, at last, care for one another and our fellow creatures as we share this place we call home.

When my moments in the church come to an end, I'll spend some time at the graves of my mom and dad, and maybe feel the same gentle Michigan breezes they enjoyed at the end of the day.

"Hey, dad, do you remember when the stupids threw me out of their bedroom, and I tried to kick their door down?"

"Mom, you were right, big breakfasts really do stick to your ribs. Oh, and uh, sorry I just called my brothers the stupids."

I'll spend a little more time with them, thank them for all they did for me, and say goodbye.

I'll climb aboard a jet and fly back home to see another sunset over the Pacific. I'll be thinking about tomorrow and our climb together to that higher moral place, where we will care for one another, for the earth and all creatures on it—all the while remembering that "With God, all things are possible."

# Starting Points

To help avert a global ecological crisis resulting from a nuclear exchange between nations, the following sections provide the reader with a number of practical ways to start:

1. Review and put into daily practice David Krieger's "100 Ideas for Creating a More Peaceful World."
2. Join and support organizations doing the day-to-day work of peacemaking.
3. Review to understand more deeply the reasons why nuclear weapons are a danger to humanity's future in "Ten Lessons You Should Learn about Nuclear Weapons" by David Krieger.
4. Study the "United Nations Treaty on the Prohibition of Nuclear Weapons" which offers the world a legal structure for aspiring to a nuclear weapons' free world.
5. On YouTube, view JFK's brilliant American University commencement address in which he addresses the question of "What Kind of Peace Do We Want?"
6. Read David Krieger's "The Road from Armageddon to Transformation" a brilliant case for the abolition of nuclear weapons.
7. Choose from the sources in the Further Reading section. Each provides important information that can contribute to humanity's journey to world peace.

# 100 Ideas for Creating a More Peaceful World

## By David Krieger

1. Be generous with your smiles.
2. Be kind.
3. Respect the Earth.
4. Walk in a forest.
5. Plant a tree.
6. Contemplate a mountain.
7. Protect the Earth.
8. Live simply.
9. Help feed the hungry.
10. Erase a border in your mind.
11. Teach peace to children.
12. Read Chief Seattle's Letter to the President.
13. Be honest.
14. Demand honesty from your government.
15. Think about consequences.
16. Commit yourself to nonviolence.
17. Support nonviolent solutions to global problems.
18. Speak up for a healthy planet.
19. Demand reductions in military expenditures.
20. Be fair.
21. Pledge allegiance to the Earth and to its varied life forms.
22. Think for yourself.
23. Ask questions.
24. Recognize your unique potential.
25. Join an organization working for peace.
26. Be less materialistic.
27. Be more loving.
28. Empower others to work for peace.
29. Oppose all weapons of mass destruction.
30. Support equality.
31. Speak out for a nuclear weapons-free world.
32. Support a Department of Peace.
33. Listen to your heart.

34. Help the poor.
35. Fight against militarism.
36. Study the lives of peace heroes.
37. Help create a community peace park or garden.
38. Commemorate the International Day of Peace.
39. Help strengthen the United Nations.
40. Support the International Criminal Court.
41. Read the Universal Declaration of Human Rights.
42. Advance the rights of future generations.
43. Be a voice for the voiceless.
44. Join an action alert network.
45. Be forgiving.
46. Laugh more.
47. Play with a child.
48. Support education and the arts over weapons.
49. Help educate the next generation to be compassionate.
50. Take personal responsibility for creating a better world.
51. Sing.
52. Write a poem.
53. Organize a church service on the theme of peace.
54. Learn about another culture.
55. Help someone.
56. Support the UN Children's Fund (UNICEF).
57. Oppose the arms trade.
58. Clear your mind.
59. Breathe deeply.
60. Sip tea.
61. Express your views on peace to government officials.
62. Fight for the environment.
63. Celebrate Earth Day.
64. Think like an astronaut, recognizing that we have only one Earth.
65. Be constructive.
66. Let someone else go first.
67. Plant seeds of peace.
68. Work in a garden.
69. Change a potential enemy into a friend.
70. Be positive.
71. Share.
72. Be a good neighbor.
73. Send a note of appreciation.

## 100 IDEAS FOR CREATING A MORE PEACEFUL WORLD

74. Tell your friends how much they matter.
75. Say "I love you" more.
76. Don't tolerate prejudice.
77. Demand more from your elected officials.
78. Walk by the ocean, a river, or a lake.
79. Recognize that all humans have the right to peace.
80. Respect the dignity of each person.
81. Be a leader in the struggle for human decency.
82. Be a friend.
83. Send sunflowers to world leaders, and call for a world free of nuclear weapons.
84. Oppose technologies that harm the environment.
85. Lose an argument to a loved one.
86. Value diversity.
87. Walk softly on the Earth.
88. Appreciate the power of the sun.
89. Speak out for global disarmament.
90. Support a democratic order.
91. Teach non-violence by example.
92. Remember that "No man is an Island."
93. Spend time in nature.
94. Boycott war toys.
95. Be thankful for the miracle of life.
96. Seek harmony with nature.
97. Remind your leaders that peace matters.
98. Oppose violence in television programming for children.
99. Listen to Beethoven's Ode to Joy.
100. Celebrate peace.

*Reprinted by permission from David Krieger*
*Founder and former president of the Nuclear Age Peace Foundation*

# Organizations and Links

For those who wish to join with millions of others around the world who are involved in the movement to abolish nuclear weapons before they abolish us, I have included a list of organizations below and their links. The descriptions were obtained in whole, or in part, from each respective website.

**Bulletin of the Atomic Scientists** is an annual report that assesses world events in order to warn the public if humanity is moving closer or moving away from bringing destruction on ourselves by our own technology. www.thebulletin.org.

**International Campaign to Abolish Nuclear Weapons** (ICAN) "is a coalition of non-governmental organizations in one hundred countries promoting adherence to and implementation of the United Nations nuclear weapons ban treaty." ICAN has 541 partners in 103 countries. ICAN was awarded the 2017 Nobel Peace Prize for its work on the United Nations Treaty on the Prohibition of Nuclear Weapons. www.icanw.org.

**International Physicians for the Prevention of Nuclear War** (IPPNW) "is a non-partisan federation of national medical groups in over 60 countries, representing tens of thousands of doctors, medical students, other health workers, and concerned citizens who share the common goal of creating a more peaceful and secure world freed from the threat of nuclear annihilation and armed violence." www.ippnw.org

**Mayors for Peace** is an international organization established in 1982 and dedicated to banning all nuclear weapons. Currently there are 7,833 member cities in 163 countries. www.mayorsforpeace.org.

**Nuclear Age Peace Foundation of Santa** Barbara (NAPF) was founded in 1982. Its mission is to educate, advocate, and inspire action for a just and peaceful world, free of nuclear weapons. The Foundation is a non-partisan, non-profit organization with consultative status to the United Nations and is composed of over 80,000 individuals and groups worldwide who realize the imperative for peace in the Nuclear Age. NAPF is a proud Partner Organization of the International Campaign to Abolish Nuclear Weapons (ICAN). www.wagingpeace.org.

**Pax Christi International** (PCI) is a Catholic Peace Movement founded in 1945 and headquartered in Brussels, Belgium. PCI has 120 member organizations worldwide. The organization promotes peace, respect for human rights, justice and reconciliation throughout the world. PCI holds special consultative status with the United Nations in New York, Geneva, and Vienna as well as UNESCO in Paris. www.paxchristi.net.

**Physicians for Social Responsibility** (PSR) has a Nuclear Weapons Abolition Program that "amplifies the health professional voice to increase and broaden grassroots support for nuclear weapons abolition and to cultivate legislative initiatives to reduce the threat of nuclear weapons." PSR has 24 chapters throughout the United States. www.psr.org.

**Soka Gakkai International** – USA "is the most diverse Buddhist community in the United States with more than 500 chapters and some 100 centers throughout the country. SGI-USA is a part of a larger SGI network which comprises more than 12 million people in 192 countries and territories around the world." SGI is involved with various peace activities including the movement to abolish nuclear weapons. www.sgi-usa.org.

# Ten Lessons You Should Learn About Nuclear Weapons

## By David Krieger

Here are ten lessons that I learned about nuclear weapons in the process of working for their abolition for the past four decades. I wish I could share these lessons with every citizen of the planet, all of whom are endangered by these weapons.

1. The effects of nuclear weapons cannot be contained in space or time. Radiation from a nuclear detonation is carried by the wind and cannot be stopped at national borders, with or without border checkpoints. Radioactive materials also have long lives. Plutonium-239, for example, has a half-life of 24,000 years and will remain deadly if inhaled for the next 240,000 years.

2. Nuclear weapons have made possible omnicide, the death of all. Omnicide is a 20th century concept created by philosopher John Somerville. It is the logical extension of suicide, homicide, genocide. Although it is a concept too final to even imagine, it must be taken seriously.

3. The survivors of the atomic bombings of Hiroshima and Nagasaki are the ambassadors of the nuclear age, having witnessed first-hand the horror of nuclear weapons use and not wanting their past to become anyone else's future. Many survivors, known as hibakusha, have made it their life's work to speak out to educate others and to rid the world of nuclear weapons.

4. Nuclear deterrence does not provide physical protection against nuclear weapons – it provides only a false sense of security and the possibility of retaliation and vengeance. Reliance on nuclear deterrence opens the door to omnicide.

5. Nine countries with nuclear weapons are playing Nuclear Roulette with the human future. Nuclear weapons are like having grenades pointed at the heart of humanity, putting

everything we love and treasure at risk. With Nuclear Roulette the odds are not with humanity.

6. Einstein warned: "The unleashed power of the atom has changed everything save our modes of thinking, and we thus drift toward unparalleled catastrophe." For ourselves, our countries and our planet, we must change our modes of thinking and end the widespread ignorance and apathy surrounding nuclear weapons. We must rid the world of nuclear weapons before they rid the world of us.

7. Nuclear weapons are an absolute and ultimate evil. Their only purpose is to kill indiscriminately – women, men and children, as well as other forms of complex life.

8. There are many ways a nuclear war could begin: by malice, madness, mistake, miscalculation or manipulation (hacking). That we have not yet had a nuclear war is more from good fortune than good planning. We have come chillingly close on numerous occasions.

9. Nuclear weapons make us all reliant for our lives and futures on the sanity and wisdom of a small number of national leaders. It is far too much power to put in the hands of any leader. We must speak out, join together and demand that these weapons be abolished before they abolish us.

10. The choice between two memes of the 20th century will determine whether humankind survives the 21st: the image of the mushroom cloud, and the image of the earth from outer space. The first is an image of death and destruction, while the second is an image of the fragility of our planetary home, the only place we know of in the universe where life exists. The choice should be clear, and it calls out to us to choose peace, not war; survival, not devastation; hope, not despair; and engagement to save our planet and the precious gift of life it harbors.

Reprinted with permission from David Krieger,
Nuclear Age Peace Foundation of Santa Barbara, CA. 2019.

# UNITED NATIONS 2017

# Treaty on the Prohibition of Nuclear Weapons

The States Parties to this Treaty,

Determined to contribute to the realization of the purposes and principles of the Charter of the United Nations,

Deeply concerned about the catastrophic humanitarian consequences that would result from any use of nuclear weapons, and recognizing the consequent need to completely eliminate such weapons, which remains the only way to guarantee that nuclear weapons are never used again under any circumstances,

Mindful of the risks posed by the continued existence of nuclear weapons, including from any nuclear-weapon detonation by accident, miscalculation or design, and emphasizing that these risks concern the security of all humanity, and that all States share the responsibility to prevent any use of nuclear weapons,

Cognizant that the catastrophic consequences of nuclear weapons cannot be adequately addressed, transcend national borders, pose grave implications for human survival, the environment, socioeconomic development, the global economy, food security and the health of current and future generations, and have a disproportionate impact on women and girls, including as a result of ionizing radiation,

Acknowledging the ethical imperatives for nuclear disarmament and the urgency of achieving and maintaining a nuclear-weapon-free world, which is a global public good of the highest order, serving both national and collective security interests,

Mindful of the unacceptable suffering of and harm caused to the victims of the use of nuclear weapons (hibakusha), as well as of those affected by the testing of nuclear weapons,

Recognizing the disproportionate impact of nuclear-weapon activities on indigenous peoples,

Reaffirming the need for all States at all times to comply with applicable international law, including international humanitarian law and international human rights law,

Basing themselves on the principles and rules of international humanitarian law, in particular the principle that the right of parties to an armed conflict to choose methods or means of warfare is not unlimited, the rule of distinction, the prohibition against indiscriminate attacks, the rules on proportionality and precautions in attack, the prohibition on the use of weapons of a nature to cause superfluous injury or unnecessary suffering, and the rules for the protection of the natural environment,

Considering that any use of nuclear weapons would be contrary to the rules of international law applicable in armed conflict, in particular the principles and rules of international humanitarian law,

Reaffirming that any use of nuclear weapons would also be abhorrent to the principles of humanity and the dictates of public conscience,

Recalling that, in accordance with the Charter of the United Nations, States must refrain in their international relations from the threat or use of force against the territorial integrity or political independence of any State, or in any other manner inconsistent with the Purposes of the United Nations, and that the establishment and maintenance of international peace and security are to be promoted with the least diversion for armaments of the world's human and economic resources,

## Treaty on the Prohibition of Nuclear Weapons

Recalling also the first resolution of the General Assembly of the United Nations, adopted on 24 January 1946, and subsequent resolutions which call for the elimination of nuclear weapons,

Concerned by the slow pace of nuclear disarmament, the continued reliance on nuclear weapons in military and security concepts, doctrines and policies, and the waste of economic and human resources on programmes for the production, maintenance and modernization of nuclear weapons,

Recognizing that a legally binding prohibition of nuclear weapons constitutes an important contribution towards the achievement and maintenance of a world free of nuclear weapons, including the irreversible, verifiable and transparent elimination of nuclear weapons, and determined to act towards that end,

Determined to act with a view to achieving effective progress towards general and complete disarmament under strict and effective international control,

Reaffirming that there exists an obligation to pursue in good faith and bring to a conclusion negotiations leading to nuclear disarmament in all its aspects under strict and effective international control,

Reaffirming also that the full and effective implementation of the Treaty on the Non-Proliferation of Nuclear Weapons, which serves as the cornerstone of the nuclear disarmament and non-proliferation regime, has a vital role to play in promoting international peace and security,

Recognizing the vital importance of the Comprehensive Nuclear-Test-Ban Treaty and its verification regime as a core element of the nuclear disarmament and non-proliferation regime,

Reaffirming the conviction that the establishment of the internationally recognized nuclear-weapon-free zones on the basis of arrangements freely arrived at among the States of the region concerned enhances global and regional peace and security, strengthens the nuclear non-proliferation regime and contributes towards realizing the objective of nuclear disarmament,

Emphasizing that nothing in this Treaty shall be interpreted as affecting the inalienable right of its States Parties to develop research, production and use of nuclear energy for peaceful purposes without discrimination,

Recognizing that the equal, full and effective participation of both women and men is an essential factor for the promotion and attainment of sustainable peace and security, and committed to supporting and strengthening the effective participation of women in nuclear disarmament,

Recognizing also the importance of peace and disarmament education in all its aspects and of raising awareness of the risks and consequences of nuclear weapons for current and future generations, and committed to the dissemination of the principles and norms of this Treaty,

Stressing the role of public conscience in the furthering of the principles of humanity as evidenced by the call for the total elimination of nuclear weapons, and recognizing the efforts to that end undertaken by the United Nations, the International Red Cross and Red Crescent Movement, other international and regional organizations, non-governmental organizations, religious leaders, parliamentarians, academics and the hibakusha,

Have agreed as follows:

**Article 1**
**Prohibitions**

1. Each State Party undertakes never under any circumstances to:

(a) Develop, test, produce, manufacture, otherwise acquire, possess or stockpile nuclear weapons or other nuclear explosive devices;

(b) Transfer to any recipient whatsoever nuclear weapons or other nuclear explosive devices or control over such weapons or explosive devices directly or indirectly;

(c) Receive the transfer of or control over nuclear weapons or other nuclear explosive devices directly or indirectly;

(d) Use or threaten to use nuclear weapons or other nuclear explosive devices;

(e) Assist, encourage or induce, in any way, anyone to engage in any activity prohibited to a State Party under this Treaty;

(f) Seek or receive any assistance, in any way, from anyone to engage in any activity prohibited to a State Party under this Treaty;

(g) Allow any stationing, installation or deployment of any nuclear weapons or other nuclear explosive devices in its territory or at any place under its jurisdiction or control.

**Article 2**
**Declarations**

1. Each State Party shall submit to the Secretary-General of the United Nations, not later than 30 days after this Treaty enters into force for that State Party, a declaration in which it shall:

(a) Declare whether it owned, possessed or controlled nuclear weapons or nuclear explosive devices and eliminated its nuclear-weapon programme, including the elimination or irreversible conversion of all nuclear-weapons-related facilities, prior to the entry into force of this Treaty for that State Party;

(b) Notwithstanding Article 1 (a), declare whether it owns, possesses or controls any nuclear weapons or other nuclear explosive devices;

(c) Notwithstanding Article 1 (g), declare whether there are any nuclear weapons or other nuclear explosive devices in its territory or in any place under its jurisdiction or control that are owned, possessed or controlled by another State.

2. The Secretary-General of the United Nations shall transmit all such declarations received to the States Parties.

**Article 3**
**Safeguards**

1. Each State Party to which Article 4, paragraph 1 or 2, does not apply shall, at a minimum, maintain its International Atomic Energy Agency safeguards obligations in force at the time of entry into force of this Treaty, without prejudice to any additional relevant instruments that it may adopt in the future.

2. Each State Party to which Article 4, paragraph 1 or 2, does not apply that has not yet done so shall conclude with the International Atomic Energy Agency and bring into force a comprehensive safeguards agreement (INFCIRC/153 (Corrected)). Negotiation of such agreement shall commence within 180 days from the entry into force of this Treaty for that State Party. The agreement shall enter into force no later than 18 months from the entry into force of this Treaty for that State Party. Each State Party shall thereafter maintain such obligations, without prejudice to any additional relevant instruments that it may adopt in the future.

**Article 4**
**Towards the total elimination of nuclear weapons**

1. Each State Party that after 7 July 2017 owned, possessed or controlled nuclear weapons or other nuclear explosive devices and eliminated its nuclear-weapon programme, including the elimination or irreversible conversion of all nuclear- weapons-related facilities, prior to the entry into force of this Treaty for it, shall cooperate with the competent international authority designated pursuant to paragraph 6 of this Article for the purpose of verifying the irreversible elimination of its nuclear-weapon programme. The competent international authority shall report to the States Parties. Such a State Party shall conclude a safeguards

agreement with the International Atomic Energy Agency sufficient to provide credible assurance of the non-diversion of declared nuclear material from peaceful nuclear activities and of the absence of undeclared nuclear material or activities in that State Party as a whole. Negotiation of such agreement shall commence within 180 days from the entry into force of this Treaty for that State Party. The agreement shall enter into force no later than 18 months from the entry into force of this Treaty for that State Party. That State Party shall thereafter, at a minimum, maintain these safeguards obligations, without prejudice to any additional relevant instruments that it may adopt in the future.

2. Notwithstanding Article 1 (a), each State Party that owns, possesses or controls nuclear weapons or other nuclear explosive devices shall immediately remove them from operational status, and destroy them as soon as possible but not later than a deadline to be determined by the first meeting of States Parties, in accordance with a legally binding, time-bound plan for the verified and irreversible elimination of that State Party's nuclear-weapon programme, including the elimination or irreversible conversion of all nuclear-weapons-related facilities. The State Party, no later than 60 days after the entry into force of this Treaty for that State Party, shall submit this plan to the States Parties or to a competent international authority designated by the States Parties. The plan shall then be negotiated with the competent international authority, which shall submit it to the subsequent meeting of States Parties or review conference, whichever comes first, for approval in accordance with its rules of procedure.

3. A State Party to which paragraph 2 above applies shall conclude a safeguards agreement with the International Atomic Energy Agency sufficient to provide credible assurance of the non-diversion of declared nuclear material from peaceful nuclear activities and of the absence of undeclared nuclear material or activities in the State as a whole. Negotiation of such agreement shall commence no later than the date upon which implementation of the plan referred to in paragraph 2 is completed. The agreement shall enter into force no later than 18

months after the date of initiation of negotiations. That State Party shall thereafter, at a minimum, maintain these safeguards obligations, without prejudice to any additional relevant instruments that it may adopt in the future. Following the entry into force of the agreement referred to in this paragraph, the State Party shall submit to the Secretary-General of the United Nations a final declaration that it has fulfilled its obligations under this Article.

4. Notwithstanding Article 1 (b) and (g), each State Party that has any nuclear weapons or other nuclear explosive devices in its territory or in any place under its jurisdiction or control that are owned, possessed or controlled by another State shall ensure the prompt removal of such weapons, as soon as possible but not later than a deadline to be determined by the first meeting of States Parties. Upon the removal of such weapons or other explosive devices, that State Party shall submit to the Secretary-General of the United Nations a declaration that it has fulfilled its obligations under this Article.

5. Each State Party to which this Article applies shall submit a report to each meeting of States Parties and each review conference on the progress made towards the implementation of its obligations under this Article, until such time as they are fulfilled.

6. The States Parties shall designate a competent international authority or authorities to negotiate and verify the irreversible elimination of nuclear-weapons programmes, including the elimination or irreversible conversion of all nuclear- weapons-related facilities in accordance with paragraphs 1, 2 and 3 of this Article. In the event that such a designation has not been made prior to the entry into force of this Treaty for a State Party to which paragraph 1 or 2 of this Article applies, the Secretary-General of the United Nations shall convene an extraordinary meeting of States Parties to take any decisions that may be required.

## Article 5
## National implementation

1. Each State Party shall adopt the necessary measures to implement its obligations under this Treaty.

2. Each State Party shall take all appropriate legal, administrative and other measures, including the imposition of penal sanctions, to prevent and suppress any activity prohibited to a State Party under this Treaty undertaken by persons or on territory under its jurisdiction or control.

## Article 6
## Victim assistance and environmental remediation

1. Each State Party shall, with respect to individuals under its jurisdiction who are affected by the use or testing of nuclear weapons, in accordance with applicable international humanitarian and human rights law, adequately provide age- and gender-sensitive assistance, without discrimination, including medical care, rehabilitation and psychological support, as well as provide for their social and economic inclusion.

2. Each State Party, with respect to areas under its jurisdiction or control contaminated as a result of activities related to the testing or use of nuclear weapons or other nuclear explosive devices, shall take necessary and appropriate measures towards the environmental remediation of areas so contaminated.

3. The obligations under paragraphs 1 and 2 above shall be without prejudice to the duties and obligations of any other States under international law or bilateral agreements.

## Article 7
## International cooperation and assistance

1. Each State Party shall cooperate with other States Parties to facilitate the implementation of this Treaty.

2. In fulfilling its obligations under this Treaty, each State Party shall have the right to seek and receive assistance, where feasible, from other States Parties.

3. Each State Party in a position to do so shall provide technical, material and financial assistance to States Parties affected by nuclear-weapons use or testing, to further the implementation of this Treaty.

4. Each State Party in a position to do so shall provide assistance for the victims of the use or testing of nuclear weapons or other nuclear explosive devices.

5. Assistance under this Article may be provided, inter alia, through the United Nations system, international, regional or national organizations or institutions, non-governmental organizations or institutions, the International Committee of the Red Cross, the International Federation of Red Cross and Red Crescent Societies, or national Red Cross and Red Crescent Societies, or on a bilateral basis.

6. Without prejudice to any other duty or obligation that it may have under international law, a State Party that has used or tested nuclear weapons or any other nuclear explosive devices shall have a responsibility to provide adequate assistance to affected States Parties, for the purpose of victim assistance and environmental remediation.[150]

[**Author's note**: The remaining Articles 8 through 20 have not been included here. Access these articles and the full document (A/CONF.229/2017/8) at:
https://www.un.org/disarmament/wmd/nuclear/tpnw/ ]

. . . DONE at New York, this seventh day of July, two thousand and seventeen.

From Treaty on the Prohibition of Nuclear Weapons, by United Nations General Assembly 2017. Reprinted with the permission of the United Nations

# Nuclear Abolition: The Road from Armageddon to Transformation

## By David Krieger

Nuclear weapons pose a grave threat to the future of civilization. As long as we allow these weapons to exist, we flirt with the catastrophe that they will be used, whether intentionally or accidentally. Meanwhile, nuclear weapons skew social priorities, create imbalances of power, and heighten geopolitical tension. Diplomacy has brought some noteworthy steps in curbing risks and proliferation, but progress has been uneven and tenuous. The ultimate aim of abolishing these weapons from the face of the earth—the "zero option"—faces formidable challenges of ignorance, apathy, and fatigue. Yet, the total abolition of nuclear weapons is essential for a Great Transition to a future rooted in respect for life, global solidarity, and ecological resilience. This will require an emboldened disarmament movement working synergistically with kindred movements, such as those fighting for peace, environmental sustainability, and economic justice, in pursuit of the shared goal of systemic change.

## Civilization at Risk

Nuclear weapons, unique in their power and capacity for destruction, pose an existential threat to humanity. Although the peril of living at the precipice of nuclear devastation is clear, progress toward nuclear abolition has been slow and uneven, and the issue of nuclear weapons appears distant or abstract to many. And yet, nuclear abolition remains vital to achieving a Great Transition in our minds and on our planet. Ignoring the problem could result in nuclear war, which could leave few, if any, humans to rebuild a better world. With so much at stake, it is more important now than ever to re-energize and broaden the movement toward nuclear abolition. Making Earth a nuclear-free zone would be a gift to all inhabitants of the planet and all future generations.

The number of nuclear weapons in the world reached a peak of 70,000 in the 1980s amidst the Cold War. Although the nearly 15,000 that exist today across nine nuclear-armed countries (United States, Russia, United Kingdom, France, China, Israel, India, Pakistan, and North Korea) is far below this Cold War zenith, it is still enough to destroy civilization several times over. The vast majority of these weapons are in the arsenals of the US and Russia, the two countries that have always led the nuclear arms race.

To grasp the scope of the risks, consider that atmospheric scientists conclude that a relatively small nuclear war in South Asia, in which India and Pakistan fired fifty Hiroshima-size nuclear weapons at each other's cities, would send enough soot into the upper atmosphere to substantially block sunlight, shorten growing seasons, cause crop failures, and lead to a nuclear famine that could take the lives of some two billion people globally. The sunlight-blocking dust generated by the detonation of, say, 300 thermonuclear weapons in a war between the US and Russia could trigger a new Ice Age, dropping global temperatures to the lowest levels in 18,000 years, and leaving civilization utterly destroyed. Those who would survive the blast, heat, and radiation of nuclear war would live in a nuclear winter of freezing temperatures and perpetual darkness. The survivors would likely envy the dead.

The history of the nuclear age reveals just how resistant nuclear-armed nations have been to real accountability, fueling a vicious cycle of ignorance, apathy, and fatigue. Only a global, systemic movement can bring the global, systemic change required. For that to be a possibility, the nuclear abolition movement must link up with the many other social forces fighting for a better world.

## The Case for Abolition

It is clear that the status quo is not working. The paradigms of arms control and non-proliferation that dominate international diplomacy assume the continued existence of nuclear weapons. However, the dangers inherent in nuclear weapons will remain whether there are tens of thousands or only a few. As long as they exist, they can be used, whether by malicious intent, miscalculation or careless accident.

Key attributes of nuclear weapons make them incompatible with a secure, sustainable world:

· Immense destructive potential. Nuclear weapons are capable of destroying cities, countries, civilization, and most complex life on the planet. The nuclear age has ushered in a new form of devastation: omnicide, the death of all. Living with nuclear weapons is like sitting on a world-encompassing keg of dynamite capable of exploding at any moment.

· Lack of discrimination between soldiers and civilians. Due to their immense destructive power, nuclear weapons cannot distinguish between armed soldiers and civilians, thus violating a basic tenet of international humanitarian law. As the world learned from the atomic bombings of Hiroshima and Nagasaki, deaths from a nuclear attack result from blast, heat, fire, and radiation, the latter especially painful.

· Concentration of power. The decision to use nuclear weapons resides with a small number of leaders, sometimes only one. In the US, the president is given the codes to launch a nuclear strike, and the same centralization of power holds in other nuclear-armed countries. No pretext exists for democratic procedure, or even a formal declaration of war. Of the nuclear-armed countries, only China and India have current pledges of "no first use," i.e., that they will not use nuclear weapons unless first attacked with nuclear weapons.

· Geopolitical imbalance. The world is divided into a small number of nuclear "haves," and some 185 nuclear "have-nots." This provides some countries with the leverage to bully other countries into submission. As a result, nuclear weapons look more attractive to all as a way of asserting geopolitical power, increasing the prospects of nuclear proliferation.

· Diversion of resources from meeting basic needs. The development, testing, deployment, and modernization of nuclear weapons impose immense costs. In recent years, many nuclear powers have embraced a crushing fiscal austerity, reducing public funding for health care, housing, education, and other services for the poor, the hungry, and the needy, while spending billions to maintain or even expand nuclear arsenals. At the same time, scientific and technological resources have been diverted from socially beneficial purposes, such as the rapid development of clean energy technologies.

· Violation of fundamental moral and ethical codes. Maintaining the nuclear option carries with it the implicit and sometimes explicit threat of mass annihilation, which no major religious, cultural, or philosophical standard of moral principles would condone. The persistence of this threat stands as a profound moral malady of our age; the only cure is unleashing the better angels of our nature in a reinvigorated campaign for nuclear abolition.

## A Brief History of the Nuclear Age

How did the world come to build and maintain, to the tune of more than $100 billion each year, such civilization-destroying weapons of mass destruction?[i] The story begins with the creation of the first nuclear weapons in the secret US Manhattan Engineering Project during World War II. This massive project was initially sparked by fears, which ultimately proved unfounded, that Germany was well on its way to developing an atomic bomb. The war in Europe, had, indeed, already ended by the time the US conducted its first test of a nuclear device at Alamogordo, New Mexico, on July 16, 1945.

Three weeks later, on August 6, 1945, the US dropped an atomic bomb on the Japanese city of Hiroshima, causing massive destruction and killing up to 90,000 individuals immediately and 145,000 by the year's end. Three days later, the US used a second atomic weapon on the city of Nagasaki, killing tens of thousands more. Later, it came to light that the US knew, through the interception of secret communications, that Japan was trying to surrender and obtain favorable terms.[ii] The two bombs were used anyway, purportedly to keep the Soviet military from moving into

---

[i] Bruce Blair and Matthew Brown, Nuclear Weapons Cost Study (Washington, DC: Global Zero, 2011), https://www.globalzero.org/files/gz_nuclear_weapons_cost_study.pdf.
[ii] Gar Alperovitz, "The War Was Won Before Hiroshima – And the Generals Who Dropped the Bomb Knew It," The Nation, August 6, 2015, https://www.thenation.com/article/why-the-us-really-bombed-hiroshima/.

Japan, while signaling to the Soviet Union and the world the coming preeminence of US military power in the postwar order.

In July 1946, less than a year after the destruction of Hiroshima and Nagasaki, the US began testing nuclear weapons in the Marshall Islands, which the US would administer as a United Nations Trust Territory starting in 1947. The US conducted sixty-seven nuclear tests in the Marshall Islands from 1946 to 1958, the equivalent power of detonating 1.6 Hiroshima bombs each day for twelve years. Marshallese children on islands far away from the tests were powdered with radioactive ash, which they played in like snow. Over the course of the nuclear age, more than 2,000 nuclear tests have been conducted, causing untold numbers of cancers, leukemia, and other radiation-induced illnesses.

By the end of the 1940s, the Soviet Union tested its first nuclear device, triggering a rapidly unfolding arms race. In 1952 and 1953, the US and the Soviet Union, respectively, detonated their first thermonuclear weapons, which, as fusion weapons, were far more powerful than the fission bombs used at Hiroshima and Nagasaki.

The world came very close to nuclear war during the Cuban Missile Crisis in October 1962 over the secret Soviet placement of nuclear missiles in Cuba. A number of incidents during the thirteen-day confrontation could have led either side to launch World War III. Ultimately, to the whole world's benefit, an agreement was reached that the USSR would withdraw its nuclear weapons from Cuba, and the US would later and secretly withdraw its nuclear-armed missiles from Turkey.

After reaching the brink, the US, UK, and Soviet Union took steps to control the nuclear arms race. First, the Partial Test Ban Treaty (PTBT) of 1963 prohibited nuclear testing in the atmosphere, outer space, and under water. The PTBT's preamble stated clearly that it sought "to achieve the discontinuance of all test explosions of nuclear weapons for all time, [and was] determined to continue negotiations to this end." But it would take another thirty-three years for the international community to adopt and open for signatures the 1996 Comprehensive Test Ban Treaty (CTBT), which has yet to secure the necessary support to enter into force.

The second treaty in the aftermath of the Cuban Missile Crisis was the 1968 Treaty on the Non-Proliferation of Nuclear Weapons (NPT), which entered into force in 1970. It aims not only to prevent the proliferation of nuclear weapons to additional countries but also, importantly, to provide for the disarmament of then existing nuclear states: the US, USSR, UK, France, and China. Indeed, the NPT could have been more accurately called the Nuclear Non-Proliferation and Disarmament Treaty. Parties agreed to "pursue negotiations in good faith on effective measures relating to cessation of the nuclear arms race at an early date and to nuclear disarmament, and on a treaty on general and complete disarmament under strict and effective international control." But a major loophole undermined non-proliferation: the treaty refers to nuclear energy as an "inalienable right." Israel, India, and Pakistan never signed the NPT, and drew upon their so-called peaceful nuclear programs to develop nuclear weapons, while North Korea withdrew from the NPT in 2003, and conducted its first nuclear weapon test in 2006.

The next two decades saw continued efforts by the Cold War superpowers to mitigate the risks of nuclear war. In 1972, the US and Soviet Union entered into the Anti-Ballistic Missile (ABM) Treaty, which set limits on the number of sites that could be protected with missile defense systems (the deployment of ABM systems had exacerbated the arms race as countries sought to build even more powerful weapons to overcome them). Then, at a 1986 summit in Reykjavík, Presidents Ronald Reagan and Mikhail Gorbachev jointly stated that "a nuclear war cannot be won and must never be fought." They came close to agreeing to abolish their nuclear arsenals, but negotiations collapsed over Reagan's insistence on developing missile defenses. With the collapse of the Soviet Union several years later, the Cold War came to an end, but bloated nuclear arsenals remain a troublesome and dangerous legacy of Cold War rivalry that has been difficult to dislodge.

The post-Cold War era has offered a mixed landscape on nuclear disarmament. In 2002, the US unilaterally withdrew from the

ABM Treaty, and soon began deploying missile defense installations in Eastern Europe near the Russian border, purportedly against a threat from Iran. But Russia is concerned that their real purpose is to take out any Russian offensive missiles that might survive a US first strike.[iii] The US abrogation of the ABM Treaty also removed restraints on stationing weapons in outer space. US withdrawal from the ABM Treaty may prove to be the single greatest blunder of the nuclear age.

This checkered history notwithstanding, there has been some progress. A series of Strategic Arms Reduction Treaties (START) have substantially reduced US and Russian arsenals. As of 2018, each country is limited to the deployment of 1,550 strategic nuclear weapons, still far more than enough to destroy most humans and other complex forms of life on the planet.[iv]

In July 2017, the United Nations adopted the Treaty on the Prohibition of Nuclear Weapons (TPNW), the result of a partnership between the International Campaign to Abolish Nuclear Weapons (ICAN), a coalition of civil society organizations, and most non-nuclear weapon states. They joined forces to assert that nuclear war would be a dead end for humanity, with a total ban on nuclear weapons the only way out. ICAN's 2017 Nobel Peace Prize builds momentum but achieving the necessary ratifications of 50 countries will take time. The US, UK, and France have vowed never to sign or ratify it, preferring to control their own nuclear arsenals rather than to cooperate in preserving a livable world—a reminder of the entrenched opposition the nuclear abolition movement faces.

## Challenges for Movement-Building

The nuclear disarmament movement reached its apex in the early 1980s, when the arms race looked bleakest. In 1982, more than a

---

[iii] The US public and leaders might more easily sympathize with this concern by imagining a scenario where Russian missile defenses were deployed at the Canadian or Mexican borders.

[iv] President Trump's criticism of this Obama-era treaty, which clouds its prospects, should also be noted. See https://www.reuters.com/article/us-usa-trump-putin-idUSKBN15O2A5.

million people took to the streets in New York to demand that the number of nuclear weapons be frozen and further deployment cease. One must wonder if the protest was so large because it asked for so little: a freeze, rather than deep reductions. Still, the movement succeeded in spreading public awareness and concern about the dangers. Once the Cold War ended, though, interest in nuclear disarmament issues rapidly faded.

Various factors have contributed to this decline in enthusiasm. First and foremost is ignorance. The awesome destructiveness of nuclear weapons lacks tangibility since they are largely kept out of the public sight and mind. As a result, many in nuclear-armed countries see them as a positive source of prestige and necessity for security. Nuclear countries boast of technological achievement and belonging to an exclusive "club." When the Indians and Pakistanis tested nuclear weapons in 1998, for instance, their people took to the streets in celebration. Such national pride undermines efforts to establish nuclear abolition policies. At the same time, the security justification—the belief that nuclear weapons offer protection—is a fallacy. In fact, countries that possess them, by posing risks to other countries, become more likely to be nuclear targets themselves.

Contrasting narratives about the bombing of Hiroshima and Nagasaki exemplify the tension between nuclear pride and punishment. Most people, at least in the US, learn in school that the atomic attacks were necessary to save American lives. A different story is told by the Japanese survivors—a story of pain, suffering, and death. These two stories, one from above the mushroom cloud and one from below it, compete for dominance as frameworks drawing lessons of the past for guiding the future. The story from above, celebrating technological achievement, serves to keep the nuclear arms race alive. The story from below awakens humanity to the extreme peril it faces. The nuclear abolition movement builds on the stories from ground-zero, those beneath the mushroom cloud.

Beyond ignorance and its cousin pride, another source of apathy is a sense of fatigue. We must use our imaginations to envision the horror of nuclear catastrophe, but it is very difficult to sustain such fear in the public mind year after year, decade after decade, in the absence of nuclear war. The world has come close on many occasions, but malice, madness, or mistake has not yet triggered the use of nuclear weapons in war since World War II. Nonetheless, it is essential that we keep shouting warnings despite accusations of being "the boy who cried wolf." Only by sounding the alarm can we build a movement with sufficient power to abolish nuclear weapons once and for all.

Even when people understand the dangers of nuclear weapons, however, they may still be paralyzed by a perceived lack of power to bring about change. With decision-making power on nuclear policy highly centralized, individuals lack influence—unless they become politically active in large numbers. Ironically, the perception of impotence becomes a self-fulfilling prophecy that impedes movement-building and effective change.

The only way to change direction is to build a strong popular movement, in the nuclear-armed countries and throughout the world, to delegitimize nuclear weapons, support the Treaty on the Prohibition on Nuclear Weapons, and oppose reliance on nuclear arsenals. Political pressure from below is our best hope for getting governments of the nuclear states to join the rest of the world in prohibiting the possession, use, and threat of use of nuclear arms.

**Toward Systemic Change**

Nuclear weapons stand as the quintessential shared risk, posing a danger to the whole of humanity. The problem cannot be solved by any one nation alone. Nuclear abolition requires collective global action—a deep shift in values and institutions lest the forces that created the nuclear age continue to prevail.

Just as no nation can succeed on its own, in our interdependent world, no movement seeking fundamental change can truly succeed on its own. However, movements are too often isolated in different issue silos, competing for support and scarce resources. This fragmentation erodes unity and long-term impact. The nuclear abolition movement must join with other movements seeking systemic global change.

Synergy is most promising between the nuclear abolition movement and the wider peace movement, the environmental movement, and the economic justice movement. Each of these movements demands a global sensibility and global action. And each calls into question the governing assumptions of society that have led us down an unsustainable path.

The most obvious opportunity for cross-movement collaboration is with the peace movement. Any war involving nuclear-armed states or their allies could lead to the use of nuclear weapons. Peace activists, of course, have often been on the frontlines protesting the expansion of nuclear arsenals. However, the peace movement in the US and globally appears to be exhausted after the long wars in Afghanistan, Iraq, and elsewhere in the Middle East that have dragged on for more than a decade.

Still, there are bright spots. New approaches to peace literacy are sprouting up.[v] Veterans groups, such as Veterans for Peace (VFP), have helped to reinvigorate the peace movement. Through their first-hand experience with warfare, the veterans bring a unique perspective, legitimacy, and energy to the quest for peace, and have demonstrated a willingness to take on the issue of nuclear abolition as well. VFP has resurrected the Golden Rule, a ship that first sailed in the 1950s to protest atmospheric nuclear weapons testing in the Pacific. Now, she sails again in support of nuclear abolition and to display the bravery and tenacity that can overcome militarism. VFP also supports such disarmament projects as the lawsuits filed by the Marshall Islands in 2014 at the International Court of Justice against the nine nuclear-armed countries.[vi] The British Nuclear Test Veterans Association and other groups work to support veterans who have suffered radiation exposure from nuclear tests.

---

[v] A program developed by Paul Chappell at the Nuclear Age Peace Foundation is making its way into school curricula. See www.peaceliteracy.org.
[vi] Although the lawsuit was dismissed, this type of action helps to forge a united front for a livable future.

The environmental movement offers another potential partner for cross-movement collaboration. Nuclear abolition has not been high on the priority list of the environmental movement. At least in the US, the movement has been preoccupied with defensive battles against an administration intent on rolling back environmental protection. Even before, it focused on tangible and immediately pressing battles while tackling such planetary-scale threats as ozone depletion and climate change.

Environmentalists have, however, sounded the alarm on the deleterious impacts of so-called "peaceful" nuclear power, particularly in the aftermath of the accidents at Three Mile Island in the US, Chernobyl in the former Soviet Union, and Fukushima in Japan. But this is just one facet of the threat nuclear technology poses to a livable planet. Without total abolition, every aspect of the Earth's living systems, as well as life itself, remains at risk, while building and maintaining these tools of total war are a drag on efforts to transition toward a sustainable economy. As nuclear energy always contains within it the possibility of nuclear proliferation, advocates of nuclear abolition must likewise get behind the fight for a renewables-driven clean economy that would render such technology unnecessary.

The economic justice movement is a third promising ally of the nuclear abolition movement. Nuclear weapons systems have consumed vast public resources since the onset of the nuclear age. The US alone has spent more $7.5 trillion on its nuclear arsenal and plans to spend $1.7 trillion more over the next three decades to modernize it. World nuclear weapons expenditures exceed $1 trillion per decade, with the US accounting for over sixty percent of the total with Russia accounting for 14 percent and China 7 percent.[vii] These resources could be far better used to provide food, clean water, shelter, health care, and education to those in need. This diversion of resources is a double whammy: we

---

[vii] Joseph Cirincione, "Lessons Lost," Bulletin of the Atomic Scientists (November/December 2005): 47, https://thebulletin.org/2005/november/lessons-lost; Kingston Reif, "CBO: Nuclear Arsenal to Cost $1.2 Trillion," Arms Control Association, December 2017, https://www.armscontrol.org/act/2017-12/news/cbo-nuclear-arsenal-cost-12-trillion. Note that this will be $1.7 Trillion when factoring in inflation.

underspend on human and ecological well-being while intensifying the threat of a nuclear catastrophe.

The militarization of the economy and centralization of power, for which nuclear weapons have been both cause and effect, are incompatible with egalitarian national economic systems. Internationally, as long as nuclear weapons give a handful of countries outsize power on the global stage, especially the ability to make credible threats, the shift toward a more democratic global economic system will be impossible.

For all these reasons, nuclear abolition serves the cause of economic justice. And it is equally true that those of us who care about the nuclear threat need to advocate for greater justice. Economic inequality within and between nations fosters polarization, migration pressure, and geopolitical conflict, thereby raising the risk of (nuclear) war. Thus, the peace movement has powerful incentives to ally with social justice movements.

Peace, a healthy environment, and economic justice will remain elusive in a nuclear world. A cooperative movement of movements would enhance the capacity of each constituent to achieve its own goals, while fostering the cross-movement solidarity that can bring a Great Transition future. With the alarms sounding, the time has come to act together with a sense of urgency.

## Armageddon or Transformation?

At the onset of the nuclear age, Einstein reflected, "The unleashed power of the atom has changed everything save our modes of thinking, and we thus drift toward unparalleled catastrophe." The splitting of the atom made new modes of thinking not only desirable but necessary. Nuclear weapons threaten the future of civilization and the human species. We can no longer think in old ways, solving differences among countries by means of warfare. Instead of absolute allegiance to a sovereign state, we must think holistically and globally. In light of the omnicide that our technologies have made possible, we must elevate our moral and spiritual awareness to forge a movement global and systemic enough to meet the challenges ahead.

Armageddon is a frightening thought, but as long as these "doomsday machines" exist, to use Daniel Ellsberg's term, it remains a possibility. The only realistic alternative to Armageddon is transformation, both of individual and collective consciousness: an "anti-nuclear revolution," to quote activist Helen Caldicott.[viii] This requires nothing less than changing the course of history; we are compelled to transform our world or to face Armageddon.

Change ultimately begins with individuals. Movements are composed of committed individuals, some of whom step forward as leaders. The task is to awaken to the urgency of the threat and mobilize. The nuclear age and the Great Transition call upon us, before it is too late, to wake up.

Reprinted by permission from David Krieger

---

[viii] Daniel Ellsberg, *The Doomsday Machine: Confessions of a Nuclear War Planner* (New York: Bloomsbury, 2017); Helen Caldicott, *Sleepwalking to Armageddon: The Threat of Nuclear Annihilation* (New York: The New Press, 2017)

# WAKE UP!

The alarm is sounding.
Can you hear it?
Can you hear the bells
of Nagasaki
ringing out for peace?
Can you feel the heartbeat
of Hiroshima
pulsing out for life?
The survivors of Hiroshima
and Nagasaki
are growing older.
Their message is clear:
Never again!
Wake up!
Now, before the feathered arrow
is placed into the bow.
Now, before the string
of the bow is pulled taut,
the arrow poised for flight.
Now, before the arrow is let loose,
before it flies across oceans
and continents.
Now, before we are engulfed in flames,
while there is still time, while we still can,
Wake up!

Reprinted by permission from David Krieger,
From *Wake Up!* A Nuclear Age Peace Foundation Book,
Santa Barbara, CA, 2015.

# President John F. Kennedy Commencement Address At American University[*]

## Washington, D.C., June 10, 1963

President Anderson, members of the faculty, board of trustees, distinguished guests, my old colleague, Senator Bob Byrd, who has earned his degree through many years of attending night law school, while I am earning mine in the next 30 minutes, distinguished guests, ladies and gentlemen:

It is with great pride that I participate in this ceremony of the American University, sponsored by the Methodist Church, founded by Bishop John Fletcher Hurst, and first opened by President Woodrow Wilson in 1914. This is a young and growing university, but it has already fulfilled Bishop Hurst's enlightened hope for the study of history and public affairs in a city devoted to the making of history and the conduct of the public's business. By sponsoring this institution of higher learning for all who wish to learn, whatever their color or their creed, the Methodists of this area and the Nation deserve the Nation's thanks, and I commend all those who are today graduating.

Professor Woodrow Wilson once said that every man sent out from a university should be a man of his nation as well as a man of his time, and I am confident that the men and women who carry the honor of graduating from this institution will continue to give from their lives, from their talents, a high measure of public service and public support.

---

[*] The reader is invited to also see and hear John F. Kennedy deliver this amazing speech at jfklibrary.org and other online sources.

"There are few earthly things more beautiful than a university," wrote John Masefield in his tribute to English universities--and his words are equally true today. He did not refer to spires and towers, to campus greens and ivied walls. He admired the splendid beauty of the university, he said, because it was "a place where those who hate ignorance may strive to know, where those who perceive truth may strive to make others see."

I have, therefore, chosen this time and this place to discuss a topic on which ignorance too often abounds and the truth is too rarely perceived--yet it is the most important topic on earth: world peace.

What kind of peace do I mean? What kind of peace do we seek? Not a Pax Americana enforced on the world by American weapons of war. Not the peace of the grave or the security of the slave. I am talking about genuine peace, the kind of peace that makes life on earth worth living, the kind that enables men and nations to grow and to hope and to build a better life for their children--not merely peace for Americans but peace for all men and women--not merely peace in our time but peace for all time.

I speak of peace because of the new face of war. Total war makes no sense in an age when great powers can maintain large and relatively invulnerable nuclear forces and refuse to surrender without resort to those forces. It makes no sense in an age when a single nuclear weapon contains almost ten times the explosive force delivered by all the allied air forces in the Second World War. It makes no sense in an age when the deadly poisons produced by a nuclear exchange would be carried by wind and water and soil and seed to the far corners of the globe and to generations yet unborn.

Today the expenditure of billions of dollars every year on weapons acquired for the purpose of making sure we never need to use them is essential to keeping the peace. But surely the acquisition of such idle stockpiles--which can only destroy and never create--is not the only, much less the most efficient, means of assuring peace.

I speak of peace, therefore, as the necessary rational end of rational men. I realize that the pursuit of peace is not as dramatic as the pursuit of war--and frequently the words of the pursuer fall on deaf ears. But we have no more urgent task.

Some say that it is useless to speak of world peace or world law or world disarmament--and that it will be useless until the leaders of the Soviet Union adopt a more enlightened attitude. I hope they do. I believe we can help them do it. But I also believe that we must reexamine our own attitude--as individuals and as a Nation--for our attitude is as essential as theirs. And every graduate of this school, every thoughtful citizen who despairs of war and wishes to bring peace, should begin by looking inward--by examining his own attitude toward the possibilities of peace, toward the Soviet Union, toward the course of the cold war and toward freedom and peace here at home.

First: Let us examine our attitude toward peace itself. Too many of us think it is impossible. Too many think it unreal. But that is a dangerous, defeatist belief. It leads to the conclusion that war is inevitable--that mankind is doomed--that we are gripped by forces we cannot control.

We need not accept that view. Our problems are manmade--therefore, they can be solved by man. And man can be as big as he wants. No problem of human destiny is beyond human beings. Man's reason and spirit have often solved the seemingly unsolvable--and we believe they can do it again.

I am not referring to the absolute, infinite concept of peace and good will of which some fantasies and fanatics dream. I do not deny the value of hopes and dreams but we merely invite discouragement and incredulity by making that our only and immediate goal.

Let us focus instead on a more practical, more attainable peace--based not on a sudden revolution in human nature but on a gradual evolution in human institutions--on a series of concrete actions and effective agreements which are in the interest of all concerned. There is no single, simple key to this peace--no grand or magic formula to be adopted by one or two powers. Genuine peace must be the product of many nations, the sum of many acts. It must be dynamic, not static, changing to meet the challenge of each new generation. For peace is a process--a way of solving problems.

With such a peace, there will still be quarrels and conflicting interests, as there are within families and nations. World peace, like community peace, does not require that each man love his neighbor--it requires only that they live together in mutual tolerance, submitting their disputes to a just and peaceful settlement. And history teaches us that enmities between nations, as between individuals, do not last forever. However fixed our likes and dislikes may seem, the tide of time and events will often bring surprising changes in the relations between nations and neighbors.

So let us persevere. Peace need not be impracticable, and war need not be inevitable. By defining our goal more clearly, by making it seem more manageable and less remote, we can help all peoples to see it, to draw hope from it, and to move irresistibly toward it.

Second: Let us reexamine our attitude toward the Soviet Union. It is discouraging to think that their leaders may actually believe what their propagandists write. It is discouraging to read a recent authoritative Soviet text on Military Strategy and find, on page after page, wholly baseless and incredible claims--such as the allegation that "American imperialist circles are preparing to unleash different types of wars . . . that there is a very real threat of a preventive war being unleashed by American imperialists against the Soviet Union . . . [and that] the political aims of the American imperialists are to enslave economically and politically the European and other capitalist countries . . . [and] to achieve world domination . . . by means of aggressive wars."

Truly, as it was written long ago: "The wicked flee when no man pursueth." Yet it is sad to read these Soviet statements--to realize the extent of the gulf between us. But it is also a warning--a warning to the American people not to fall into the same trap as the Soviets, not to see only a distorted and desperate view of the other side, not to see conflict as inevitable, accommodation as impossible, and communication as nothing more than an exchange of threats.

No government or social system is so evil that its people must be considered as lacking in virtue. As Americans, we find communism profoundly repugnant as a negation of personal freedom and dignity. But we can still hail the Russian people for their many achievements--in science and space, in economic and industrial growth, in culture and in acts of courage.

Among the many traits the peoples of our two countries have in common, none is stronger than our mutual abhorrence of war. Almost unique among the major world powers, we have never been at war with each other. And no nation in the history of battle ever suffered more than the Soviet Union suffered in the course of the Second World War. At least 20 million lost their lives. Countless millions of homes and farms were burned or sacked. A third of the nation's territory, including nearly two thirds of its industrial base, was turned into a wasteland--a loss equivalent to the devastation of this country east of Chicago.

Today, should total war ever break out again--no matter how--our two countries would become the primary targets. It is an ironic but accurate fact that the two strongest powers are the two in the most danger of devastation. All we have built, all we have worked for, would be destroyed in the first 24 hours. And even in the cold war, which brings burdens and dangers to so many nations, including this Nation's closest allies--our two countries bear the heaviest burdens. For we are both devoting massive sums of money to weapons that could be better devoted to combating ignorance, poverty, and disease. We are both caught up in a vicious and dangerous cycle in which suspicion on one side breeds suspicion on the other, and new weapons beget counterweapons.

In short, both the United States and its allies, and the Soviet Union and its allies, have a mutually deep interest in a just and genuine peace and in halting the arms race. Agreements to this end are in the interests of the Soviet Union as well as ours--and even the most hostile nations can be relied upon to accept and keep those treaty obligations, and only those treaty obligations, which are in their own interest.

So, let us not be blind to our differences--but let us also direct attention to our common interests and to the means by which those differences can be resolved. And if we cannot end now our differences, at least we can help make the world safe for diversity. For, in the final analysis, our most basic common link is that we all inhabit this small planet. We all breathe the same air. We all cherish our children's future. And we are all mortal.

Third: Let us reexamine our attitude toward the cold war, remembering that we are not engaged in a debate, seeking to pile up debating points. We are not here distributing blame or pointing the finger of judgment. We must deal with the world as it is, and not as it might have been had the history of the last 18 years been different.

We must, therefore, persevere in the search for peace in the hope that constructive changes within the Communist bloc might bring within reach solutions which now seem beyond us. We must conduct our affairs in such a way that it becomes in the Communists' interest to agree on a genuine peace. Above all, while defending our own vital interests, nuclear powers must avert those confrontations which bring an adversary to a choice of either a humiliating retreat or a nuclear war. To adopt that kind of course in the nuclear age would be evidence only of the bankruptcy of our policy--or of a collective death-wish for the world.

To secure these ends, America's weapons are nonprovocative, carefully controlled, designed to deter, and capable of selective use. Our military forces are committed to peace and disciplined in self- restraint. Our diplomats are instructed to avoid unnecessary irritants and purely rhetorical hostility.

For we can seek a relaxation of tension without relaxing our guard. And, for our part, we do not need to use threats to prove that we are resolute. We do not need to jam foreign broadcasts out of fear our faith will be eroded. We are unwilling to impose our system on any unwilling people--but we are willing and able to engage in peaceful competition with any people on earth.

Meanwhile, we seek to strengthen the United Nations, to help solve its financial problems, to make it a more effective instrument for peace, to develop it into a genuine world security system--a system capable of resolving disputes on the basis of law, of insuring the security of the large and the small, and of creating conditions under which arms can finally be abolished.

At the same time we seek to keep peace inside the non-Communist world, where many nations, all of them our friends, are divided over issues which weaken Western unity, which invite Communist intervention or which threaten to erupt into war. Our efforts in West New Guinea, in the Congo, in the Middle East, and in the Indian subcontinent, have been persistent and patient despite criticism from both sides. We have also tried to set an example for others--by seeking to adjust small but significant differences with our own closest neighbors in Mexico and in Canada.

Speaking of other nations, I wish to make one point clear. We are bound to many nations by alliances. Those alliances exist because our concern and theirs substantially overlap. Our commitment to defend Western Europe and West Berlin, for example, stands undiminished because of the identity of our vital interests. The United States will make no deal with the Soviet Union at the expense of other nations and other peoples, not merely because they are our partners, but also because their interests and ours converge.

Our interests converge, however, not only in defending the frontiers of freedom, but in pursuing the paths of peace. It is our hope-- and the purpose of allied policies--to convince the Soviet Union that she, too, should let each nation choose its own future, so long as that choice does not interfere with the choices of others. The Communist drive to impose their political and economic system on others is the primary cause of world tension today. For there can be no doubt that, if all nations could refrain from interfering in the self-determination of others, the peace would be much more assured.

This will require a new effort to achieve world law--a new context for world discussions. It will require increased understanding between the Soviets and ourselves. And increased understanding will require increased contact and communication. One step in this direction is the proposed arrangement for a direct line between Moscow and Washington, to avoid on each side the dangerous delays, misunderstandings, and misreadings of the other's actions which might occur at a time of crisis.

We have also been talking in Geneva about the other first-step measures of arms control designed to limit the intensity of the arms race and to reduce the risks of accidental war. Our primary long range interest in Geneva, however, is general and complete disarmament-- designed to take place by stages, permitting parallel political developments to build the new institutions of peace which would take the place of arms. The pursuit of disarmament has been an effort of this Government since the 1920's. It has been urgently sought by the past three administrations. And however dim the prospects may be today, we intend to continue this effort--to continue it in order that all countries, including our own, can better grasp what the problems and possibilities of disarmament are.

The one major area of these negotiations where the end is in sight, yet where a fresh start is badly needed, is in a treaty to outlaw nuclear tests. The conclusion of such a treaty, so near and yet so far, would check the spiraling arms race in one of its most dangerous areas. It would place the nuclear powers in a position to deal more effectively with one of the greatest hazards which man faces in 1963, the further spread of nuclear arms. It would increase our security--it would decrease the prospects of war. Surely this goal is sufficiently important to require our steady pursuit, yielding neither to the temptation to give up the whole effort nor the temptation to give up our insistence on vital and responsible safeguards.

I am taking this opportunity, therefore, to announce two important decisions in this regard.

First: Chairman Khrushchev, Prime Minister Macmillan, and I have agreed that high-level discussions will shortly begin in Moscow looking toward early agreement on a comprehensive test ban treaty. Our hopes must be tempered with the caution of history--but with our hopes go the hopes of all mankind.

Second: To make clear our good faith and solemn convictions on the matter, I now declare that the United States does not propose to conduct nuclear tests in the atmosphere so long as other states do not do so. We will not be the first to resume. Such a declaration is no substitute for a formal binding treaty, but I hope it will help us achieve one. Nor would such a treaty be a substitute for disarmament, but I hope it will help us achieve it.

Finally, my fellow Americans, let us examine our attitude toward peace and freedom here at home. The quality and spirit of our own society must justify and support our efforts abroad. We must show it in the dedication of our own lives--as many of you who are graduating today will have a unique opportunity to do, by serving without pay in the Peace Corps abroad or in the proposed National Service Corps here at home.

But wherever we are, we must all, in our daily lives, live up to the age-old faith that peace and freedom walk together. In too many of our cities today, the peace is not secure because the freedom is incomplete.

It is the responsibility of the executive branch at all levels of government--local, State, and National--to provide and protect that freedom for all of our citizens by all means within their authority. It is the responsibility of the legislative branch at all levels, wherever that authority is not now adequate, to make it adequate. And it is the responsibility of all citizens in all sections of this country to respect the rights of all others and to respect the law of the land.

All this is not unrelated to world peace. "When a man's ways please the Lord," the Scriptures tell us, "he maketh even his enemies to be at peace with him." And is not peace, in the last analysis, basically a matter of human rights--the right to live out our lives without fear of devastation--the right to breathe air as nature provided it--the right of future generations to a healthy existence?

While we proceed to safeguard our national interests, let us also safeguard human interests. And the elimination of war and arms is clearly in the interest of both. No treaty, however much it may be to the advantage of all, however tightly it may be worded, can provide absolute security against the risks of deception and evasion. But it can--if it is sufficiently effective in its enforcement and if it is sufficiently in the interests of its signers--offer far more security and far fewer risks than an unabated, uncontrolled, unpredictable arms race.

The United States, as the world knows, will never start a war. We do not want a war. We do not now expect a war. This generation of Americans has already had enough--more than enough--of war and hate and oppression. We shall be prepared if others wish it. We shall be alert to try to stop it. But we shall also do our part to build a world of peace where the weak are safe and the strong are just. We are not helpless before that task or hopeless of its success. Confident and unafraid, we labor on--not toward a strategy of annihilation but toward a strategy of peace.

From John F. Kennedy Presidential Library and Museum<br>https://www.jfklibrary.org/archives/other-resources/john-f-kennedy-speeches/american-university-19630610

# Notes

1. C. G. Jung, *The Portable Jung,* introduction and edited by Joseph Campbell, trans. R. F. C. Hull (New York: Penguin Books, Ltd., 1980), 636.

2. Jonathan Granoff, Contributor, "Ronald Reagan, Republicans and Nuclear Weapons" *Huffpost,* updated November 30, 2012. https://www.huffpost.com/entry/president-ronald-reagan_b_1927491.

3. John F. Kennedy, "JFK Commencement Address at American University, Washington, D.C., June 10, 1963." JFK Library. https://www.jfklibrary.org/archives/other-resources/john-f-kennedy-speeches/american-university-19630610.

4. Jonathan Schell, *The Fate of the Earth and The Abolition* (Stanford, CA: Stanford University Press, 2000), ix.

5. John Hersey, *Here to Stay* (New York: Paragon House Publishers, 1988), viii.

6. Herman Wouk, *The Winds of War* (New York: Little, Brown and Company, 2002), Preface to 1st Ed.

7. John F. Kennedy, "JFK News Conference 55, May 8, 1963," JFK Library. https://www.jfklibrary.org/archives/other-resources/john-f-kennedy-press-conferences/news-conference-55.

8. "Berlyn Brixner," Atomic Photographers Guild, accessed August 25, 2021. https://atomicphotographers.com/photographers/berlyn-brixner/.

9. Richard Rhodes, *The Making of the Atomic Bomb* (New York: Simon & Schuster, 2012), 672–676.

10. Robert R. Holt, "Meeting Einstein's Challenge: New thinking about nuclear weapons," April 3, 2015, *Bulletin of the Atomic Scientists*. https://thebulletin.org/2015/04/meeting-einsteins-challenge-new-thinking-about-nuclear-weapons/.

11. Tim O'Brien, *The Things They Carried* (New York: Mariner Books, 2009), 36.

12. John F. Kennedy, *Prelude to Leadership: The Post-War Diary of John F. Kennedy* (Washington D.C.: Regnery Publishing Company, Inc., 1995), xxiv.

13. Fulton J. Sheen, *Peace of Soul* (New York: McGraw-Hill Book Company, 1949), 1.

14. Hersey, *Here to Stay*, 85–103.

15. Nigel Hamilton, *JFK Reckless Youth,* (New York: Random House, 1992), 250–254.

16. Rhodes, *Atomic Bomb*, 672.

17. Rhodes, *Atomic Bomb*, 676.

18. Rhodes, *Atomic Bomb*, 676.

19. United Nations, Charter of the United Nations and Statute of the International Court of Justice, United Nations Publications, 2015, 2.

20. Robert Dallek, *An Unfinished Life: John F. Kennedy 1917–1963* (New York: Back Bay Books; Little, Brown and Company, 2003), 116.

21. Dallek, *An Unfinished Life*, 116.

22. Dallek, *An Unfinished Life*, 116.

23. Clifton Daniel, *Chronicle of the 20th Century,* North American Edition, (Mount Kisco, NY: Chronicle Publications, Inc., 1987), 695.

24. John Abbot Willis, *The Nations at War: A Current History* (New York: Leslie-Judge Company, 1917), 78–79.

25. Daniel, *Chronicle of the 20th Century*, 700.

26. "Life is Worth Living [21/02/1953]" (web page) British Universities Film & Video Council, February 21, 1953. http://bufvc.ac.uk/shakespeare/index.php/title/av36814.

27. Daniel, *Chronicle of the 20th Century*, 730.

28. Rosemary Sullivan, *Stalin's Daughter: The Extraordinary and Tumultuous Life of Svetlana Alliluyeva* (New York: HarperCollins Publishers, 2015), 186–187.

29. Daniel, *Chronicle of the 20th Century*, 808.

30. Daniel, *Chronicle of the 20th Century*, 808.

31. Daniel, *Chronicle of the 20th Century*, 829.

32. Philip Nash, *The Other Missiles of October: Eisenhower, Kennedy, and the Jupiters, 1957–1963* (Chapel Hill/London: University of North Carolina Press, 1997), 67.

33. "First Kennedy–Nixon Debate, 26 September 1960," JFK Library, CBS Studios, Chicago IL, https://www.jfklibrary.org/asset-viewer/archives/TNC/TNC-172/TNC-172.

34. "First Kennedy–Nixon Debate, 26 September 1960."

35. "First Kennedy–Nixon Debate, 26 September 1960."

## Notes

36. "CPD: October 21, 1960 Debate Transcript," The Fourth Kennedy-Nixon Presidential Debate, Commission on Presidential Debates. https://www.debates.org/voter-education/debate-transcripts/october-21-1960-debate-transcript/.

37. "CPD: October 21, 1960 Debate Transcript."

38. USG:1-W (excerpt) JFK Victory Speech at Hyannis Armory – *YouTube,* Hearst Metrotone News Inc. November 9, 1960, JFK Library YouTube channel video, 1:44. https://www.youtube.com/watch?v=ZPB4Hl2AVhY.

39. Thurston Clarke, *Ask Not: The Inauguration of John F. Kennedy and the Speech that Changed America* (New York: Penguin Books, 2011), 191.

40. Clarke, *Ask Not*, 199.

41. Clarke, *Ask Not*, 200.

42. Clarke, *Ask Not*, 200.

43. Thomas Merton, *Conjectures of a Guilty Bystander* (Garden City, New York: Image Books edition, by special arrangement with Doubleday & Company, Inc., 1968), 58.

44. Amy Tikkanen, "Tsar Bomba | Soviet thermonuclear bomb." *Britannica,* October 23, 2020. https://www.britannica.com/topic/Tsar-Bomba.

45. William L. Shirer, *Berlin Diary 1934–1941, The Rise and Fall of the Third Reich* (New York: Barnes & Noble Books, 1997), 77.

46. John Hersey, *Hiroshima* (New York: Bantam Books, 1966), 5.

47. Hersey, *Hiroshima*, 1.

48. Hersey, *Hiroshima*, 6.

49. Hersey, *Hiroshima*, 7.

50. John F. Kennedy, *The Burden and the Glory,* Allan Nevins, ed. (New York: Harper & Row Publishers, 1964), 99.

51. Jung, *The Portable Jung*, 636-637.

52. Stacey Bredhoff, *To the Brink: JFK and the Cuban Missile Crisis.* (Washington, DC: The Foundation for the National Archives, 2013), 40.

53. Theodore C. Sorensen, *Kennedy* (New York: A Bantam Book/Published by arrangement with Harper & Row Publishers, Inc., 1966), 792.

54. Robert F. Kennedy, *Thirteen Days: A Memoir of the Cuban Missile Crisis,* foreword by Arthur Schlesinger, Jr. (New York: W. W. Norton and Company, 1999), 19.

Notes

55. Jonathan Rauch, "Firebombs Over Tokyo," *The Atlantic,* July/August 2002 Issue. https://www.theatlantic.com/magazine/archive/2002/07/firebombs-over-tokyo/302547/.

56. Daniel Ellsberg, *The Doomsday Machine: Confessions of a Nuclear War Planner* (New York: Bloomsbury USA, imprint of Bloomsbury Publishing Plc., 2017), 263.

57. Ellsberg, *Doomsday Machine*, 262.

58. "Survivors of Hiroshima and Nagasaki," Atomic Heritage Foundation, July 27, 2017. https://www.atomicheritage.org/history/survivors-hiroshima-and-nagasaki.

59. *Listening In: The Secret White House Recordings of John F. Kennedy,* selected and introduced by Ted Widmer, foreword by Caroline Kennedy (New York: Hyperion, 2012), 145–157.

60. Ellsberg, *Doomsday Machine*, 2–3.

61. Ellsberg, *Doomsday Machine*, 135.

62. Ellsberg, *Doomsday Machine*, 136–142.

63. Dallek, *An Unfinished Life*, 346.

64. Kennedy, *Thirteen Days*, 35.

65. *Listening In,* Widmer, 147–155.

66. *Listening In,* Widmer, 155.

67. Kennedy, *Thirteen Days*, 77.

68. Dallek, *An Unfinished Life*, n.p.

69. Kennedy, *Thirteen Days*, 53–54.

70. Kennedy, *Thirteen Days*, 54.

71. Kennedy, *Thirteen Days*, 54.

72. Kennedy, *Prelude to Leadership,* 49.

73. Hersey, *Hiroshima*, 47.

74. Hersey, *Hiroshima*, 46.

75. Hersey, *Hiroshima*, 59.

76. Ellsberg, *Doomsday Machine*, 209.

77. Ellsberg, *Doomsday Machine*, 213–217.

78. Ellsberg, *Doomsday Machine*, 213–217.

79. Ellsberg, *Doomsday Machine*, 216.

80. Ellsberg, *Doomsday Machine*, 216.

81. Ellsberg, *Doomsday Machine*, 216.

82. Ellsberg, *Doomsday Machine*, 216–217.

83. Robert S. McNamara, *Blundering into Disaster: Surviving the First Century of the Nuclear Age* (New York: Pantheon Books, 1986), 11.

84. Kennedy, *Thirteen Days*, 91.

## Notes

85. Sorensen, *Kennedy*, 833.

86. David Krieger, *In the Shadow of the Bomb: Poems of Survival* (Santa Barbara, CA. A Nuclear Age Peace Foundation Book, 2018), 7.

87. Kennedy, *Burden and the Glory*, 62.

88. Kennedy, *Burden and the Glory*, 63.

89. Kennedy, *Burden and the Glory*, 184.

90. Jim Polk and Alicia Stewart, "'I Have a Dream': 9 historical facts about MLK's speech and march," *CNN,* January 21, 2019. https://www.cnn.com/2019/01/21/us/mlk-i-have-a-dream-speech.

91. Polk and Stewart, "About MLK's speech."

92. Martin Luther King, Jr., *A Testament of Hope: The Essential Writings and Speeches of Martin Luther King, Jr.*, James Melvin Washington, ed., (HarperSanFrancisco, A Division of Harper Collins Publishers, 1986), 220.

93. Kennedy, *Burden and the Glory*, 68.

94. David Claerbaut, *Duffy Daugherty: A Man Ahead of His Time* (East Lansing, MI: Greenstone Books, 2018).

95. For an account of Coach Daugherty's historic effort to integrate players into college football, see Maya Washington's brilliant documentary *Through the Banks of the Red Cedar*. (www.mayawashington.net).

96. Pierre Salinger, *With Kennedy* (Garden City, NY: Doubleday & Company, Inc., 1966), 5.

97. Salinger, *With Kennedy*, 8.

98. Salinger, *With Kennedy*, 9.

99. Kennedy, *Burden and the Glory*, 75.

100. Kennedy, *Burden and the Glory*, 64

101. Kennedy, *Burden and the Glory*, 75.

102. Salinger, *With Kennedy*, 10.

103. Salinger, *With Kennedy*, 10–11.

104. Salinger, *With Kennedy*, 11.

105. Salinger, *With Kennedy*, 11.

106. Thurston Clarke, *JFK's Last Hundred Days: The Transformation of a Man and the Emergence of a Great President* (New York: Penguin Press, 2013), 360.

107. "National Security Action Memorandum [NSAM]: NSAM 263, South Vietnam*,*" October 11, 1963, JFK Library. https://www.jfklibrary.org/asset-viewer/archives/JFKNSF/342/JFKNSF-342-007.

108. Dallek, *An Unfinished Life*, 668.

## Notes

109. "Folder, 'NSAM # 273: South Vietnam, 11/26/1963,' National Security Action Memorandums, NSF, Box 2," DiscoverLBJ. https://www.discoverlbj.org/item/nsf-nsam-b2-f08.

110. "Folder, NSAM # 273: South Vietnam, 11/26/1963."

111. James W. Douglass, *JFK and the Unspeakable: Why He Died and Why It Matters* (New York: Simon & Schuster, 2008).

112. Daniel, *Chronicle of the 20th Century*, 925.

113. Lyndon B. Johnson, "Special Message to the Congress on U.S. Policy in Southeast Asia," August 5, 1964, The American Presidency Project. https://www.presidency.ucsb.edu/node/238756.

114. Muhammad Ali, with Richard Durham, *The Greatest: My Own Story* (Graymalkin Media, 2015), 137.

115. Arthur M. Schlesinger, Jr., *Robert Kennedy and His Times* (Boston: Houghton Mifflin Company, 1978), 874.

116. Schlesinger, *Robert Kennedy*, 874–875.

117. Evan Thomas, *Robert Kennedy: His Life,* 1st Touchstone ed. (New York: Simon & Schuster, 2002), 391.

118. Larry Tye, *Bobby Kennedy: The Making of a Liberal Icon.* (New York: Random House, a division of Penguin Random House LLC New York, 2016), 437.

119. Chris Matthews, *Bobby Kennedy: A Raging Spirit* (New York: Simon & Schuster, 2017), 304.

120. James W. Douglass, *The Non-Violent Cross: A Theology of Revolution and Peace* (London: The Macmillan Company, Collier-Macmillan LTD., 1969), 6.

121. Tye, *Bobby Kennedy*, 441.

122. "Patton (1970) - George C. Scott as General George S. Patton, Jr.," *IMDb,* under Quotes, first lines, accessed September 2, 2021, https://www.imdb.com/title/tt0066206/characters/nm0001715.

123. Jack Newfield, *Robert F. Kennedy: A Memoir* (New York: Berkley Publishing Corporation, 1978), 337.

124. Kennedy, *Burden and the Glory*, 63.

125. C. G. Jung, first published 1933, *Modern Man in Search of a Soul,* trans. W. S. Dell and Cary F. Baynes (New York: Harcourt, Brace & World, Inc., 1966), 204.

126. Margaret Hartmann, "Trump Thinks About Nukes a Lot, Doesn't Know Much About It," August 20, 2017, *Intelligencer.* https://nymag.com/intelligencer/2017/08/trump-thinks-about-nukes-a-lot-doesnt-know-much-about-them.html.

127. Granoff, "Ronald Reagan."

## NOTES

128. "Status of World Nuclear Forces" (webpage), Federation Of American Scientists, accessed September 15, 2021, https://fas.org/issues/nuclear-weapons/status-world-nuclear-forces/.

129. James G. Blight and David A. Welch, *On the Brink: Americans & Soviets Reexamine the Cuban Missile Crisis,* 2nd Edition by Noonday Press (New York: Farrar, Straus and Giroux New York, 1990), xiii.

130. McNamara, *Blundering into Disaster*, 15.

131. McNamara, *Blundering into Disaster*, 37–75

132. McNamara, *Blundering into Disaster*, 13.

133. McNamara, *Blundering into Disaster*, 13–14.

134. McNamara, *Blundering into Disaster*, 15.

135. James W. Douglass, *The Nonviolent Coming of God* (Maryknoll, NY: Orbis Books, 1992), xii.

136. Granoff, "Ronald Reagan."

137. Donald Trump, "President Trump delivers first address to UNGA," September 19, 2017, YouTube video, 42:49. https://www.youtube.com/watch?v=rTGMu8BrzS8.

138. Cynthia Lazaroff, "Dawn of a new Armageddon," *Bulletin of the Atomic Scientists,* August 6, 2018. https://thebulletin.org/2018/08/dawn-of-a-new-armageddon/.

139. Jonathan Schell, *Fate of the Earth*, 230.

140. Wayne W. Dyer, *10 Secrets for Success and Inner Peace* (Carlsbad, CA: Hay House, Inc., 2001), 21.

141. Christine M. Bochen and William H. Shannon, eds., *Cold War Letters: Thomas Merton* (Maryknoll, NY: Orbis Books, 2006), xxxi.

142. Kennedy, "Address at American University."

143. Kennedy, *Burden and the Glory*, 77.

144. United Nations General Assembly, "Treaty on the Prohibition of Nuclear Weapons – UNODA," July 7, 2017, A/CONF.229/2017/8, United Nations. https://www.un.org/disarmament/wmd/nuclear/tpnw/.

145. "The World's Nuclear Weapons," International Campaign to Abolish Nuclear Weapons, accessed September 8, 2021, https://www.icanw.org/nuclear_arsenals.

146. Jung, *The Portable Jung*, 638.

147. Kennedy, *Burden and the Glory*, 66.

148. Eleanor Coerr, *Sadako and the Thousand Paper Cranes* (New York: Puffin Books. Published by the Penguin Group, 1977), n.p.

## NOTES

149. Kennedy, "Address at American University, Washington, D.C., June 10, 1963 - JFK Library," JFK Library. https://www.jfklibrary.org/archives/other-resources/john-f-kennedy-speeches/american-university-19630610.

150. United Nations, "Treaty on Prohibition of Nuclear Weapons."

# Sources Consulted/Further Reading

You may find these additional sources useful in reaching a deeper understanding and commitment to the cause of universal peace.

Arenadt, Hannah. *On Violence* (San Diego, CA: A Harvest Book, Harcourt Brace & Company, 1970).

Chomsky, Noam. *Who Rules the World?* (New York: Henry Holt and Company, LLC, 2016).

de Saxe, Maurice. *Reveries on the Art of War,* trans., ed., Brig. General Thomas R. Phillips (Mineola, NY: Dover Publications, 2007).

Dobbs, Michael. *One Minute to Midnight: Kennedy, Khrushchev, and Castro on the Brink of Nuclear War* (New York: Vintage Books, A Division of Random House, Inc., 2009).

Douglass, James W. *Gandhi and the Unspeakable: His Final Experiment with Truth* (Maryknoll, New York: Orbis Books, 2012).

Douglass, James W. *Lightning East to West: Jesus, Gandhi, and the Nuclear Age.* (Eugene, OR: Wipf & Stock Publishers, 2006).

Einstein, Albert. *The World as I See It,* (n.p. Snowball Publishing, 2014).

Falk, Richard and David Krieger. *The Path to Zero* (Boulder, CO: Paradigm Publishers, 2012).

Gandhi, Mohandas K. *Gandhi on Non-Violence,* edited, and with an introduction by Thomas Merton (New York: New Directions Publishing Corporation, 1965).

Graff, Garrett M. *Raven Rock* (New York: Simon & Schuster, 2017.

Hawkins, David R. *Power vs. Force: The Hidden Determinants of Human Behavior* (Carlsbad, CA: Hay House Inc., 2012).

Kelsey, Morton. *Discernment: A Study in Ecstasy and Evil* (New Jersey: Paulist Press, 1978).

Kelsey, Morton. *Encounter with God: A Theology of Christian Experience* (Mahwah, NJ: Paulist Press, 1987).

Krieger, David, ed. *Hope in A Dark Time: Reflections on Humanity's Future,* foreword by Archbishop Desmond Tutu (Santa Barbara, CA: Capra Press, 2003).

Merton, Thomas. *The New Man* (New York: The Noonday Press, 1961).

Merton, Thomas. *Passion for Peace: Reflections on War and Nonviolence,* William H. Shannon, ed. (New York: Crossroad Publishing Company, 2006).

Merton, Thomas. *Raids on the Unspeakable* (New York: New Directions Publishing Corporation, 1966).

Michael, Chester P. and Marie C. Norrisey. *Arise: A Christian Psychology of Love* (Charlottesville, VA: The Open Door Inc., 1981).

Pope Francis in Conversation with Austen Ivereigh, *Let Us Dream: The Path to a Better Future* (New York: Simon Schuster, 2020).

Pope Francis, *Laudato Si': On Care for Our Common Home* [Encyclical] (Huntington, IN: Our Sunday Visitor, 2015)

Pritikin, Trisha T. *The Hanford Plaintiffs: Voices from the Fight for Atomic Justice,* foreword by Richard C. Eymann and Tom H. Foulds, introduction by Karen Dorn Steele (Lawrence, KS: University Press of Kansas, 2020).

Roberts, Priscilla, ed. *Cuban Missile Crisis: The Essential Reference Guide,* (Santa Barbara, CA: ABC-CLIO, LLC., 2012).

Rohr, Richard. *A Lever and a Place to Stand: The Contemplative Stance, The Active Prayer,* foreword by James Martin, SJ (Mahwah, NJ: Hidden Spring, 2011).

Rohr, Richard. *The Universal Christ: How a Forgotten Reality Can Change Everything We See, Hope For, and Believe* (New York: Convergent Books, 2019).

Salmon, James; SJ; and John Farina, eds., *The Legacy of Pierre Teilhard de Chardin* (Mahwah, NJ: Paulist Press, 2011).

SOURCES CONSULTED / FURTHER READING

Scarry, Elaine. *Thermonuclear Monarchy: Choosing Between Democracy and Doom* (New York: W.W. Norton & Company, 2014).

Schweitzer, Albert. *Albert Schweitzer: Reverence for Life – The Inspiring Words of a Great Humanitarian,* foreword by Norman Cousins (Kansas City, MO: Hallmark Cards, Inc., 1971).

Sorensen, Theodore C. *Decision-Making in the White House: The Olive Branch or the Arrows,* foreword by John F. Kennedy (New York: Columbia University Press, 1963).

Stern, Sheldon M. *The Cuban Missile Crisis in American Memory: Myths versus Reality,* Stanford Nuclear Age Series (Stanford, CA: Stanford University Press, 2012).

Sumiteru, Taniguchi. *The Atomic Bomb on My Back: A Life Story of Survival and Activism,* compiled by Hisashi Tomokuni (Montpelier, VT: Rootstock Publishing, 2020).

Teilhard, Pierre de Chardin. *The Future of Man* (n.p. An Image Book Published by Doubleday, 2004).

Tuchman, Barbara W. *The Guns of August,* foreword by Robert K. Massie (New York: Ballantine Books, 2004).

Wink, Walter. *Engaging the Powers: Discernment and Resistance in a World of Domination* (Minneapolis, MN: Fortress Press, 1992).

Wink, Walter. *Jesus and Nonviolence: A Third Way* (Minneapolis, MN: Fortress Press, 2003).

Wink, Walter. *Naming the Powers: The Language of Power in the New Testament* (Philadelphia, PA: Fortress Press, 1984).

Wink, Walter, ed., *Peace Is The Way: Writings on Nonviolence from the Fellowship of Reconciliation* (Maryknoll, NY: Orbis Books, 2000).

Wink, Walter. *The Powers That Be: Theology for a New Millennium* (New York, NY: A Galilee Book, Doubleday, 1999).

Wink, Walter. *Unmasking the Powers: The Invisible Forces That Determine Human Existence* (Philadelphia, PA: Fortress Press, 1986).

Wink, Walter. *When the Powers Fall: Reconciliation in the Healing of Nations* (Minneapolis, MN: Fortress Press, 1998).

# Acknowledgments

This story covers a span of seventy-five years, involving a lot of people and a lifetime of memories. I have kept the actual names of those most important to the story: family members, friends, college athletes, and political leaders. I have also kept the actual names of my first teacher, Sister Agnes Carmel of the Sisters of St. Dominic, and a man whom I did not know, named Moses. For others more peripheral to the story, like long-ago teachers and classmates, I have given substitute names. Each of the events in the story I've described happened. Admittedly I may have added a touch of *Hungarian blarney* to add a little sparkle to the storytelling. I say, if the Irish can do it, why the hell can't we?

I want to express my deep appreciation to those who provided encouragement and help in the creation of this book. Rich Appelbaum, Nancy Barron, Ralph Baxter, Jaime Bognar, Stan Bognar, Hector Briones, Regina Chow, Brian Clark, Cheryl Clark, David Coelho, Carol Copp, Jim Copp, Barbara Cragg, Bill Cragg, Sister June Mary Deswysen, Shelley Douglass, Joe Esseff, Pat Esseff, Pat Gallinagh, Virginia Garland, John Garman, Laurie Garry, Susan Garon, Julie Garvey, Lisa Gosdschan, Fr. Larry Gosselin, Jean Holsten, Clinton Jones, Sandy Jones, Dianne Kenny, Rob Laney, Sandra Lommasson, Larry Markworth, Marc Maxwell, Hal Maynard, Carmen Mendevil, Sister Theresa Nightingale, Joe Nolan, Kristin Nugent, Jill Overton, Melissa Lovinger Owen, Jimmy Patrick, Trisha Pritikin, Adib Setareh, Audrey Stech, Juanita Walker, Carol Warner, Geof Whittaker, Lisa Wysel, Sandra Yanez, and Lindsay Young.

The late Father John Leonard was the first to encourage me to write the book and harangued me over many years to complete it. The late Father Chester Michael, founder of the Spiritual Direction Institute, Inc. of Charlottesville, Virginia, rekindled my deepening concern about the ongoing nuclear danger and, in his own inimitable direct way, asked me what I was going to do about it. I owe a debt of gratitude to Elizabeth Alegri, who reviewed the earliest drafts, and expressed more enthusiasm about the initial work than I did. Elizabeth steadfastly withheld my first cup of morning coffee, until I produced evidence that another chapter was forthcoming. My brother Tom refreshed my memory of family history and folklore. Debbie Jenae's marvelous analytical skills provided recommendations that improved each chapter markedly, and completed the manuscript's final editing. Sandy Cambeilh reviewed initial drafts and helped me keep my sense of humor along the way.

James Douglass, who has served as a mentor to me, convinced me that the project should have my highest priority. Richard Falk provided invaluable feedback, and encouragement when it was needed most. David Krieger has worked tirelessly for forty years to awaken the public to the dangers of the nuclear age. He not only gave his counsel to this project but provided crucially important information for inclusion in this book. Sean Hirshberg has provided needed guidance about how best to make the book available online, and his technical expertise went on to make it so. Artist Steve Simon made available an image of his magnificent painting of Sadako Sasaki. Sandy Jones offered her marvelous artistic ability to create the cover for the book.

I owe a special debt to the board and staff of the Nuclear Age Peace Foundation, and to Beatrice Fihn, Executive Director of the International Campaign for the Abolition of Nuclear Weapons (ICAN) and its members throughout the world for their groundbreaking work at the United Nations, the *Treaty on the Prohibition of Nuclear Weapons*.

My thanks would be incomplete without acknowledging my two canine assistants, Sunny and Josey Marie, who on a daily basis, tested my resolve to stay at the keyboard, by throwing every possible distracting obstacle in my way. Extra Chewies for you both!

I want to thank our three children and their wonderful spouses, who enrich my life and the lives of those around them with their boundless energy and life-giving spirit: Bobby and Mayet, Holly and Sean, Nicholas and Amber. Lastly, I want to thank Mary Ann, my wonderful wife of fifty-two years. In initial drafts, over countless hours, she suffered through some of the most primitive

## Acknowledgments

sentences ever constructed by a *homo sapien.* She was the first to tell me so. Mary Ann is, and will always remain, the love of my life.

# About the Author

**Francis Charles Bognar** was born in 1946, a few months after the United States dropped the atomic bomb on Hiroshima and Nagasaki. He is the sixth child of a loving, Catholic, Hungarian immigrant family. In 1963 he attended Michigan State University, followed by minor and major seminary training in philosophy, theology and spirituality at St. Paul's Seminary in Saginaw, Michigan and Notre Dame Seminary in New Orleans, Louisiana. On discerning that his vocation was a career in the helping professions rather than the priesthood, he left seminary life to return to college. He graduated with a bachelor's degree in psychology from Loyola University in 1969. He married his wife, Mary Ann, and accepted a commission as a 2nd Lieutenant in the U.S. Infantry. In military service he trained as a Psychological Operations Officer and served as a General Staff Officer at V Corps, Frankfurt, Germany. In the evenings he worked to earn a master's degree in counseling psychology from Ball State University. As the Vietnam war deepened, he applied as a conscientious objector, finished his tour, and received an honorable discharge. Returning to civilian life he continued his education earning a master's and doctorate in public administration from Nova University of Fort Lauderdale, Florida. He graduated from the Spiritual Direction Institute of Charlottesville, Virginia in 1993 where under the direction of Father Chet Michael, he studied works of Thomas Merton, Teilhard de Chardin, Carl G. Jung, and Reverend Morton Kelsey. He served over forty years in social services as a counselor, licensed marriage and family counselor, and administrator, primarily with Catholic Charities agencies. He served on the board of the Nuclear Age Peace Foundation, a partner organization of the International Campaign to Abolish Nuclear Weapons (ICAN), a coalition of nongovernmental organizations world-wide, which received the 2017 Nobel Peace Prize for its work on the United Nations *Treaty on the Prohibition of Nuclear Weapons*. He later served as NAPF's board's chair and vice chair.

## About the Author

The author believes that our world is at an existential crossroads, the moment of choice, when we must make the decision of placing our faith and future in the possession and advancement of nuclear weapons, or in renouncing them. Our collective decision will impact everything we treasure, and everyone we love. He has written *A Great Flash of Light* to help sound the alarm on the closeness of nuclear danger and help set a direction to reach a nuclear weapons' free world.

# About the Author

**Francis Charles Bognar** was born in 1946, a few months after the United States dropped the atomic bomb on Hiroshima and Nagasaki. He is the sixth child of a loving, Catholic, Hungarian immigrant family. In 1963 he attended Michigan State University, followed by minor and major seminary training in philosophy, theology and spirituality at St. Paul's Seminary in Saginaw, Michigan and Notre Dame Seminary in New Orleans, Louisiana. On discerning that his vocation was a career in the helping professions rather than the priesthood, he left seminary life to return to college. He graduated with a bachelor's degree in psychology from Loyola University in 1969. He married his wife, Mary Ann, and accepted a commission as a 2nd Lieutenant in the U.S. Infantry. In military service he trained as a Psychological Operations Officer and served as a General Staff Officer at V Corps, Frankfurt, Germany. In the evenings he worked to earn a master's degree in counseling psychology from Ball State University. As the Vietnam war deepened, he applied as a conscientious objector, finished his tour, and received an honorable discharge. Returning to civilian life he continued his education earning a master's and doctorate in public administration from Nova University of Fort Lauderdale, Florida. He graduated from the Spiritual Direction Institute of Charlottesville, Virginia in 1993 where under the direction of Father Chet Michael, he studied works of Thomas Merton, Teilhard de Chardin, Carl G. Jung, and Reverend Morton Kelsey. He served over forty years in social services as a counselor, licensed marriage and family counselor, and administrator, primarily with Catholic Charities agencies. He served on the board of the Nuclear Age Peace Foundation, a partner organization of the International Campaign to Abolish Nuclear Weapons (ICAN), a coalition of nongovernmental organizations world-wide, which received the 2017 Nobel Peace Prize for its work on the United Nations *Treaty on the Prohibition of Nuclear Weapons*. He later served as NAPF's board's chair and vice chair.

## About the Author

The author believes that our world is at an existential crossroads, the moment of choice, when we must make the decision of placing our faith and future in the possession and advancement of nuclear weapons, or in renouncing them. Our collective decision will impact everything we treasure, and everyone we love. He has written *A Great Flash of Light* to help sound the alarm on the closeness of nuclear danger and help set a direction to reach a nuclear weapons' free world.